Rumi's
Love Affair

Rumi's
Love Affair

Anandmurti Gurumaa

FULL CIRCLE
HIND POCKET BOOKS

RUMI'S LOVE AFFAIR

© Gurumaa Vani, 2010
First Paperback Edition, 2010
ISBN 978-81-7621-198-7

Published by
FULL CIRCLE
Hind Pocket Books Pvt. Ltd.
J-40, Jorbagh Lane, New Delhi-110003
Tel: +011 24620063, 24621011 • Fax: 24645795
E-mail: contact@fullcirclebooks.in • website: www.fullcirclebooks.in

Cover Designed by: Gurumaa Vani

Designing & Typesetting: SCANSET
J-40, Jorbagh Lane, New Delhi-110003

Printed at Tan Prints (India) Pvt. Ltd., Distt. Jhajjar, Haryana

PRINTED IN INDIA
10/10/01/10/21/SCANSET/DE/TP/TP/NP295/NP295

Anandmurti Gurumaa

Mesmerising Persona
Piercing Eyes
A Crystal Clear Mind
Wisdom Personified
Anandmurti Gurumaa — A New Age Buddha

Anandmurti Gurumaa — a contemporary mystic master — is a beacon of light to those on the path of spirituality, meditation, love and wisdom. With her characteristic humility, Anandmurti Gurumaa says, "I have nothing new to offer in terms of words; but much to offer in terms of 'the understanding of the spirit' and its essence."

Anandmurti Gurumaa teaches all the important essential precepts that we must understand and internalise, if we are to progress on the path of spirituality. Anandmurti Gurumaa is an embodiment of love, grace, compassion, understanding and equanimity. At the same time, she is modern and dynamic in her thinking and outlook. Her pragmatic teachings empower the seeker with the wisdom to live with absolute harmony.

Redefining Spirituality

Anandmurti Gurumaa says: "The spiritual path is a warrior's path where you have to wage a war against your own darkness, your own ignorance — not to fight with your own mind but to understand it so as to transgress it. It is like the seed that is always there but flowers only in the right climate, rich soil and with the loving nurturing of a gardener."

Anandmurti Gurumaa is a constant source of wisdom and serves as a platform for inner transformation. "Things are difficult only up to the point where you do not wish to change," according to Gurumaa. The most amazing thing is that you may not wake up even after a lot of hard work, and yet for another, the door may open in a flash. This mystery cannot be understood by the mind, it can be known only through experience.

Anandmurti Gurumaa on Meditation

Demystifying the concept of meditation for the common man, Anandmurti Gurumaa has developed several meditation techniques that can be followed by anyone in day to day life. The art of meditation helps to connect with our inner bliss and to be peaceful, devoid of any past or future worries. The unique meditation techniques developed by Anandmurti Gurumaa encompass both, the timeless wisdom of the east and the highest technical approach of the west, helping the seeker enjoy the best of both worlds. Anandmurti Gurumaa conducts worldwide meditation camps where she personally teaches the art of meditation. The benefits of meditating in the company of a living enlightened master are enormous compared to meditating alone.

Anandmurti Gurumaa's crusade against the ills of society

With her mystic vision, wisdom, rationality and cosmic intellectualism, Anandmurti Gurumaa stands as a constant source of inspiration for one and all. She is working zealously towards the upliftment of women. Devoid of any fear and with great enthusiasm, Anandmurti Gurumaa through her divine utterances and 'Shakti' revolution has been waging a war against the exploitation of women, the ill-treatment meted out to widows, forced female infanticide, the dowry system and the prevalent discriminatory treatment of the girl child in our society.

Anandmurti Gurumaa motivates women to fortify their energy and respect themselves as women. In order to not confine her teachings to mere words, Gurumaa in her true crusader spirit has launched the project 'Shakti – An initiative to empower the girl child'. For more details, please visit: www.gurumaa.com.

PREFACE

In the November of 2003, Anandmurti Gurumaa travelled to Turkey. The purpose: To study firsthand the mystical rites of Sufism. Right from the start, the endeavour witnessed miracles. From the flight that was never expected to take off, but to everyone's surprise did; the near magical appearance of master players of the Ney; an unexpected invitation to attend Sema and to participate in Zikr, it turned out to be an all encompassing magical journey. In a country where she did not speak their language and only few locals spoke English, where she had no contacts, where the weather was biting cold and vegetarian food a rare find, Gurumaa was adventurous enough to enjoy it all. In the end they were witness even to the secretly conducted ceremony of 'the whirling dervishes'.

After several insightful discussions and debates with Turkish Sufis – with the help of interpreters of course – Gurumaa returned, carrying back with her to India, the riches of the Sufi tradition. She then proceeded to disseminate this wealth, conducting meditation camps on Sufism. These camps served as a basic introduction to the mystical Sufi tradition of Jalaluddin Rumi and Sufism.

Never before had the common man in India been exposed to Sufism – a privilege thus far limited to the English speaking elites, who could pour over the several translations of Rumi's works available worldwide. However, so far even they did not have access to a master who would teach them the precise technique of Zikr – the Sufi meditation.

This book is a compilation of Gurumaa's discourses given during the Sufi camps. Although the essence of Sufism's divine wine can't be framed in words and presented as a book yet this book is a gesture to give the readers a glimpse of that which is indescribable.

Those who would enjoy this book are suggested to listen to Rumi's poetry narrated with enchanting music in the album called 'Rumi – Love at its Zenith' and experience the reverberating Sufi chants & meditation in 'Zikr – Call of a Sufi' by Anandmurti Gurumaa. For more details, log on to www.gurumaa.com.

CONTENTS

1. Who is a Sufi?   12

2. Remove the Dross from your Mind   33

3. Pay the Price of Being a Disciple   54

4. At the Feet of the Master   73

5. The Fire of Love   92

6. Purify Thyself   104

7. Illumine Your Heart   128

8. The Master is an Embodiment of Love   139

9. The Search   155

10. Surrender   188

11. Divine Intoxication is Essential   204

12. Allah! The Most Benevolent   225

13. Message of Love   237

CHAPTER 1

WHO IS A SUFI?

Bismillah-ir-Rehman-ir-Rahim
Ya Allah salamat, Ya Rasool salamat
Ya Sufi salamat, Ya Sufi salamat

Shower your blessings, O Allah
Shower your blessings, O Mohammad
Shower your blessings, O Sufi

O Allah, I seek thee
O Allah, O God of Gods
Where can I find you?

Let me take you all on a mystical journey – a journey of Sufism. Let us first understand who a Sufi is and who is capable of becoming a Sufi. When we try to define the word 'Sufi', we find it has many meanings and many applications. Before I take you to the depths of the meaning of the word 'Sufi', I would like to explain a tenet that is basic to the understanding of any spiritual or religious matter.

I am often asked why I talk of Sufism when I am not a Muslim. "Why do you even want to talk on this subject?" is the common query. Here we need to understand the fundamental principle that it is not necessary to be a Muslim in order to be a Sufi. It is not at all necessary to abide by the rules and regulations of the Muslim religious code, because the word 'Sufi' means 'love', and there is no religion in the world, leave alone Islam that is devoid of love.

Love is the 'rooh' (true-self) of the 'Sufi'. Just like body is dead without its rooh similarly without love all religions are dead. Behind this body, heart and mind is our true 'self'; also known as 'rooh' in Arabic, Persian and Urdu. The word 'Sufi' is not a proper noun; it is not the name of a person bound by a particular set of rules, epics or laws. A Sufi is a person whose rooh ascends to the Almighty's abode; one who is in love and is compassionate, is a Sufi.

The Hindu religion would become static if it did not contain the essence of love and devotion. The rooh of Judaism is Haseed; of Buddhism it is Zen – Buddhism gets its fragrance from Zen.

As we all know, fragrance cannot be imprisoned – it is impossible to do so. You just cannot imprison a fragrance! You may grow flowers in your garden, but their scent reaches your neighbour's house. You cannot tell a flower that you are the master of its fragrance: "This is my fragrance, I own this perfume." You cannot command the wind to desist from carrying the scent of the flowers of your garden to the neighbour's house. Neither the wind nor the flowers will obey you!

The fragrance of the flower of Islam is the Sufi movement. Disregarding the limitations imposed by the walls between, the perfume of the flowers in your garden reaches homes afar. You grow tuberoses in your garden, but their scent reaches distant colonies. When the jasmine flower blooms in your garden, its perfume envelops the homes of even those neighbours you are not on good terms with. The tiny dainty flowers of jasmine have no idea who your friend is, and who your enemy.

Similarly, the flower of Islam blooms in the garden of religious conviction, but the essence of the flower of Islam – the Sufi – transcends all boundaries. Just as the body is dead without its rooh, every religion is life-less without love; love is the rooh of religion. So then who is a Sufi? A Sufi is love! And what is Sufism? It is the path of love.

There is yet another meaning of the word 'Sufi'. Those who wear clothes made of suf are called Sufi. 'Suf' is the wool made from the hair of sheep, goat or camel – and the person who wears a robe made of suf is called a Sufi. There was a time when Sufis were recognised by the robes they wore. A Sufi by the name of Idris Shah once said, "Animal skin? That cannot be a defining characteristic of Sufism. Such a lowly definition! One who wears clothes made of animal skin is a Sufi?"

In my view, the statement: 'one who wears robes made of suf is a Sufi', is correct if viewed in a certain perspective. However, there is a mystery to its meaning and only one who understands that mystery will understand this statement in its correct perspective. He who wears suf is a Sufi – this has a profound meaning!

Man is born with some baser qualities which are very overpowering. You don't make yourself hungry – hunger just happens; so you arrange for food. Your body feels the heat and the cold, so you arrange to protect yourself from them. There is yet another hunger that rises in a well-fed, healthy body, and that is to acquire financial security in order to meet all these needs. So there is a hunger for wealth too. Once you have arranged for food, clothing and shelter, once you have satiated your hunger and secured a dwelling, a third kind of hunger arises – that for sex.

Whether educated or uneducated, animal or human, every being experiences these three types of hunger: hunger for food, shelter and sex. It is obvious, it is natural and it is universal! It doesn't have to be taught to anyone.

These three traits are inherent in animals and human beings alike. One, who has managed to kill the animal within, that is, he who has managed to kill the beastly instincts in him, he then wears a symbolic robe of animal skin. This is to announce to the world that the animal inside him exists no more. This animal skin that you see, this suf robe that is on his body, is proof of the fact that his baser instincts are sublimated.

Remember, it is not sufficient to be born a human being. We may have a human form, but unless we kill the animal instincts within, and unless we break away from them, we cannot really be called human beings.

Bhojan, bhog, bhay, nidra
Eh nar pashu samaan

Food, sex, fear, sleep
Make a man into animal

It is said that the person who only eats, seeks pleasure, suffers from fear and sleeps, is like an animal. If he eats, he will sleep too. Food grains produce lethargy in the body. If you eat more than what is required, you feel lazy even in the daytime. When you eat at night, you feel sleepy due to the effect of food. Sleep is also a natural requirement of the body, so food and sleep are inter-connected. The fear of losing your food or shelter is also natural; it is there in animals as well as in human beings. Physical desires also come along with all these. A person who does only these four things in life – eat, seek physical pleasure, fear, and sleep – cannot be called a human being; he is merely an animal. Only someone who manages to rise above these animal-like traits can be called a human being. And Sufism is only for human beings, not for animals.

The important question is: Are you an animal or a human being? Introspect while reading these words: Are you an animal or a human being? Having a human body or form does not necessarily mean possessing a human identity. In other words, though you are a human being, you don't possess human traits. Is a usurper an animal or a human being?

A famous saying lists the three basic causes of all quarrels: wealth, women and land. Anyone who fights over these is not a human being. Remember this! And be aware of who you really are – an animal or a human being! Whoever manages to kill the animal instinct within, is a Sufi. Addressing the basis of Idris Shah's doubts – how a man wearing an animal skin can be called a Sufi – I say that a person wearing a suf robe can be called a Sufi, because his outer veil, his dress speaks of his inner condition. Whoever has risen above his inner beastliness is a Sufi – he wears coarse cloth.

If we try to understand the meaning of the word Sufi in Persian, we find a very interesting comment in their dictionary.

It says: A Sufi is a Sufi! So who is a Sufi? First we said a Sufi is one who is a lover of God. Then we said that the one who wears suf robes is a Sufi. Just as the Almighty is infinite and mysterious, similarly a Sufi is a mystery. That which can be defined by words is not a mystery. How can that which can be contained by the limitations of words be a mystery?

So who is a Sufi? A Sufi is one who treads on the path of a mysterious discovery; who is in love with an unseen, mystical power. Can God be seen? No! The world can be seen; creation can be seen, but not the creator. One who loves the unseen and whose love cannot be understood, is a Sufi. So who is a Sufi? The one who sets out on a mystical journey is a Sufi; he who is in love with God is a Sufi; he who wears clothes made of suf is a Sufi.

We can carry on describing and explaining the meaning of the word 'Sufi' – there is no end to it. I feel that the definition in the Persian language is the most appropriate. Who is a Sufi? A Sufi is a Sufi – no less, no more. Who is a Sufi? A Sufi is the one who is a Sufi! It is like a riddle that one has to solve.

Remember that whatever I say will mostly be in riddles. I am going to leave many blank spaces for you to fill. Let me warn you that this is a difficult journey, a very mysterious and difficult journey that you will undertake. Therefore your preparation should be honest and strong. It is not easy to understand the mystery of Sufism.

Who is a Sufi? The word Sufi means purity, clarity and piety. A person who is not pure and pious cannot be a Sufi. This means that anybody who wants to tread the path of Sufism will have to pay special attention to the purity of the body and the mind.

What state is your mind in? How polluted is it? How much darkness lies within? How many vices have made a home in your mind? As long as there is darkness and negativity in your mind, you cannot become a Sufi. I invite you to understand Sufism and become a Sufi yourself.

I would like to clarify at the outset that I am not going to discuss Sufism but Sufi! Someone questioned how I could speak on Sufism? My answer is: I can speak on Sufism because I myself am a Sufi, and only a Sufi has the right to speak on Sufi. Remember, I am going to discuss Sufi and not Sufism. While a flower is visible, its fragrance remains hidden. A sect can be seen but Sufi cannot be seen. There is a famous saying in Turkey: One who is seen and recognised is not a true Sufi.

The Sufi, Al Hillaj Mansoor was once asked, "What is the height of Sufism? What is the highest experience in Sufism?"

Mansoor replied, "Come tomorrow and you will see for yourself."

"See? See what? Why can't you give me the answer in words right now?"

Mansoor laughed and said, "Whatever can be described in words is not Sufism. Come tomorrow and see for yourself."

The next day when the man reached Mansoor's dwelling to 'see' his reply, what does he see there? Mansoor had been arrested; he was tied with a rope and was being dragged. People said he was going to be executed. Why? Because Mansoor kept repeating, 'An-al-haq'. An-al-haq means: I am the One; I am God. This is irreverence! This is blasphemy! A profusely bleeding Mansoor was being stoned. And Mansoor? Well! He was laughing! In the crowd of spectators, Mansoor's eyes recognised the person who had questioned him and he shouted, "See, this is the height of Sufism."

The man who had asked the question was upset because when Mansoor looked at him, the crowd started looking at him. He immediately stepped back and merged with the crowd for fear of being recognised and killed.

But Mansoor kept on laughing. The scaffolding on which Mansoor was made to stand was drenched with his blood. People were still throwing stones at him but he did not stop laughing. The executioner raised his sword, and the head rolling down the steps called out, 'An-al-haq!' Even after the beheading, the sound of An-al-haq echoed. This is the highest experience where death becomes a celebration.

Why was Mansoor laughing? He was laughing because he knew that the one these people were trying to kill was not his real self.

"The executioner's sword cannot reach the real 'me'. What a game these mortal beings are playing! They are trying to kill 'me', but the sharp-edged sword that can touch 'me' or even wound 'me' has not yet been made. If at all, they will kill this body. By destroying this perishable body, these fools think that they can kill 'me'!"

That is why Mansoor was laughing. The ecstasy in Mansoor's laughter is the height of Sufism.

So then who is a Sufi? The person for whom both life and death are a celebration is a Sufi. A Sufi can view his whole life objectively as a celebration, only because his mind is quiet and in his heart, resides only, God's love. Remember, if you want to become a Sufi, you have to lay open your heart onto the feet of love. A person with a cluttered mind can only listen to talks on Sufi and Sufism, but can never become a Sufi. I am giving you an open invitation to become a Sufi and not just to learn about Sufism.

Who is a Sufi? A Sufi is the one whose heart is full of love and whose mind is clean and unblemished. Sufis have developed a few techniques for keeping your mind clean and pure. They say the first quality that a man should possess for treading on this path, is khushu. The word 'khushu' means humility or egoless-ness. Now look at yourself intently. Are you humble? Are you without ego? Remember, a man either has an ego or he does not have an ego; one can never claim to be less egoistic than another. There is no measure of ego. It is wrong to say that another person has a bigger ego while I have a lesser ego, because ego is either present or not present. A man is either dead or alive. To say that a person is half-dead is not correct. If a man is alive, it can be certified; if he dies, a death certificate can be obtained from the municipality. But no certificate can be granted for a half-dead condition. You are either physically alive, or dead – there is nothing in between.

So you either have an ego or you do not have an ego. One who is an egoist can never tread on the path of Sufism. Nothing less will work; no compromise. This is not the wisdom of Vedanta, wherein you can recite with me 'Shivoham' (I am God, I am the Truth). To become a Sufi, you will have to fulfill certain conditions: egoless-ness, purity and total absence of conceit.

Who is a Sufi? A Sufi is the one who is devoid of ego and does not bear any spite or hatred towards anyone. One, whose mind is attached or tied to anybody or anything, cannot be a Sufi. The one, who is detached from all sorts of bonds and attachments, in true sense, is a Sufi. The journey to become a Sufi begins with humility. Kabir, a Sufi, says:

Roda hoye raho baat ka taj mann ka abhimaan

Casting aside your pride
Be as a stone by the wayside

One must aspire to be like a stone lying on the wayside. This small stone is kicked around by thousands of people. So a harjan, i.e. true devotee of God, needs to be like a stone lying on the wayside – devoid of any ego. Now look within! Do you ever feel like a stone lying on the road? No! You do not consider yourself less than God! You consider yourself to be the very best: best in knowledge, understanding, wealth, strength, body and beauty. You have several reasons to consider yourself better than others.

But, says Kabir, "Who is a true devotee? Who can be a Sufi? He who is like the stone lying by the wayside; the one who is kicked around by thousands, can be a Sufi" But then again Kabir says:

Roda hua to kya hua
Panthi ko dukh de
Harjan aisa chahiye
Jyon dharni mein kheh

So what if you have become a stone, you hurt passerby
God's devotee should be as dust on earth

So what if one has reduced oneself to a state as devoid of ego as a stone? The stone lying on the ground may at times hurt the passer-by. How can anybody who causes pain to someone be a humble devotee of God?

Do you hurt anybody with your words or your behaviour? If yes, then you cannot be a Sufi. One who never causes pain to anybody and whose conduct never hurts anybody, is a Sufi. Sometimes, though not deliberately, yet unintentionally, we do hurt people. If someone is heavily built or obese, you say, "What a fatso you have become!" You may say it in jest, but the person concerned may not find it funny. Sometimes you imitate a person behind his back; copy the way he walks or talks or eats. For you it may be fun — just a joke — but the person feels hurt when he gets to know about it.

So who is a Sufi? Certainly not one who causes pain to another; leave alone doing so deliberately, he cannot even think of doing so unintentionally. Not even unknowingly! And we cause pain to others deliberately! The one who even unknowingly does not cause pain to others is a Sufi.

What should a God's devotee be like? Like dust and sand, says Kabir. But then he goes on to add:

Kheh bhayi to kya hua
Jo ud laage ang
Harjan kaisa chahiye
Jyon paani sarbhang

So what if you have become dust
You sully people's body
How should be the devotee of lord
As lucid as water

So what if you are completely devoid of pride, and have become like dust and sand? Dust particles, when blown by the wind, get into the eyes and dirty the body. So it is not enough to be like dust. Not even dust! Become more humble, come down even further!

What should a God's devotee be like? Like water. Water has the characteristic of taking the shape of the utensil that contains it. One who can easily be moulded is a Sufi.

But we mortal beings fight over petty things. There are arguments even when deciding the menu for a particular meal. Who will sit in a particular wooden chair in the office — there can be a tiff over this! The favourite chair in your drawing room is exclusively for you, and if someone else sits in it, there is a fight.

One who has given up all contentions; one who has cast

himself in the Sufi mould will say, "Never mind, you be happy. If you are happy sitting on this chair, then please sit here. What matters is your happiness." Be simple and pure like water.

You may have many qualities, but one quality that is missing is simplicity and straight-forwardness. Children are simple and pure, but adults have become very complicated. All the time you are pre-occupied with thoughts like: 'This person said this; that person troubled me. Right now I will not get into a conflict with him, but later on I will do something that will trouble him immensely.'

One who plays such dirty politics, whose mind is polluted... how can he be a Sufi? Who is a Sufi? The one whose mind has no impurities. Who is a Sufi? The one whose heart is filled with love. If you only want to read about Sufi, you are free to do as you please. But when you have a chance to become a Sufi yourself, then why restrict yourself to just reading? Why not become a Sufi? Why just read and listen to talks on humility? Why not become humble? Why just read books and discourses on purity of the heart and mind? Make yourself pure; it is this purity, this piety, this clarity that makes you a Sufi. Do not just read or listen, try to imbibe these qualities.

Who is a Sufi? He who has the first trait of khushu, i.e. humility and absence of ego.

It is very good if you want to become a Sufi, but then you need to possess another quality and that is karamat – the virtue of charity, the ability to give. One who cannot donate, cannot give or distribute and is only interested in taking, cannot be a Sufi. So, who is a Sufi? The one who just gives! These are small things, yet I would like to explain them through simple examples.

There is one chair and two people are standing. The one who is not a Sufi will take the seat first. The one who wants to be a Sufi will offer the seat to the other person. Learn to give! One who gives is a Sufi. And it is equally important that we are not proud of the fact that we donate. In fact, when you donate something, you should be thankful to the other person for being kind enough for accepting whatever you gave. When you give something to someone, you mention it a hundred times. Even if you do donate, you boast about it repeatedly. Even if you give something to your own relatives, you mention it a hundred times. The one who talks about his charity makes it worthless.

Emperor Suleiman used to observe a rule: every morning he would stand in front of his palace and give alms to the poor and the needy, according to their requirement, whatever it may be – food, money, clothing. So there used to be long queues outside his palace to receive alms. One day a beggar asked for food grain; a bag full of grain was given to him. The man bowed and greeted him, "King Suleiman, may you be victorious, nobody is as generous as you! There is nobody as virtuous as you! You are the greatest!" Thus he kept singing the king's praises. Initially the king felt awkward and even embarrassed, but when he said, "There is no one as generous as you," his eyes became moist with tears.

The beggar was alarmed. He could not understand what he had said to make the king cry. "Your honor, please forgive me if I have made a mistake."

Suleiman said, "Certainly I have made a mistake, there must be some fault somewhere, something wrong in the manner of my giving that you consider me great and yourself worthless. Whatever God has given me, is his wealth placed in my custody, and it is for his men that he has bestowed this upon me. I only work as a medium of distribution; who am I to give? God gave me birth in the family of kings. Had it been the Almighty's wish, I would have been born in a hut. So if he has sent me to a king's house, it is not because there is something great about me. He has assigned me the task of serving his people; I am here to serve you all. The one who serves is a humble servant, not a master. So, O' child of God, if you want to shower blessings, do it in the name of the Almighty and not in the name of a mortal being like me. Do not call me great; I am not great. Instead, remember Him who is truly great."

Who then who is a Sufi? The one, who has a passion for giving; the one, who gets happiness by giving and the one who wants to donate. When I say 'one who wants to distribute', it implies not expecting anything in return. Often you enjoy giving and you do give, but somewhere deep inside, you expect something in return – if only to be remembered by the beneficiary of your largesse.

The one who expects something in return has not really given; he has not really made a true donation yet. Priests say that if you donate in this world, you will get the returns in the other world. Give a piece of bread to the needy here, and after death when you are crossing the 'river of fasting' (a belief held by some that man is subjected to this after death), you will be provided food in the other world. So if a businessman distributes food grains amongst the poor here, it is not because he feels for the poor but because he wants to ensure some food for himself in the other world, so that he doesn't have to go hungry then.

Your priest says, "Donate; donate everything in the name of the deceased – cots, beds, quilts." If you ask why, they tell you: "Donate so that your loved ones who have gone to heaven get a cot, bed, quilt and everything there. So please donate for them."

When I first witnessed the rituals carried on in the name of the deceased, I was shocked! Many things were donated, and on enquiring about it I was told: "We have to give these to him."

"To whom?" I asked.

"To him, the brother from the gurudwara," they said.

"Why should we give him? And what about these utensils, new clothes, all these food items, fruits and sweets?"

They told me that everything had to be given to him, because whatever is given to him here, would be provided to our dear departed one in the other world."

I have heard of courier services, but what kind of a courier service is this? All the things that the priest from the gurudwara had taken were unloaded and arranged in his house. They were all there; I saw them even a week later – the things had not been delivered to their supposed destination! When would the goods be delivered to the person who had gone to the other world? What kind of a courier service is this? Everything was lying here and yet we are told that our loved ones will get them in the other world! These things will never reach them!

Such donations cannot be considered donations in the right

sense of the term. Wherever there is an expectation of any kind of return, it cannot be considered a donation. Above all, you even donate with the desire of earning spiritual merit. One who has the expectation of earning virtue in return for a donation cannot be considered a true donor.

People do have the intention of giving. Sometimes when they feel very emotional towards me, they want to give me something. But they are particular about their cheques or envelopes being handed over only to me. They are hesitant to hand it over to my people and insist that I see the cheque or the envelope personally. They give me some reason or the other for this; they ask me to see if the cheque is properly made. Then finally I have to agree and say, "Ok, let me see." These people are unable to understand – though they all love me – but if you can't offer something to your guru – who you have full faith in – without making it obvious, then it would be foolish to expect you to give anything to anybody else without showing off.

Who is a Sufi? One who enjoys giving and one who feels happy giving to others. One who is happy distributing is a Sufi.

Khushu, karamat... and a third quality is sijjat. Who is a Sufi? One who has sijjat.

Sijjat means basic, fundamental, original, truthful and authentic. One who is not double-faced; the person who is the same before you and behind your back; one who does not bow his head before you while planning to stab you in the back; one who is not unscrupulous – is a Sufi. So sijjat means truthful and authentic.

Along the path of life, you may come across many people with whom you are not compatible. So what do you do? You can do either of two things: The first option is to carry on as though you are enjoying their company. But at some point in time, this kind of pretence becomes evident and a problem in itself. A meaningful relationship is one in which the hearts are compatible; where they are not, there should be no relationship at all. So where there is actually no relationship, why pretend that good relations exist? There should be truthfulness; where your nature is not in harmony with another's, all you have to do is fold your hands very humbly and tell that person: "Your thinking differs from mine, so it is better to part ways."

Is it very difficult to say such a small thing? Is it such a big problem? Why do we go on pretending? Finally we start enjoying this pretence to the extent that it appears real. Isn't it better to speak the truth rather than carry on the formality of enjoying each other's company, despite the fact that your thoughts and your views are not in harmony? When we fraternize like this, we actually hurt each other. Instead of going through this pain, isn't it better, to very politely, very humbly, suggest a parting of ways. Muster the courage and say it!

Someone came up to me and said, "A friend of mine is antagonistic to you and speaks against you; I feel very bad about it." I told him that every man has the right to speak his mind. The Indian Constitution too has given us the right to freedom of speech. His friend too has the freedom of speech like everyone else – he has the right to express his views.

"If you don't appreciate his views, why do you listen to them? I am putting this very simply to you and it will save you a lot of trouble if you adopt it in the right manner. You say you don't appreciate his views – when your views are not in harmony, how can he be your friend? Friendship is always between like-minded people. People can be friends only when they have similar choices, similar thoughts.

In such a situation, it is a good idea to tell him the next time you meet: "There was a time when our views were similar. We were good friends and had great times together, but now I have changed and so have my ideas. Your views are still the same. My path has changed and there can be no agreeable discussion between us. I thank you for the time we spent together, but now since our views differ, we may not be able to get along."

Is it very painful to say this much? But you are concerned about society; you have got so used to unrealistic behaviour and to telling lies that you find it difficult to get rid of this dishonesty. You wonder how you could ever get yourself to say something like this!

Someone said, "It may be possible to speak the truth if the

people concerned are outsiders or just friends, but what should we do if they are our own people, our family? If the people at home keep talking such nonsense then what do we do?"

Remember, only those of you who are courageous will be able to walk with me, only those who have the courage to speak the truth. Only those of you can walk with me, who, for the sake of truth, are ready to distance themselves even from their loved ones. Those of you, who do not have this courage, won't be able to walk onto this path, with me.

A lady said to me, "I do not tell my husband when I come to your place. I make the excuse of going to my parents' house and come to the ashram. I worry about being caught someday."

I said, "Isn't he your husband? Are husband and wife not supposed to understand each other and take care of each other's likes and needs? Isn't this the basis of a marital relationship? Tell me, isn't it so?"

She said, "Yes, it is."

I said, "If so, then explain to your husband that now you find joy in religious discourses; you find bliss in meditation. Tell him that it will make you all the more happy if he shared in your joy as well. In case he does not want to, then he is free to do as he pleases. But then, you too have your freedom?"

She said, "My husband will pull me by my hair and throw me out of the house."

"If your husband can throw you out over such a small thing, it will be better for you to walk out instead of giving him a chance to throw you out." What kind of a husband is he who does not respect his wife? Who cannot give due regard to his own wife! What kind of a husband is he who does not give you space to pursue spiritual happiness?

I have said this several times, your marriages are not arranged on the basis of compatible views or thinking. Your marriages are fixed after seeing the house, money, status and caste. It is never seen whether ideas match or not. Is it not so? Neither views nor conduct are matched before forcing two people to live together. Now what do these people do? As they cannot relate to each other, they keep fighting – all their lives! Ninety percent of couples fight constantly. It doesn't matter on what issue they fight, but the fact is that they are always fighting.

Sijjat! I would like to repeat that making an effort, to become a Sufi, is an act of courage. Becoming a Sufi is not an easy task, only courageous people can take up the task and only courageous people can succeed. There are three basic tenets to the foundation of Sufism: khushu, karamat and sijjat. Anybody who feels the presence of these three traits in his life, realises that he has made a beginning on the path of Sufism. But one who doesn't feel the presence of these things in his life is still far from his destination.

There is another meaning of the word 'Sufi' and that is friend. The word 'Sufi' originally comes from the Greek word, Sophia. Sophia means wisdom or the power of discernment. So who is a Sufi? One who is prudent – note that I am not saying 'knowledgeable'. One can gain knowledge from books or libraries; one can gain knowledge by listening to lectures and discourses. One who has amassed information does not automatically become a Sufi; one who has intellectual knowledge does not become a Sufi.

Who is a Sufi? The one who has the power of judgment. One who possesses the essence, the wisdom, is a Sufi. It does not matter if you acquire a huge quantum of bookish knowledge; it is of no use. What is important is your power of discernment, your ability to be judicious, and this comes from an understanding of the essence of wisdom. Knowledge of the English language is of no use; knowing several English words does not make you proficient in the language, unless and until you know how to use those words.

A child from a middle-class family was admitted to a public school for better prospects. The father had studied in a government school, and wanted to fulfill his desire for public school education through his child. So the child was put in a public school. One day, both father and son set out in a car and on the way they met with an accident. It was a minor accident, no one received any serious injury, but the other car got a dent. The owner of that car seemed to be well educated. He came out of his car fuming and started abusing in English.

Our man, being unable to understand what the other fellow was saying, called his son. "Pappu, come here!"

The boy came running and said, "Yes daddy?"

"I did not send you to an English medium school for no reason. This gentleman is going on in English, you too say something."

The son came forward confidently and began, "There was a crow. The crow was thirsty. The crow was flying in the sky looking for water. He found a pot which was filled with water.... ." He started off with the story of the thirsty crow!

The well-read English-speaking gentleman was flabbergasted, for this made no sense. He again started abusing in English. Well, the thirsty crow story isn't very long so it was soon over! The gentleman got even more annoyed on seeing how stupid these people were. He shouted, "Go and get admitted in a mental asylum! What on earth are you talking about?"

Once the story got over, the child started reciting an application letter: "To, The Principal, Dear Sir, I was sick, therefore I could not come to school, and for the next four days, I will be........." And so he recited an entire leave application!

There are many people who have this kind of knowledge. They have accumulated knowledge, but do not possess the judgment required for its correct usage. A Sufi is not knowledgeable, a Sufi is discerning.

Kabir says he has found a master who is discernment personified. "I have found a guru who is the personification of discernment." Who is a Sufi? One whose mind is not burdened with the theoretical knowledge of epics and scriptures, but is full of wisdom; the one who is discerning. The word Sufi is derived from the word sophia. There is yet another word that is derived from it, and that is 'philosophy'. But there is a mistake here: sophia actually means wisdom, but the other word 'philosophy' means a 'system of thoughts'. One who thinks or reflects all the time and gets caught in a web of his own thoughts – like a spider – is called a philosopher. He goes on thinking, and in the process, misses out on the actual meaning of the words. He gets lost in the labyrinth of the hollow knowledge of words, and loses touch with the real world.

A Sufi is not the one who gets lost in literal knowledge. A Sufi is one who is able to extract the essence of that knowledge. So remember one thing, an essence is an extract; it is always small in quality. An abundance of words can be very impressive but their substance may be miniscule in reality. A garden full of flowers may be huge, but the perfume prepared from all the flowers in the garden can be filled in a small bottle. You can even claim to carry a whole garden in a small bottle! A rose garden may be very large, but when we extract the essence of all the roses to make perfume, its quantity is minute.

Similarly, in the context of literal knowledge, we find that Kabir, Ravidas and other Sufi poets never attended any school, college or university. Neither did they have any understanding of faculties, nor did they hold any degrees. But they had something that even degree-holders lack, and that is wisdom. They had wisdom and a deep understanding of life, of the true 'self' and of the Almighty. The one, who has the power of right judgment and of reasoning, is a Sufi.

One last meaning of the word Sufi that we come across is friend. Who is a Sufi? One who has only God as his friend. Friendship with whom? Only with the Almighty. He does not become friends with anybody else. One who has found a friend in God, in the Almighty, is a Sufi.

Once I met a dervish in Turkey with whom I had very long discussions. There was a translator with us, because the dervish spoke only Turkish. So I was talking in English and our translator was interpreting our conversation and conveying it to him. And the talks which started at midnight lasted till 2:30 in the morning! Sufis say that days are meant for worldly people and nights for Sufi. A worldly man keeps awake during the day and a Sufi at night! It was a tedious affair as whatever I said had to be translated for him, and his reply also had to be translated for me – naturally it was time-consuming. So finally in the end, he put his hand over his

29

heart – a Sufi is connected to the heart, he loves from his heart; he remembers his God from the heart and he is connected to his sheikh – the son of God – through his heart – and said, "I am fortunate to have found a friend." And he immediately made it clear that by 'friend' he did not mean a worldly friend but a Sufi. I am not a man, nor did I know his language; I am not a Muslim, yet this ascetic calls me a friend! What he was saying was: "A Sufi has found a friend, i.e. another Sufi."

Rasool Mohammad sahib is called Mustafa which means a friend or well-wisher. To every Muslim, Mohammad sahib is a Mustafa; he is a friend. Why is he a friend? Because he is the link between man and God; Allah is also a Mustafa, a friend. I would like to repeat, a friend is a person with whom your ideas and thoughts are in consonance; one with whom you share and get joy out of the interaction.

Mind you, a dervish, a Sufi, is not one who can be recognised. There was another Sufi by the name of Hamid. It is said that once he had a dream and in the dream God asked him: "Should I announce to the world that you are a Sufi?" Please remember that these stories I tell you about Sufi are parables. We are not concerned with the authenticity of these tales; we are concerned with the gist, the substance. So do not get caught up in words. You must not expect God to appear in your dream tonight or the next night, thinking that if God could talk to Abu Hamid, why can't he talk to you. This is a story and we have to grasp its essence. So first listen to the story; the substance will come of its own. I will not even need to tell you; you will understand it on your own, for I expect you to be intelligent.

So Abu Hamid dreams of God, who asks him: "Should I announce to the world that you are a Sufi?" Abu Hamid bowed to him and said, "If you want to kill me, then certainly you may announce that I am a Sufi. After what happened to Al Hillaj Mansoor, I will also meet the same fate. What happened to Shams Tabreez will happen to me as well. This world cannot tolerate a living Sufi. So if you want to grant me the same fate as you gave Mansoor……"

Remember, Abu Hamid did not say that the world killed Mansoor; that people are against religion and God; that people are enemies of Sufis. He did not say that the executioner killed Mansoor. Abu Hamid said, "God, you killed him. Whatever fate you granted to Mansoor, if you want to grant me the same fate, then yes, you may make the announcement."

I repeat this important Turkish quotation: One who can be recognised cannot be a Sufi. If, by some good luck, you ever happen to meet the ascetic with whom I had this discussion, you may well bang your head in amazement! Except in Sema – the congregation of Sufis – if you see him elsewhere, you will find him wearing trousers and a shirt, dressed up smartly and looking very handsome. A very well dressed man indeed! Also a chain smoker!

The day I met him, we ate together while talking. Let me inform you that he is a married man with children! He is a professor in a university and also a musician – he plays the ney. So we met, talked and had dinner. After dinner he sought my permission to smoke. "May I smoke?" he asked.

"I have no objection if you want to smoke."

He thanked me, lit a cigarette and started smoking. While drawing on his cigarette, he started talking about Sufism. So, who is a Sufi? He whose heart does not love anyone other than God Almighty. Or else he loves those who have a similar love for God. There is either of two things: he loves God, or he loves those who love God – such a man is a Sufi.

So who is a Sufi? One whose constant refrain is the name of the Almighty; one whose heart sings only one song; one who is forever calling out to God; one who lives within the confines of his body but is not bound by it; one who lives in society, but is far removed from social norms.

Let me repeat: you are very fortunate that this day, this moment, you have set out on a journey with me, of knowing who a Sufi is? You may not realise it, but these special words are meant only for special ears. This deep understanding, this essence and wisdom is not available on TV. All of you who undertake this journey must remember that it is a very different and unusual journey, for you are going to learn a new language, a new dialect, a new form; everything will be new. In order to enjoy this novelty, stop expecting the same old language and the same old behaviour that you are used to. This is a new and novel journey.

The heart that reverberates with the name of God, the heart that echoes the name of Allah – that is the heart of a Sufi. The first and foremost principle is to never speak without the permission of your revered one. For the one who is quiet, a day will come when his master will say: "Mind! Quiet!" And the mind will obey.

Who is a Sufi? They say: One, who loves God or loves those beings, who love God, is a Sufi. In other words, being a Sufi means being in love. I repeat, one who is bound by the walls of religion cannot be a Sufi. Again, it is not necessary to be a Muslim in order to be a Sufi; to be a Sufi, all you need is love. Therefore, Meera, Jesus, Guru Nanak and Namdev are all Sufis.

Who is a Sufi? A Sufi is a Sufi! To be a Sufi you don't have to be limited by narrow walls or compartments or labels of religion. The earth can be divided by walls, but no wall bisects the sky. Who is a Sufi? One who is like the sky and not one who is like the earth. Open, expansive, vast, unlimited, boundary-less, and intense: like the sky is he! And with this expansive heart and mind, his voice, his rooh and his heart calls out.

O Allah, O God of Gods
Where can I find you?

CHAPTER 2

REMOVE THE DROSS FROM YOUR MIND

Sufi is not the name of a person, Sufi is the name of love. There is a clause in the New Testament, that says that God created this world, with all his love. He was so overwhelmed by love that he created the universe. And when his love grew boundless, he felt the desire to be known and understood; to be sought. That is why he created human beings. God created man with all his heart. Why? Because God loves mankind.

This is a very beautiful explanation of the reason this world came into being. Why did this world come into existence? When God was overwhelmed with his own love, his love overflowed and became the basis for the world's existence. When the world came into being initially, all its features were inert. Earth, water, wind, fire, sky, celestial bodies; this entire universe was totally inert. A mountain stood in its place, water just flowed and the sky was in its place. This inert world didn't satisfy Him; He wasn't happy with His own creation. When He didn't find any happiness in His own creation, then He created man. The existence of human beings is the greatest proof of God's love. He loves us and we are here because He wants us to be here.

There is another saying: God has loved man for ages, while man came to love God only later. First God loved us; His love came first. It is only because of His love that we exist. Man started loving God much later, therefore God's love will always be deeper than that of man. The very reason of our existence is His love;

we are here because He loves us. Those who say: 'We think of God often but He never thinks of us', are ignorant. The fact is that God always remembers us and the surest proof of this is our very existence. We would not exist if He didn't remember us or if He didn't love us. God doesn't need to prove that He loves His beings; it is human beings who need to prove whether or not they love the Almighty.

Let me take the understanding of Sufi a little further. Who is a Sufi? What is Sufism? Being a Sufi means being in love with the Almighty. The name of the love-relationship with God is Sufism. Even before man starts loving his Master, the Master already loves his beings. The affair of this love-relationship has existed ever since the creation of the universe, and the very fact that the world exists, exhibits His love. It is because of love that all the creatures in this world exist; that this whole universe exists. So what is Sufi? Love! Sufi existed even before the world came into being. Remember that by Sufi I mean love. The moment you hear the word 'love', you start wondering what it means! We will never be able to understand the true meaning of anything if we try to understand it intellectually.

There was Sufi by the name of Baha-ud–din. Someone asked him, "How did you realise God? How did you find Him?" Baha-ud-din replied, "By not darkening the portals of my mind but by brightening my heart with love. It was by not blackening the book of my mind, but by making my heart radiant with love." This statement has many very deep meanings.

When we think about God or when we pronounce the word 'Almighty', the word starts to resonate in some part of the mind. The moment the word 'God' comes to mind, we begin thinking about our religion, religious scriptures and their related tenets. For example, a Hindu, on hearing the word 'God', thinks of Krishna, Ram, Shiva, etc. Or he starts reflecting on the principles of the Vedas. The moment a Sikh hears the word 'God', it has a different connotation for him. To begin with, he would rather take the name of 'Waheguru' than of God. He will start recollecting verses from the scriptures, but not those of the Gita or Upanishads, but of the Guru Granth Sahib.

When a Jaina hears the word 'Almighty', the discourses of their 23 'teerthankers', of Lord Mahavir, and the sermons of religious leaders echo in his mind. The minute a Muslim hears the word 'God', he will not show much attachment to the word in the first place, and would insist that you say 'Ya Allah'. And the moment the word 'Allah' is spoken, the verses of the 'Quran Sharif' will start resounding in his mind.

If an average Hindu – many of you may claim to be devout Hindus – is asked to recite the Gita, he will not be able to do so. All you know is that the Bhagavad-Gita is our sacred scripture. If a Muslim were asked to recite the complete Quran Sharif, he too will find it difficult to do so. I asked one of them to do this and he replied, "It is good enough if one memorises just what is required for offering namaaz." He further added, "The Hadith says that if one can't remember the entire namaaz, at least one should say, 'La Ilaha Illallah, Mohammad Rasool Allah'. If one is of low intelligence and cannot remember the entire namaaz, reciting just this much will do. But if one totally lacks intelligence, then he may just say 'Allah Allah'."

When a Buddhist hears the word 'Almighty', he is reminded of the Buddha – with closed eyes and a smiling face – that too of Sakya Muni; he knows nothing of other Buddhas! In case he is born in Tibet or China, he may know of 'Padmasambhava' or of 'Amitabha Buddha'. If someone is more knowledgeable, he may take the name of 'Maitreya Buddha', and then start reciting verses from the Buddhist scriptures.

So whether one is a Buddhist, Jain, Hindu, Sikh, Muslim or even a Christian, the moment a person hears the word 'Almighty', he remembers his respective religion and its scriptures, thus sullying the portals of his mind. The word 'Almighty' has been reduced to a mere word!

For you God is not a living 'Truth'. It is merely a word; and you decide which language this word – God – should belong to! You want to make a choice of scriptures too. You are happy with that; you don't even want to hear anything else.

A long time ago, a satsang (discourse session) was organised in Kanpur. The gentleman who invited me there was associated with a temple as well as a gurudwara. One day the satsang was held in a temple and the next day in a gurudwara. After the first day's satsang, the organisers of both the satsang committees made a request: 'Please give more time to us. Bring her again to our satsang'. But I had only six days. How was one to accommodate both? So it was decided that the morning satsang would be held in the temple, and the evening one at the gurudwara. During the gurudwara satsang, I would speak in Punjabi, and during the temple satsang I would speak in Hindi. Naturally I would discuss the teachings of the 'Guru Granth Sahib' while sitting in the gurudwara, and while in the temple, I would discuss the verses and principles of the Gita and the Upanishads.

Consequently, a debate arose in the whole of Kanpur; people started wondering who I really was! There was something wrong they felt! Which party did I belong to? Was I a Sikh or a Hindu? 'Who is she?' was the constant refrain. When the Sikhs heard me, they felt that nobody had discussed Sikhism with such depth and conviction till then; this is what they felt at that time. When I sat in the temple, Hindus were thrilled listening to my devotional songs and discourses. Then a secret meeting was held between the two committees and they asked each other, "Who is she? If she is a Hindu, she should stay in the temple and need not come to the gurudwara. And if she is a Sikh, then why does she go to the temple?"

By the sixth day, the problem arose that those who got attached to me began coming along wherever I went. As a result you could see Sikhs with their swords and turbans in the temple. Imagine! Orthodox Sikhs sitting in a temple – it seemed so odd and in the gurudwaras, staunch Hindus with saffron marks on their foreheads were sitting and listening to me!

This whole episode was given a political colour. At last I was questioned directly: "You may please clarify who you are? There is a lot of confusion; a fight may erupt or a riot may take place."

I asked in amazement, "Why a riot?"

"No, you don't know but plans are being made to draw

swords. If you happen to be a Hindu, you will be stopped from speaking in the gurudwara, as you do not have the right to speak there. Only a Sikh can preach to the Sikhs and only a Hindu can preach to the Hindus. Who is this person trying to preach to both? What sort of politics is going on? Who are you? Please speak for yourself!"

"If you really want a reply, I am neither a Hindu nor a Sikh." They said, "Then are you a Muslim? Now it is clear, you are a trouble-maker."

"If it comforts your heart, then know that I am not even a Muslim."

They asked again, "Then who are you?"

I said, "In this entire world, more than 350 different religions are practiced. You may not even know the names of all of them. Even if you name all of them one by one and ask me if I belong to any of them, my answer will still be in the negative; I will still deny it."

"But then who are you? You are neither a Hindu, Sikh, Muslim, Jain, nor Buddhist; neither a Gnostic nor an Agnostic. Then who are you?" I said, "The only answer I have is that I am love; wherever I find the fragrance of love, that place is mine own."

People befriend each other on the basis of caste, religion and state. If you go abroad or even to South India, the moment a Punjabi sees another Punjabi, he is happy. 'Wow! I am a Punjabi, you too are a Punjabi!' Or 'I am a Sindhi and you are a Sindhi as well!' And when abroad, they feel happy saying, 'I am an Indian, and you too are Indian!' They feel good, they feel happy.

In the same way, I am only 'love'; wherever I find love, those people are mine and I belong to them. And so I am a Hindu, a Muslim, a Sikh, a Buddhist, a Jew and a Jain. I am everything; I am all of these because I am none of these. Till such time as one feels he is 'something' or 'someone', he can't be everything. But when he becomes nothing, then he becomes 'everything'. I am everything!

Sufi is love, just love. This love existed even before the world came into existence; it will be there after the world perishes, and it is present even today. Someone once asked, "When did the Sufi religion come into being?" If we consider the history of Islam, then I would say that Sufism began with Prophet Mohammad.

It is said that in the year 610 A. D., Mohammad Sahib stayed in a cave on a hill named 'Hira' and worshipped God there. It should be kept in mind that Prophet Mohammad was born in a tribe of idol worshippers. It is believed in Hindu mythology that there are 33 crore deities. I sometimes feel like asking who these deities are; if not 33 crore, tell me the names of at least one crore! Please teach me something as I would love to learn and acquire knowledge! If you come across a fundamentalist Hindu some time, do ask him this question. But you must ask in all humility and without sarcasm, for this is no joke. But ask you must: Who are these 33 crore gods and goddesses!

Well, idols were also worshipped in the tribe where Mohammad sahib was born. Every man had made an idol for himself. Hundreds of idols were kept at a common site, which was like a temple, and people used to worship them. But Mohammad Sahib would go and sit in his cave in solitude and think. He would ask himself, "Who is God? Where is he?"

Just remember one thing: we think with our mind. How much does a mind know? We get to know this world through our sense organs – we see it with our eyes, hear with our ears, smell all the scents through our nose, taste with our tongue, and touch and feel with our hands – yet, if someone questions you about the visible world, it will be difficult for you to answer! How much do we really know about the world we live in? Very little indeed! I ask you, how much knowledge do you have about the body in which you live?

Forget about the body, let us talk about the brain. There are hundreds and thousands of neurons and cells in the left and right hemispheres of the brain; because of them our body is able to function. But what happens when someone's blood pressure shoots up? What happens inside when some nerve gets so tense that a man becomes paralysed, and is unable to even speak?

What actually goes wrong? We do not know anything about our own body; just as we do not know anything about the visible world. How then can we know anything about the Almighty who is invisible? It is very difficult to understand this; it is a huge mystery!

The Prophet was not satisfied with what he saw and what was happening around him. Disappointment and inquisitiveness were the motivating factors that drove him to solitude, and for hours he would sit alone in contemplation. Suddenly one day something happened in this solitude – some vital energy awakened within him. This was such a tremendous experience that his whole body started trembling; he was frightened. He came back in that frightened state and covered himself with a blanket. His wife asked, "What happened?"

He replied, "I don't know. Either I have been possessed by some hidden power or maybe I have become a poet. But I do not really understand what is happening."

A very unusual experience – his whole body was trembling and burning. It is said that the advice his wife gave him at that moment was very precious. She said, "Just stay here; do not go out; do not even talk to anybody yet. Whatever is happening is for the good." She knew her husband well – he was a noble person, a helper of the needy, and he had a pious and pure heart. I have described the quality of karamat – one who gives and derives joy from giving, and also of khushu – one whose heart is pious and pure; one who is humble and devoid of ego.

Mohammad sahib's wife said, "Do not worry, there must be some mystery in whatever is happening, so whatever is happening is happening for the good." It is said that in a span of 23 years, the verses of the Quran Sharif were nazil, or they descended upon him – that is, they revealed themselves to him.

Again the same thing comes to light: there is a mythological belief that an angel by the name of Gabriel used to come and impart knowledge to Mohammad Sahib. One has to find a way to relate the occurrences of the past, and it is a fact that if things are not explained in this manner, man would not be able to understand what had actually happened. The word 'nazil' means

39

'to descend'. It is believed that the verses of the Quran 'descended' on Mohammad Sahib.

Here another thing needs to be understood: the persons, who go through these profound experiences, have their own mind and understanding. Whoever Mohammad sahib discussed these verses with, lacked the kind of understanding required to grasp them in totality. So only that much was conveyed to them, as much as could be understood by them.

When someone special goes through such an experience, others cannot understand by merely looking at him that he has had such an experience. Whatever happened, happened inside the cave of Hira. Whatever occurred, occurred within the heart of Mohammad sahib. But other people started noticing the change in attitude, behaviour and mannerisms of Mohammad sahib.

Now this kind of incident has occurred elsewhere with other people too. What happened to Guru Nanak sahib's inner self when he had enlightenment, is known only to him. Those around him have only documented his behaviour, his way of talking, his manner of worshipping, eating, rising, etc. This is how all the customs of various religions come into being.

In my view, Mohammad sahib and Guru Nanak went through the same experience. There was no difference in the experience of enlightenment that took place within them. But their personalities were different, their language, life style and environment were different too – vastly different. Fighting wars, killing and dying were the norm in the time of Mohammad Sahib. That is why the various clauses of the Quran Sharif carry instructions on the way one is supposed to behave in civil society. Man has been advised to stay away from sin – those who sin will be punished and those who don't will be rewarded.

Similarly, it has been written in the eighty thousand mantras of the Vedas, that if you sin, such and such a thing will happen to you; if you perform virtuous acts, certain other things that will happen to you are listed out. The methods of performing virtuous acts are written therein. If you want to perform a sacred fire ritual – or a yajna – an elaborate ritual to appease the deities

– then you need to follow certain principles. And if you commit sins, then there are seven hundred different types of hell that are described as punishment.

There are unimportant descriptions aplenty in there too. But these unimportant things needed to be told because Mohammad sahib lived amongst people whose level of comprehension was low. It is just like having to explain to a child or answer his question. A child asked, "Where have I come from?"

The father replied, "You have come from your mother's stomach."

"Where have you come from?"

The father said, "I have come from my mother's stomach."

"So then where did mother come from?"

"She came from her mother's stomach."

The confused child then asked, "Everybody comes from some stomach or the other, then who's was the first stomach? I came from mother's stomach, mother came from grandmother's stomach and grandmother came from her mother's stomach. Then who was that first woman from whose stomach we all have come?"

Finally the father asked, "Why do you want to know?"

Then the child revealed his reason, "I just want to ask, why all of us have been thrown out? Why weren't we allowed to stay inside? Now we have to go to school! We were better off inside."

If one has to explain to a child, the complete process of a child's birth, it would be very complicated and difficult. The level of understanding of the people who lived around Mohammad sahib wasn't very high. That is the reason why very little has been documented about whatever was achieved by Mohammad sahib. And whatever has been written is about the norms of society, about its rules and regulations – regarding marriage, behaviour in society, about brotherhood, trade and other such things. Everything about principles, rules and regulations is written down.

So now I can safely differentiate between Islam and Sufism. Those who understood what actually occurred in Mohammad sahib's life became Sufis, and those who simply followed the rules and regulations and the various norms of civil society as described by him, became followers of Islam. That is why it is said that Sufi is related to the heart; if you too had the amount of love as Mohammad sahib, then you too would be closer to Allah than any Muslim.

Rabia-al-Basra embarked on her first pilgrimage; the journey was long, difficult and tough. On completing that difficult journey, when she finally reached Mecca, seeing Kaba-e-Sharif, she said, "What my eyes are seeing is just a house made of bricks and stones. But my Lord! I do not want this concrete house of yours, I want you." What will I get from this house?"

But you are satisfied just seeing the house. A Hindu is content with the sight of a temple; a Sikh is satisfied at the mere sight of a gurudwara; the mere sight of a mosque satisfies a Muslim. One who is satisfied by seeing only the house made of concrete may be a religious person, but the one who asks for nothing but God is a Sufi – he is interested only in the resident and not in the building; he is concerned with the one who lives in the house and has no interest in the building.

Please keep this in mind: the resident of various houses is the same; though the appearance of the houses may differ, the owner remains the same. Just as I may have stayed in hundreds of homes ever since I got a physical form – somewhere for a few years, at others for a few months or even for a few weeks or days. If ever I narrate or write my autobiography, then maybe it will be known in how many houses I have lived. I changed houses, but 'I' didn't change. Is the house valuable or the person who resides within? In the same way, one who is concerned with the outer buildings and the scriptures is at best religious. But the one who is in constant search of, and is always anxious to meet the 'one' residing in the house – we call him a Sufi. So if we see from the point of view of Islam, the first ever Sufi was Mohammad sahib – he was the first one.

Sufism is divided into two branches. In one they first utter the name of the Almighty and then that of Rasool – God's messenger – this is a practice amongst Sufis – here I am talking of a Sufi and not of a Muslim. Similarly, there is a practice in Turkey and Iran in which whenever a Sufi settles down to a discussion, he will first remember God and then utter the name of Mohammad sahib. In Turkey, another name is remembered and that is of Hazrat Mevlana Rumi. After that they start whatever adulation they wish to perform.

There is yet another stream among Sufis who remember only God. Why? Why not Mohammad Sahib? They say: 'He who gave to Mohammad sahib will give to us too.' Among them are Al-Hillaj Mansoor and Shams Tabreez. Mevlana Rumi however, is not one of them; his worship begins with Allah's name and then he remembers Prophet Mohammad, and then the rest of his prayers begin.

Shams Tabreez and Al-Hillaj Mansoor were not of this mind. When asked why they did not remember Prophet Mohammad, they questioned in reply, "Does God talk only to apostles, prophets and Sufis? Will he not talk to us lesser men? Won't he talk to me? Remember, he is as much my God as he is of Moses; he is as much my God as he is Adam's or Prophet Mohammad's. Then why should I not talk directly to him?" This is the reason why these two do not utter anyone else's name.

I mentioned Mansoor earlier. He used to sing 'An-al-haq'. Haq means Truth and An-al means Just One. So An-al-haq means that there is just one Truth and that Truth is 'I'. What is required to start the sequence of reaching the top and climbing up to the zenith, is love. So do not darken your mind with mere words!

What difference does it make? How does it matter if someone offers his prayers in Hindi, Punjabi, Sanskrit, and Arabic or in Persian? Your prayers are mere words. Words! Just words!

The Sufi Baha-ud-Din was once asked, "How did you achieve God?" He said, "By illumining the heart. Learning the scriptures by rote only leads to darkening of the mind. On the path of Truth, I stayed away from words and I illumined my heart." "Illumined with what?" He answered, "With love."

So love is the rooh of Sufism. We have to live from the heart and not from the mind.

Remember, Sufism is not the path of knowledge – not in the least. Rather you will have to discard all the knowledge that your mind has accumulated. You will not really succeed unless you discard that rubbish. The knowledge that is filled in your mind is hollow, as demonstrated by the following story.

Once a pet shop recruited a young boy. A lady came into the shop and purchased a rabbit. She said to the shop owner, "My name is Mrs. Verma and I live in house No. 210, lane No. 5. Please deliver this rabbit at my address." She paid the money and went away. The owner of the shop told his new helper, "Son, will you take this to her house?" The boy replied, "Certainly, sir!"

"Alright! Take the van out, take this rabbit and deliver it to Mrs. Verma's residence."

So the boy took the rabbit and started off. After going some distance the van skidded as it was raining. While the boy was trying to prevent it from slipping further, it fell into a pit. As he was pulling the van out of the pit, the rear door opened and the rabbit ran off. On seeing this, the boy called out, "Go, my dear, how far will you go? The address is with me. Silly thing! He has gone without the address. How will he reach when the address is with me!"?

Now how is the rabbit bothered about the address? He is not interested in Mrs. Verma's house or even the lane in which she lives. But the boy had very painstakingly secured only the address and not the rabbit!

You too have only secured the addresses. Someone recites the Sukhmani Sahib – a religious scripture of the Sikhs; someone the Sunderkaand – a chapter of the Ramayana; another person remembers the Hanuman Chaleesa – a chant in praise of Hanuman, a Hindu god; yet another remembers the Quran Sharif – the Muslims' holy text. These are just addresses of God's house, whereas a Sufi is like the rabbit that has managed to escape. You can preserve the addresses and keep them with you!

I know a particular gentleman who has been reciting a sacred text every day for many years now. Well! That is very good and I don't oppose it. He reads it every day; early in the morning one can hear him recite:

Tum maat pita hum baalak tere
Tumhari kripa mein sukh ghanere

O Lord! You are our mother and father
We are thy children
We dwell in thy shade of bliss

He was reading it yesterday, two years back, and ten years back and even now he is reciting the same. So I asked him one day why it was that in so many years he hadn't been able to realise that God is both mother and father to us?

"Haven't you realised yet that remembering him gives the greatest of joy?"

He replied, "Yes, I know."

I asked him why he recited the text when he already knew. For how long would he be required to recite the same thing? Till he has learnt it by heart? And so he carries on with:

Charan saadh ke dhoy dhoy peeyo
Arap saadh ko apna jeeyo
Saadh ki dhoor karo ishnan
Saadh upar jaaiye kurbaan

Let's wash feet of sage and partake holy water
Let's offer our heart to the sage
I wish to bathe in dust of sage's feet
I wish to offer my life to sage

I asked again, "Then why don't you actually offer your life? Why are you still reciting?" He said, "If I stop reciting, then what do I do?"

Similarly, you too go on reading or reciting only for the sake of it. What good will it do you? You are not going to achieve anything this way, yet you continue to read; it has become a habit; it has become a disease. The whole day you just sit and read the scriptures. When are you going to search for the one you have been reading about? When will you start moving towards Him?

Remember, you will need a guide to move in His direction – that is a fact. The one whom we call satguru, i.e. the one who helps in our final liberation, is called a sheikh in Sufism. Now that we are talking about sheikhs, let me tell you about the way Sufis greet or extend salutation. One method is the same as ours, that of touching the head to the ground – it is exactly the same. But there is another very nice way of wishing – that of Turkish Sufis; it is not new and has been in practice for several years. Sufism is the 'ism' of love and of affection. When one falls in love, the heart feels pain and that is a must! One who does not have any feelings in the heart, does not really bear a heart in his bosom; it is a mere stone! One whose heart feels some vibrations, some beams of light emanating from within, should know that his journey has begun. And he in whose bosom these waves have begun radiating, what does he do? He puts his hand on his heart!

If your stomach aches, you put your hand on your stomach; you hold your head if your head aches; hold your hand if the hand hurts; hold your leg if the leg hurts; hold your knee if the knee pains, and put your hand on your eyes in case your eyes hurt. Similarly, what would he hold whose heart aches with love for the Almighty? Therefore the mureed (disciple) places his right hand on his heart and then bows his head. This is the salutation of the Sufi.

Someone once said, "I don't feel anything in my heart – no pain or desperation; not even a ray of light. Nothing! What should I do?" He was told to keep his hand on his chest and to try to find his heart. Maybe someday he will find a heart inside his chest. Put your hand on your chest and look for your heart, and also pray to God: "Where has my heart gone? Please help me find it. Unless I find my heart, how will I find the love in it?"

After keeping your hand on your heart, bow your head. Why? It is said that if you don't bow your head, your journey will not begin. Now listen to this carefully:

Jab khudi ko chhodega, tu hi khuda ho jayega
Har kadam rakhega jo, woh rehnuma ho jayega
Apne dil se gar jafa ko aur jabr ko chhod de
Ishq ki kashti ka khud tu hi mallah ho jayega

Once you leave your ego, you are God
Every step of yours will be ultimate destination
If you discard harshness and adultery from heart
Then you are the anchor of your life's boat

That is why the Sufi greeting requires that they place the hand on the heart and let the head bow down. Place your hand on your heart with the wish that His love is born in it. If that love already exists, then there will be such a yearning, that it will be impossible to not place the hand on the heart.

I'll search thee today
I'll search thee tomorrow
Through thick and thin
Through pain, through sorrow

I know not where to look
But I'm always at the ready
For my heart aches, body is drained
Yet spirits high and breathing steady

To realise this fact one needs to contemplate and to meditate. What is meditation? It is one thing to want to realise the Truth, but how does one get there? Here Sufis use another word – tareeqat, i.e. 'the right way'. For example, it is fine if you want to go to Delhi, but what is the right way to get there? How to go – walking, by scooter, by bus or by car? Someone said, "There is no way; there is neither a bus nor a scooter, nor even a car; even my legs are not able to move, but I still want to go to Delhi. Then how to reach Delhi?"

I will discuss this topic later. Right now we need to accept whether or not we have the characteristics required for becoming a Sufi: a pure and pious heart, humility etc. Once someone asked an esteemed Sufi, "How do I become humble?" He pointed his finger to the toilet of the shrine and said, "Go and keep cleaning it until I call you." Now if this person belongs to a good family and is well read, how would he feel if asked to clean other people's filth?

It is very easy to demand something, but if you are told the way to fulfill the demand, will you be able to accept it? Once a king went to a Sufi and said, "I too want to become a Sufi." The Sufi said, "Certainly, you must become a Sufi. But do you know that in order to become a Sufi, you need a Sufi's grace?"

The king said, "That is the reason why I have come to you; you are a Sufi. Please shower your grace on me so that I can become a Sufi."

"Alright! I will talk to you for some time, and if you are able to answer all my queries correctly, I will help you become a Sufi."

The king asked, "What kind of answers am I supposed to give?"

"You just have to say that you trust me. Whatever I may say, you just have to say that you believe me."

The king said, "This is not difficult at all." And so the conversation began.

"Come and sit in front of me."

The king sat down and the Sufi started speaking.

The first thing the Sufi said was, "I was there before Moses."

The king said, "I believe you."

"I was there before Jesus Christ."

The king replied, "I believe you."

"I was there even when you were born," said the Sufi.

"I believe you," said the king.

Now the Sufi said, "Your father was a poor farmer."

The king was annoyed, "You seem to have gone mad! My father was not poor and he was never a farmer."

Then the Sufi said, "Now you can go! No one can make you a Sufi."

He did not abuse him, did not say anything offensive; all he said was that nobody could ever make him a Sufi. As long as the Sufi talked about other things, the king said he believed him, but the moment he said something about his father, he was not able to accept it. When the king got up and started to leave, the Sufi said, "Ok, I will give you one last chance. Remain standing and respond to this one."

"I am a liar."

The king said, "I believe you."

"Now I can assure you that you can never be a Sufi," said the Sufi.

Everybody wants to reach the destination. Well, that is very good! But who will undertake the journey to reach the destination? And who will clear the obstacles on the path? You must introspect, you must sit in solitude. You don't have to find a cave for yourself like Prophet Mohammad – that is not required. It will suffice for you to go and sit in your inner cave of silence. When we close our eyes, it is as good as sitting in a cave. So you must sit in your cave and try to introspect. The first thing you have to do is find out how pure your mind is and wherever you find impiety, try to remove it. It is not very difficult to find for it is there in abundance.

Farid says:

> **Kale mainde kapade**
> **Kala mainda vesh**
> **Gunahi bharia mai phiran**
> **Log kahen dervish**

> I wear black and black is my being
> I have committed mistakes yet people call me a dervish

> **Farida je tu akl latif, kale likh na lekh**
> **Apande girebaan mein sar neevan kar dekh**

> If wise be thou
> From critiques abstain
> Introspect, look within yourself
> Refrain from putting blame

Once you identify the dross within, how do you remove it? The fact is – in fact it is a secret – that the moment you identify the dross, you are also shown the way out. Right now, even if you see the dross within, you feel your mind is polluted because of another's fault and not your own. We try to blame others: "I am not bad; someone created a situation in which I was forced to commit a wrong deed. I was never bad; I am not bad and I can never be bad." Do not rest your responsibility on others; own up to it. And if you evaluate objectively – being detached from your mind and keeping a watch on your mind as a mere witness – you will find every facet of your mind opening up to you. And as the veils lift, you will start coming out of them.

Nobody will fall into a pit knowingly with their eyes open. In order to fall into a pit, you need to be unconscious or have your eyes shut. Consciously, knowingly, nobody falls into a pit. You have to lose your awareness to fall down. Introspect consciously and with full awareness. Do not try to stop or control yourself. Do not make a conscious effort to think good thoughts; just let your mind loose. Sitting quietly in a solitary place, observe your mind and the flow of its thoughts without obstructing it. Do not control or repress it. Do not try to curb its thinking. Do not worry that you have come to the ashram to hear about Sufism and here your mind is wandering off into all kinds of thoughts! 'Oh no! Dear mind, please do not think of all these things': Do not try to rein in your mind like this.

Have you ever washed your clothes with your own hands? Clever, intelligent people always fold even dirty linen. But when they have to wash them, they open every fold. And when they wet the clothes and soap them, they first pay attention to the stained portions. The stains are given an extra scrub with a little extra soap. The rest of the garment is generally cleaner; it is usually at a specific place that it is dirty. But unless you spread the cloth, you will not be able to see the stain. Today I am giving you a task: just spread the cloth of your mind, stretch it and then try and locate all the stains on it. And if you are able to locate them objectively, then you may ask me how to get rid of them. You will have to identify the stains yourself; I cannot do it for you. Because if I do, you will say, "See, she is pointing a finger at me." I cannot commit this crime, so I assign the task to you. You make your confessions; I will not investigate or interrogate you. Try to find the stains yourself, and when you do find them, you may come and ask me. Someone said, "Should we ask in front of everyone?"

It is more beneficial to ask in front of others than in solitude. Why? Because when you ask before others, you get rid of the false sense of dignity and pride that you have built – your false ego will crumble. Everybody will hear you – at least all those sitting there at that moment will hear you. It is said that all are naked in the bath – then why do you want to hide your dirt in this community bath of the mind?

This experiment can be quite an experience. You should not only write down what you feel but also stand up and say it in the presence of others. You may wonder if I am trying to humiliate you. It is always better to be humiliated in your own eyes than before others. Reproach your mind yourself. I am not trying to make you feel guilty by pointing out how much dross there is in your mind. Not at all! Then why am I asking you to do this? I am doing this because the day you accept your shortcomings before others, you become free from the burden of this lie and this hypocrisy, and it is only then that you attain true humility. Remember, the mind plays complex games, and this exercise is necessary to free yourself of the complexities of the mind.

A man was travelling in a train. He said to the person sitting in front of him, "Brother, I have heard that people are robbed in trains these days. Thieves offer drugged biscuits to passengers and loot their luggage. One should not talk unnecessarily to strangers or accept eatables from them. So brother, where are you going?"

"Bombay."

"I am also going to Bombay."

After two minutes he took some biscuits from his bag and offered them to his co-passenger. "Would you like some?"

"Do you think I am mad?"

"I just asked…just in case you'd like some. After all, it is only polite to offer; it is good that you didn't accept, for it means that you are very intelligent and have understood things well. Now let me tell you another thing I have heard. When people fall asleep in the train, their goods are stolen. Even if you are in a reserved compartment, the moment you close your eyes…! Everybody is awake till around midnight, but after that sleep just overtakes one!"

Now the poor co-passenger started staring at his luggage. Though he was listening, his eyes were on his luggage. Having parted with this information, our man went to sleep. But the other gentleman could not sleep. What if this guy himself was a thief? Then he felt that if he were a thief, he wouldn't have said all that he did – yet somehow he felt uneasy and just did not manage to sleep. With great effort he kept his eyes open. He splashed water on his eyes and drank tea from his thermos flask as the danger period of twelve to four in the night arrived – a time when even great yogis may feel sleepy! And our friend sitting in front of him was fast asleep and happily snoring. Deep in his mind, he kept thinking that maybe this man was a decent fellow after all and that he unnecessarily doubted him. Then it occurred to him that even if he were not a thief, there could be other people on the train who were! So it was safer to keep awake!

Finally our friend woke up at around six o'clock, stretched himself gently like a maiden and said, "Thank you sir!"

"What do you mean?"

"Since you kept awake, my luggage was safe."

"What do you mean?" he repeated.

"Well what can I do? I always fall asleep on a train, so in the past my luggage has been stolen. Then one day I thought over it and got a novel idea. I decided to give this pep talk to the person sitting next to me. Then he would be unable to sleep and end up guarding my luggage along with his own. So that is why I am thanking you."

The gentleman was aghast at this revelation. 'Here I was thinking that he was a thief but he turned out to be a gentleman.' Then they reached Mumbai and while getting off the train, our man asked, "Brother, when are you going back to Delhi? I will book my ticket for the same day. It is difficult to find a gentleman like you these days."

If you have the slightest doubt that the person sitting in front is a thief, you will definitely be very cautious. If you know he is a cheat, won't you be on your guard? You have to find the thief living in your mind; you have to look for the cheat within you. You have to look for it, find it and guard against it.

Don't forget that you have to guard against your own mind. When you identify and locate the problem areas you are looking for, you can ask me what to do about them and how to rid yourself of them. The courageous ones will come forward and ask directly – even in the presence of others; even in a large gathering. Some of you, being first time aspirants and therefore unused to such brutal self effacing honesty, may be cowardly or may not muster up enough courage. Maybe you thought you would sit and enjoy being acquainted with Sufism, but here you find an inquisition in progress! Remember that in this court, you are the criminal, the judge, the lawyer and also your own witness; I am nobody. I will not pass judgment on anyone; I will not be an arbitrator because I don't pass verdicts on people.

CHAPTER 3

PAY THE PRICE OF BEING
A DISCIPLE

As long as the mind is alive, it is bound to suffer disorders and perversions. The mind is not new, it is millions of years old. It is only now that you have started gaining wisdom, but the seeds that have been sown in your mind are old. So it is foolish to expect the seeds sown over thousands of years to be destroyed in just a few days or months of irregular practice, and that too with the practice being restricted to a few hours in the ashram!

It is important to understand that your physical body may be twenty, thirty or forty years old, but your mind is millions of years old. The mind has been in existence since the world has been in existence. And ever since, it has been accumulating samskaras – subtle impressions – from which arise desires. Therefore it is not possible to rid the mind of impurities by just working on the mind's surface alone.

How do we rid ourselves of these aberrations? How do we get rid of sexual desires? How is it possible to be free of anger? How to get rid of doubts? There is only one solution: The very source of these thoughts – the mind must die! As long as the mind is alive, these aberrations will surface somewhere or the other, no matter how often you suppress them. This game will carry on for all eternity.

In Urdu, a disciple is called mureed and a master is called murshid. Mureed means one who has set out on a journey to kill his own mind. When the mind is dead, then what is left? The death of your mind will give you a new lease of life; this is not possible as long as the mind exists.

It makes no difference whether you fill the mind with knowledge or allow it to remain ignorant. A so-called knowledgeable person is as full of desires as an ignorant one. The amount of anger in an ignorant person is as much as in a person who attends satsang regularly. And those who attend satsang have another reason to be proud: they consider themselves superior to others by virtue of attending satsang! They feel they know more than others, understand more than others. This is even worse than being ignorant!

The root cause of all-evil is the mind, so we will have to kill the mind. In order to kill your mind, you must sing the prayer: "God, we no longer seek knowledge; we desire the death of the mind. We don't seek knowledge, for knowledge becomes an unnecessary aid to additional pride. We set out to kill our pride but end up increasing it. We don't want pride, but freedom from pride. And that is possible only if the mind dies."

Who will dare to perish one's ego in path of love
The one who will do so will reach the ultimate

Fana – to perish, is a word coined by Sufis. In English fana would translate as annihilation; in Hindi it would mean 'destroyed at the root'. That the mind perishes totally is the only cure for all its ailments. As long as the mind exists, its shadows – desire and passion – will exist. How is one to get rid of his shadow, how to achieve this remarkable feat? As long as the body exists, its shadow will be there. Similarly, as long as the mind exists, desires will be there; it is the nature of the mind to think. The very objective of the mental apparatus is to think – about what is, and even about what is not!

The mind does not have a stomach – it is a stomach! The stomach is just an organ, a very small one! In Hindi, the entire abdomen is called 'pait'. Beyond the stomach is the thirty-two foot long intestine! The abdomen comprises of other organs too: liver, pancreas, gall bladder and kidney. Amongst all these, there is a small organ that is the stomach. But the mind has no stomach, or you can say that the mind itself is a stomach; its form is infinite. The mind does not exist in any particular part of the body. Where is the exact physical location of the mind in the human body?

If you place your hand on your head, that is where the brain is; a neuro-surgeon opens the skull to perform surgery on it. You may put your hand on the chest, but there you have the heart on which a by-pass or transplant surgery is performed in which the entire heart is replaced. Then what is the mind; where is the mind? It is very difficult to pinpoint the physical location of the mind. Sometimes people end up saying that there is no such thing as the mind, or, they go to the other extreme and say that mind is everywhere – from head to toe the mind is everywhere. You call your entire body 'me', but if I ask you which part of your body is actually this 'me', you will not be able to answer. You cannot put your hand on any particular part of the body and say: 'this is the real me and the rest of the body is not me.'

Just as we call our whole body 'me', similarly, the subtle body of the mind is present throughout the physical body. The moon and stars, earth and sky, trees, rocks and mountains, all exist in the mind. Don't think of the mind as something small. All that is visible in this world exists in our mind. That is why your mind weaves a similar world while dreaming; the world of dreams does not have an iota of the reality of the physical world, yet it appears to be as real. The creator of this dream world is your own imagination, your own mind. Infinite is the power of the mind!

Do not consider the thoughts and desires arising in such a powerful mind to be petty. They are not petty – they are of tremendous significance. The mind has a much greater depth than that perceived by you at the superficial level.

If you have been to Himachal Pradesh, you would have seen the cedar tree. Some of them are a hundred feet tall, and for every hundred feet above the soil, a tree is a hundred feet below as well, for if it does not go so deep into the soil, it cannot rise up to that height. Similarly, whatever you know of your mind, it is, in reality, many thousand times that. This is why, very soon, the devices for controlling the mind, are also engulfed by the mind.

Listening! Listening to an able guru could have been an effective way of killing the mind, but you use the words of your guru only to strengthen the mind. Why else would someone feel the need to say that he has been attending my discourses since 1999? The way it was said, I was expected to be obliged! Who is keeping track? Who is counting the years? It is the mind seeking triumph! It is the mind keeping an account of the years!

This is why, at different times, masters have had to devise new methods; ones, which are different from the old methods of practicing spirituality – for you, start using the old methods only to strengthen your mind.

This is what happens when we give a medicine with sedatives to relieve a patient of a particular ailment. He is unable to give up the medicine even after the illness is cured because he has become addicted to it. Even though there was pain earlier, there is no pain now. Surgery was performed and a pain-relieving injection was administered. The post-surgical pain subsided in 3-4 weeks, but then the patient got addicted to the medicine. There is no problem now – no pain – but the patient continues to buy the medicine. When he suffered from a cough, cough-syrup was given along with a course of antibiotics. The cough was cured, but the intoxication and the sleep he got was so pleasant that it became impossible for him to give it up – even though he was cured!

A research was conducted to find out which medicines have the highest sales. The study revealed that those medicines that are not really required are sold the most – and that too over the counter! But the strange thing is that people who buy these medicines have no ailment at all! When questioned, one man admitted that he was buying them for himself. He does not take the medicines because he is suffering from an ailment, but because it gives him a good, intoxicated feeling! A new disease is born! When the medicine itself becomes the cause of an ailment, how does one treat it!

Sitting with the guru and listening to him could be a solution – in fact it is one – but you use it in such a way that it does not remain a solution anymore. Such is the thief that the mind is! It never confronts you face-on, but reveals itself in parts. That is why you see only half- truths. For example, people say: 'Gurumaa is very expensive.' This is true! Yes, I am very expensive! But then I have always said very clearly in open forums that those whose financial and economic needs are not taken care of go to gurus only to ask for money. It is their necessity! Such people do not visit them for spiritual purposes, but to acquire wealth – it is their need and their reality! I will never advise a hungry man or one who does not have a proper house to live in, to stop work in order to listen to me. That would be a sin! After all, who is religion for? What is religion for?

This is like asking for whom poetry is meant? Who should be interested in listening to classical music? Well! Only someone who has no worldly compulsions and has all the time in the world can sit and listen to poems or read a collection of Ghalib or Meera's verses!

But a person who has many obligations and is troubled by hunger has no interest in poetry. Even if you present him with a collection of Ghalib's poems, he may sell it as junk to get money for his next meal!

I will not go into much detail here, but would like to explain in brief. When classics like the Upanishads were written in India, society was very prosperous. Look at Krishna's era – children would break pitchers full of milk and curd just for fun! And today you have to buy even drinking water! If you buy a bottle of water and an unknown co-passenger says, "Sir, may I have some water?" you feel the pinch. "This is too much, I have bought this bottle for ten rupees and this person is asking for water!" But there was a time when people used to set up water dispensers for public consumption outside their homes. In this very country, if even a stranger knocked on one's door, he was welcomed as God. And today, if our own parents come visiting from the village, we look forward to their return for we just can't bear the expense!

The eras of Ram and Krishna were very prosperous. Though poor people like Sudama existed during Krishna's time, for every exception like him there were friends like Krishna who quietly turned his hut into a palace. Economically, it was a very prosperous period. And any society that is economically sound becomes a haven for the development of art forms such as poetry, sculpture, music and dance. It is not that I am allergic to the poor, but yes, I am allergic to poverty.

At the school level, there are a large number of students these days as the fee in government schools is very low – maybe just two rupees or even less. Sometimes even this is waived off! Therefore millions of children come to study in government primary schools. But by the time they come to the high school level their numbers reduce. At the college level, the number reduces further; in the university, every professor has just three or four students studying with him. Nowhere does it happen that there are a large number of students for M.Phil. or Ph.D.! There are never more than two or three students for Ph.D. Similarly, millions of students appear for the pre-medical examination, but just a few clear it and even fewer get admission. As the degree of learning gets higher, the number of candidates keeps decreasing.

My work is not like that of a government school – though when I come to your town, I do wind up setting up something akin to a government school – isn't it so? Perhaps ours is the only satsang where no special consideration is given to the rich; where there is no separate queue for businessmen. Here they are not even given a separate time for meeting – in my ashram, everyone is equal. Those who come early sit in the front rows and those who come later may sit at the back. Industrialists who come and sit with common people often ask, "Why isn't there any separate arrangement for us?" I say very humbly, "Forgive me! This is a government school – open to all. This is not a public school; it is just a government school without bias or prejudice!

Many people tell me – some directly and some indirectly – that other gurus charge some amount, when they come for giving discourses; they ask how much I charge? I tell them that I charge so much that they need not even bother to call me, for I ask for 'you' from you! Will you be able to pay up? Will you be able to give of yourself? If not, then don't call me!

Now that we are talking about this, let me show you how kind I am! In various places like Assam, Ganganagar, Rajasthan and Shimla, and to some extent in Mumbai too, the expenses were borne by us. I wanted to hold a satsang in Shimla so I went ahead and did so. When I felt like going to Ganganagar, I went there. I even held a satsang like this in Jalandhar! The religious benefactors of the whole city held meetings, wondering that if they had not given money, then who was organising the satsangs! And when they came and asked me, I said, "He who kept lengthening Draupadi's sari has arranged for this huge pavilion too!"

But when it is a question of a meditation camp, then I will not run a government school; there your ability – including your financial ability – will be considered. Till such time as your financial condition is sound, don't worry, for I am still close to you.

Why do those who are poor want to remain poor? If you get an opportunity and if you have the courage to do physical labour, then all doors will open for you. So first get rid of your laziness and understand your responsibilities. First get your own house in order. After that if you are unable to spare even a thousand rupees in a whole year – for your own spiritual progress – it just shows how incompetent you are!

Millionaires as well as municipal sweepers come to us to seek this wisdom. Sometimes people offer to sponsor the session for those who cannot afford to pay. But this is taken amiss, and the standard reaction is: 'What do you think we are? Lazy, good for nothing fellows? Young boys and girls collect money giving tuitions at home; they do not want Gurumaa to bear their expense. They insist on paying their own fee. If Gurumaa does not take donations, then why should the ashram pay for us?'

Even so, the donation that I make will not cover your registration fee. This is like potluck – everybody contributes so the entire expenditure is not one donor's responsibility. Everybody contributes so nobody can claim to have borne the entire expenditure. In that sense I am a true communist!

Another game played by the mind is of raising doubts; see how it renders the medium of the guru worthless! For several years, when I observed a life of poverty, not bothering about anything, people around me would say: 'Poor thing! What does she know.'

Then on a whim I decided I would let things be the way they are. Whatever is, is not mine, then why talk of something that is not mine? We are so ignorant of the medium that is the guru, that if a guru is poor, we wonder if he has any worldly knowledge. And if he is rich, then too we doubt his credentials!

Baba Bulleh Shah says:

Mein kithhe gujara jhat saiyan
Meri karta hi rakhey pat saiyan

How do I prove my worth to the world?
How can I make it be?
But God knows my true worth
I owe only him my loyalty!

The mind does not allow us access to the wisdom of the guru; it raises doubts here as well. If we expose the mind to wisdom, it becomes proud of wisdom: 'Who knows more than me?' Given a chance, you too would love to give discourses. The only things missing are a microphone, satellite cameras and a loving audience. It's just a matter of getting a chance; everyone suffers from the need to sermonise. We gain wisdom to overcome pride, but wisdom itself becomes a cause of arrogance. Let me tell you a strange thing: Shukhdev used to wear a single loincloth; he was a true Sufi. And Rishi Yagyavalk had ten thousand cows with gold-plated horns in his ashram! He was also a Sufi! If we talk of sensuality – he had two wives! You are unable to handle even one, while he had two! But Yagyavalk was a Sufi. Kabir was as much a Sufi as Yagyavalk, but look at Kabir's lifestyle! His lived a life of poverty. And as for Yagyavalk's lifestyle, it was so lavish that one may nurture a doubt, for he attained divine wisdom after a certain age!

What would you say of Shri Rama's guru Vasishtha? It is said that Vasishtha's ashram was extremely beautiful, with lovely gardens, dancing peacocks, pigeons sitting on branches and cuckoos singing melodious songs – a peaceful and secure atmosphere full of love. There were hills, streams and springs – all within the ashram premises.

Once when King Vishwamitra came to meet Vasishtha on

seeing the magnificence of the ashram, he forgot the purpose of his visit. Later he learnt that Vasishtha had a magical cow called Nandini, which fulfilled all requests given by one who served her.

Vishwamitra had more than ten thousand soldiers with him when he reached the ashram. On reaching there he told Vasishtha's wife that he wished to meet the guru, and asked when he should come. She said, "Please come now." Vishwamitra's Commander-General said, "Lady, the king has thousands of soldiers with him and it is already lunchtime. I think it will be better if we go back to our camp, and return after lunch".

But the sage's wife Arundhati said, "No! All of you please come and eat with us." When this was narrated to Vishwamitra he said, "Here is a sage, leading the life of a pauper, how will he arrange food for ten thousand people? Have you gone mad?" All the same, having said this, he still went out of curiosity. Lo and behold! What was served was not simple food but a variety of dishes including various sweetmeats. One would not find such food even in a palace! And even if one did, it would require elaborate preparation. He was amazed at this spectacle and wondered how it was possible. And then he learnt that Vasishtha had the magical cow, Nandini. From then on, Vishwamitra's only aim was to somehow get that cow. "What will this sage do with a cow?", he thought, "After all, all he has to do is remember God!" But Vasishtha is as much a Brahmveta (the one who knows his true-self) as Sanaka, Sanandana, Sanatan – again, who use to wear just loincloth!

When a person achieves wisdom and consciousness, his surroundings, attitude and mannerisms all become incomparable. If you try to understand his inner nature or inner state by his outer appearance, it will be impossible to do so.

A strange incident happened when Shukhdev's father said, "Go, and be blessed by the great king Janak" to Shukhdev who had completely renounced the world; this incident in the history of India has no parallel in the whole world. Usually it is the other way round – the renunciate guru has worldly disciples. But here the guru is a king living in a palace and the disciple is an ascetic. A doubting Shukhdev reached the king's palace, but as long as he harboured doubts, Janak refused to even look at him. He met him only after he was convinced of his suitability, after having tested him.

Here I would like to narrate another incident. There was a sheikh in Crimea whose name was Alhat-ed-Din. He was a famous sheikh and had several followers. The word sheikh also means teacher. One night he was sitting next to a pond when a Sufi by the name of Shams Tabreez passed by. Shams Tabreez wondered what this man was doing sitting next to the pond so late at night. So he went unto him and asked, "What are you doing? Who are you?" The man replied, "I am sheikh Alhat-ed-Din and I am meditating on the shadow of the moon in the water."

Shams Tabreez asked, "Do you have a crick in your neck that you find it difficult to look straight at the moon? The real moon is visible in the sky and you are looking at its shadow in the pond?" Alhat-ed-Din raised his head, and what did he see? The radiant face of Shams Tabreez in the moonlight... and his head bowed involuntarily in reverence. He was astonished and wondered why being a sheikh he was bowing to this man! And then he remembered the words of a wise man who had told him, "The moment you meet your master, your head will automatically bow in reverence."

Alhat-ed-Din got up immediately and said, "Will you make me your disciple?" One miracle had already taken place – his head had bowed involuntarily in reverence. Now the magnetism pulling his heart towards Shams was saying that this man was no ordinary man but a man of God.

He asked, "Will you make me your disciple?"

Shams said, "Yes, but only if you fulfill one of my requirements."

"Please order! What is your condition?"

"My condition is that you get a decanter of liquor and sit and drink with me in the open market! Only then will I make you my disciple."

On hearing this, Alhat-ed-Din was aghast. He was highly respected in society, and his knowledge and intelligence were acknowledged by the whole city – everyone called him sheikh. How could he possibly sit and drink shamelessly in the market place? After all, his religious beliefs were at stake!

Alhat-ed-Din said, "This is not possible. How can I do this?"

Shams Tabreez said, "Well, then you may go. You can never be my disciple. You are not worthy of being my disciple because my disciple has to be courageous. One who does not have courage can never be my disciple. You say you want to be my disciple, but you don't understand that when a Sufi asks you to go and bring liquor, he means the liquor of God's love. How can one who does not understand such a small thing be my disciple? What did you think? That you are pious and I am not! That your character is pure and mine is not! Go, you cannot be my disciple!"

I do not place any conditions before you. If I do, you too will fail like Alhat-ed-Din. That is why I say that you can call me your guru, but I will not say so even after the initiation ceremony. It is only when I feel that you have become worthy of being my disciple, will I say that you are my disciple. Till then I am only permitting you to call me your guru.

But Shams Tabreez did not allow Alhat-ed-Din even this much. Without pre-conditions, this relationship can neither be established, nor accomplished, nor carried forward. The fact is – as Sufis say – no guest will come and take a seat in the house of a person whose courtyard is not clean. Do you not clean your courtyard for your guests? Do you not clean your house for his sake? And God is a guest who is dearer than all guests. So unless and until you clean your mind for the supreme guest, He will not come or even step in, leave alone take a seat!

So this is the state of your mind! But your mind is unable to accept this reality. It is forever sinking in a quagmire of negativity. Sullied by this dirt, you can never become one with the glowing Almighty. Light and darkness can never exist together. Where there is light, there can never be darkness; where there is darkness, light cannot exist. And the mind is darkness personified! That is why it is said that you should free yourself of your mind.

Guru Nanak says:

Mann mare dhaat mar jaye
Bin mann muye kaise hari paye

The mind must perish
To kill all desires
Without killing mind
How can one attain God

Even when the body ages, the mind remains young; that is why an eighty-year-old does not feel ashamed molesting a ten-year-old girl! It is important to eat food when hunger strikes; but you don't think about food after satisfying your appetite. To tell you the truth, you will never think about food if you eat properly. A book on Ayurveda says that a single bite should be chewed thirty-two times before swallowing. Tonight when you eat, try to follow this rule. Take a bite, chew it thirty-two times and then swallow it. If you do this, the food you eat will become so smooth and liquefied, that your body will digest it very easily; your health too will improve.

The problem is that you are unable to concentrate on your food as much as required because you are impatient. You feel so hungry that you neither chew nor eat – you simply swallow your food. And because you do not eat properly, the desire for food remains unsatiated even after a meal!

This topic needs to be elaborated on, but I will deal with it in detail later. Similarly, for a person who has lived his sexual life with contentment and concentration, the physical act becomes like food that is eaten properly – contented, the desire does not resurface for long.

All those who have experienced the union of man and woman with love, and not with beastly passion, are contented. But the one who tries to fulfill only the physical needs of the body, will never reach a state of contentment. Somewhere it boils down to the fact that the relationship of love with your spouse was never

65

grounded. So all that you had was a physical relationship, and a relationship that is only physical never satisfies the hunger of the mind. If someone eats mindlessly without actually tasting the food, he will feel the desire to eat every two or four hours; he will also feel like eating a lot. The same is true for sex.

Shri Ram loved his wife Sita dearly. The truth is that where a swayamwara is held, the woman is given a chance to select a man of her choice. Much before the swayamwara, Ram and Sita had made a commitment to each other in the royal palace of King Janak. Their hearts had united and they had accepted each other in their lives. Sita even prayed for him in the temple of the royal garden, though he had not come there as royalty – and the swayamwara was for royalty only. Even so, Sita prayed for the man she had seen that day to be her husband.

During the swayamwara ceremony, Ram was the only one who managed to break Shiva's bow, and having fulfilled this condition laid down by King Janak, he married Sita. Their hearts had already united with love even before their marriage took place. With their marriage, not only did their bodies unite but they became one with each other. They were fulfilled with each other.

When they were staying in the forest, they did not live as man and wife. Ram had told Sita that they would observe celibacy in the forest and she had agreed, saying that it was enough for her to be with him: 'I have no physical needs that can be fulfilled by union only. Your proximity is enough for me. Being able to see you and serve you will give me joy and happiness.'

During their stay in the forest, the demoness Surpnakha came to Shri Ram in the guise of a beautiful woman and proposed to him. Her purpose was to establish a physical relationship, but he refused saying that his wife was with him and he did not need anyone else. Inspite of seeing deep emotions, love and surrender in the extremely beautiful woman Surpnakha, Ram said, "No, in this life my wife is my only companion. Apart from her, I do not belong to anyone. You are very beautiful and have deep love for me; and even though my father married thrice, I cannot marry you. The reason is that I am contented in my marriage."

If sex is devoid of the tinge of love, the mere act of sex can never give satisfaction to the mind. Our mental state is always aware of its sexuality. Even if it feels satiated for sometime, after a while desire will arise again.

Now, what is the way out of this muddle? Here is an aphorism and an incantation for you. The aphorism is to be aware of the mortal nature of your body as well as the ephemeral reality of your life. As you go into the depths of this thought process, you will realise that not only can the desire for sex be overcome, but also the hunger for food.

Love! Divine love! A spark of divine love kills all the desires of the mind. It puts an end to all the endeavours of the mind. Remember that you are asked to fill your being with His name, and not to just repeat it. Establish His name in your heart; become His devotee.

Who is a mureed? One who has managed to conquer and kill his own mind. To kill your mind, the best method is to think of your body as being lifeless. Look at the perishable nature of this world and contemplate on it.

**Farida garv na keejiye
uncha dekh aawas**

**Aaj kaal bhoyen letna
Upar jamey ghaas**

Farida don't be egoistic for your bigger house
A day would come when you will be under the ground

The day is not far when you will be buried in the earth and grass will grow on you. With the passage of time, your tombstone will break off; someone might walk away with some part of it, then who will know that a human being was buried here?

Once I had gone to Kolkata and stayed at someone's house. It was quite warm at night so I opened the window. The hostess came and said, "We never open this window." When I asked why, she said, "Just turn around and see." When I looked I found there was a Christian cemetery outside. She said, "We are scared. Even if the wind blows from the cremation ground, it seems all the dead are blowing at us. We just don't open this window." I said, "Don't worry, living people are scared of the dead, but one who is already dead is not scared, so don't worry."

Those who are alive are scared of the dead. But to tell you frankly, why be scared of the dead? One should be scared of the living! Beware of the living man! A dead person is just dead. You feel scared of the dead because of the horror movies that you have seen or scary novels that you have read, which show the dead rise at night to haunt you. You feel scared because of the stories that are there in your mind. Otherwise, why fear the dead?

A famous director of Indian cinema by the name of Tulsi Ramsay once came to meet me in a satsang in Mumbai. He heard me with great faith and became devoted to me. He finally managed to reach unto me after a great deal of effort and told me that he specialises in horror films. I said, "Well, then I am your biggest business rival, because I teach people to be fearless. Your job is to scare and my job is to rid people of fear." He said, "That is precisely what I have come to learn from you – how to become fearless and secure."

Why fear the dead? One should not fear the dead. Instead, it is prudent to fear the living, because you never know the hands that salute you today may even strangle you tomorrow! History is a witness to this: human beings have killed many Sufis. We need not go far, for the person who had Jesus killed was none other than his own disciple; he sold his master's life for twenty coins – for a mere twenty gold coins!

It is believed that Jesus lived in the forest with twelve disciples. They had reached a stage where they all looked quite similar, sporting the same kind of clothes, long beards and long hair. No one could identify Jesus. Soldiers used to wonder how they would recognise him. Then this disciple said, "Do not worry. I will go and kiss my master's cheek so you will know it is he"

Jesus knew this was going to happen. That night was one of great uncertainty; if he wanted he could have left that place and saved himself, but he stayed on. He thought to himself, "If this is

His wish, then why should I try to save my body? Why make an effort? O Lord! If you wish this body to die, then let it die." So when the disciple came close, he first held Jesus' hand and then hugged him and then he kissed him on his cheek. Jesus had tears of pity in his eyes. He said, "You are cheating me with this kiss. A deceit, wherein you embrace me, kiss me and then hand me over to my killers." This man was also a disciple but he became a killer. The disciple did not die himself, but became the cause of his master's death!

This is why it is difficult to work with a living guru and why we find the gurus who do not exist anymore to be great. Since they are not alive now, our vanity does not interfere. The fact is that accepting another man to be greater and more wise than oneself is more difficult than consuming poison. That is why man is hesitant to go to a living guru, and even if he does, he keeps raising doubts. Or else he goes to the guru but keeps deceiving himself as well as the guru.

Sufi has suggested ways and means to solve this crisis of the mind. The best of all these is zikr, which means to remember. We start the process of remembering with our tongue, then with our breath, and finally it becomes a part of our mental state. And then comes the turn of taking a great leap. A leap of what? Remember what I said earlier? Khushu, Karamat, Sijjat! But this is not going to happen in a single day. Learn to give – everyday. Practice humility – everyday. Everyday add fuel to the flame of love in your heart. Accept your sins, but not in order to feel guilty; you have to free yourself of the ignorance in which these sins are committed.

Sufism discusses what sin is; Moses lists them as: stealing, coveting another's spouse, lying, usurping, going back on your word, coveting another's property, etc. He listed ten sins and gave the 'Ten Commandments'. He said that whoever follows these commandments will be a good human being. Remember that Sufism is for human beings and not for beasts!

But Sufism went far beyond Moses; Sufis said that there is only one sin – not ten but only one, and as long as you have that in you, you are like a serial criminal. There is only one sin and only one crime – and that is unconsciousness! Lack of awareness is the only sin! If you discard unconsciousness, there is no scope for sin to occur. If you come out of this stupor, then there is no room for sin.

To get rid of this stupor, remembrance is suggested. What is remembrance? Zikr or remembrance is the use of various incantations or mantras. In Arabic, there are ninety-nine names of God. If I ask any Muslim to repeat all the ninety-nine names, they will be in a fix! Actually there are not ninety-nine, but nine hundred and ninety-nine names, just as the 'Vishnu Sahasranama' is a compilation of the thousand names of Vishnu. Guru Arjan Dev has also written a sahasranama, i.e. a thousand names of God.

Every word has a particular effect; every sound that emanates from a word has a specific effect. We can produce love, anger, greed, separation, pleasure, happiness and pain etc., in anybody's heart, merely through words or their sounds. If I speak the language of music, flat notes awaken feelings of love, empathy, anguish and of separation, etc. The vibrations of each word have their specific impact, and to feel this effect, zikr is used.

What is remembrance? It is not the repetition of words or sounds. Zikr is the entire process of experimenting with sounds, and feeling and understanding their impact and effect on our consciousness. This is the first lesson of zikr! Let me tell you again: zikr is done from the heart. The remembrance has to be from the heart and the heart has to be pure. It does not matter how much impurity you have accumulated, but when you set out on the path of zikr, at that moment your heart should be pure. Temporary virtuosity does arise within you, when sitting face to face with the guru, and we will make use of this purity and virtuosity. The chant is 'Hu'. 'Hu' means: It is the one. Which 'one' are we talking about? Now let us see the definition: One who is truth, one who is bliss, one who is consciousness, one who is all-pervasive, and one who is the king of the world, the one who is in the beginning and in the end, the one who is in the now.

It is not 'Allah Hu', but only 'Hu'. If I say 'Hu' in Sanskrit, it would mean existence; it means: Who, how and what is? When the mind is involved then there are several definitions, but the fact is that 'Hu' means whatever 'is', whatever exists! Allah brings Islam into it; Ram brings Hinduism into it, and if you say Waheguru, then it involves Sikhism. So keep all religious labels aside! Remember, a Sufi doesn't say 'Allah Hu' – he says only 'Hu'.

There is a particular style of saying 'Hu'. You don't have to say it from your throat – it should come straight from the diaphragm. In simple terms, it should come from the navel. The sound should have depth; it should not come from the throat but from the navel. To raise the sound from the navel, to lift it straight from the stomach, you will have to take a deep breath, otherwise you will not be able to say it properly.

Then, after taking a deep breath, you are not to release it in one go; you have to exhale twice in short bursts. It should be a combination of a loud aspiration and a deep breath. You will know the difference when you try to utter the word 'Hu' with a loud and deep breath.

[Gurumaa showed us the difference by demonstrating it, first bringing the sound from her throat, and then from within the stomach. You have to inhale through the mouth, and then while exhaling from the mouth you have to chant the word 'Hu'. She again brought the sound from the throat and said, "This sound is coming from the throat. You can keep doing it this way, but you are not going to gain anything from it].

Before starting zikr you must pray and thank God for the opportunity to learn the secret practice of Sufis. Someone said, "It just occurred to me how much effort Sufis have made to show us the right way." Some other time I will tell you, how much effort I had to make – in spite of being in the position of Gurumaa – to earn the wealth that I am handing over to you.

In spite of my position, I spent five weeks in Turkey – an unknown country – where I did not know a single word of the language; with an unknown sheikh about whom I knew nothing and who did not know my language. I searched for him and spent time with him. I laughed to myself: 'I have become a student once again.' It was necessary to stay close to the sheikh in order to learn their secrets; to achieve this closeness, it was necessary to stay there.

It became easy to learn their secrets in a short time by staying in close proximity to them, as the sheikh soon realised that the person sitting in front was a Sufi herself. That made things easier, as one Sufi communicates with another with ease. You will learn about my efforts in attaining this wealth for you, if at some point of time I present my memoirs in a book.

Each day new methods are devised to bring you out of your state of mental unconsciousness. You are fortunate to have this opportunity to learn the art of zikr. Close your eyes, take a deep breath, and pronounce the word 'Hu' while exhaling – remember that the sound has to come from the navel – from deep within your stomach – and not from your throat. Before starting zikr, pray to the Almighty.

CHAPTER 4
AT THE FEET OF THE MASTER

Many people do not understand what I have said so far about zikr, and are often found doing exactly what they are told not to. What makes you think it is so easy to understand? It is not easy at all! Had it been so, you wouldn't be in the state you are in! Learn to give time, and the best way to devote time is to read carefully and attentively.

Ganesha has the head of an elephant – it is a symbol! The elephant's big ears and small mouth indicate that we should hear more and talk less. An elephant's ears are really large! Because human beings do not have big ears, the elephant's head has been selected as a symbol of Ganesha. The idea is to make man understand that we should learn to hear more and talk less. But one who talks more and listens less, is a lesser animal than even an elephant. So listen more and talk less; this too is a way of practicing meditation, a means of accomplishment.

Many people complain about their anger. They talk with rage, quarrel, and thus make their environment tense. This tension will disappear automatically if you reduce talking. If you keep quiet, how will anybody be bothered by your fury, pity or affection? When you grumble, abuse others or misbehave with them, then they are upset. That is but natural! But if you just keep quiet, you will not cause any trouble to the other person. And if you remain quiet, the other person has nothing to respond to!

Another thing you have to understand is that in zikr you can't break the chant for even a moment, and that is why you have to breathe only through the mouth and not through the nose. A small gap occurs in the chant if you breathe from the nose and then say the mantra.

Do not think that this is as simple as the mystical chant of 'Om'. Do not think that just because you know how to recite Om, you will be able to do this too – do not make that mistake. While doing pranav, we breathe in through the nose, and it is only while exhaling that we pronounce the sound of the word Om. But we are not practicing Om here. Here we have to breathe in through the mouth and simultaneously make the sound from the mouth. There has to be a continuous chain of this utterance; there is no break in between, at least a discernable break. You may say that there is a break of 0.1 second; otherwise it is a constant, continuous, uninterrupted utterance of the mantra.

During this chanting, any other action is strictly prohibited. Crying, laughing, moving… any type of action is wrong. Some people stand up – that is wrong! Only if you follow the way faithfully will you tread the correct path. If you try to do things your way, then you will not succeed. First you have to become worthy of learning this technique, and therefore you are not permitted to perform any other action. Even if the body wants to, you are not allowed to move while practicing 'Hu'. Whatever energy is generated by the utterance of 'Hu' needs to go straight inward; we can't allow it to go towards the body. If any action takes place in the body – like crying or moving – then some fraction of the energy generated is diverted towards that activity. But we do not have to allow our energy to flow outward; whatever energy is generated – all of it – has to be collected and sent inward.

Try to understand it thus: Have you ever seen a flautist? While playing a clarinet or a saxophone, or any wind instrument for that matter, we need to blow into it with one end of it inside the mouth. But a flute is only brought up to the lips – it is not placed inside the mouth; it just about touches the lips! There is a certain way of blowing into it – the lower lip is gathered up a little, and the upper lip is rounded and then lowered from one side; then we breathe into it.

Remember, the flute is not actually played; we breathe into it. When a flute or a piece of bamboo is breathed-into properly, only then do musical notes emanate from it. It would be incorrect to say that a person plays the flute. If a flute player himself says that he plays the flute, it means he is a novice and has no understanding of the instrument. A flute is not played; it is only brought up to the lips, lightly touched and then breathed into. As the air goes in, musical notes start coming out.

It is not known who first invented the flute – Shri Krishna's era is said to be five to five and a half thousand years old! The flute became famous with him alright, but he did not create it; it was already there.

Sufis too have a musical instrument, which is called ney. It is not known who actually created this instrument – some Sufi made it. Like the flute, the ney too is brought to the lips and the player just breathes into it. So it is said that the ney is not played; when your breath is regulated, the ney will produce the right sound. And when will the breath be regulated? When the heart is pure! The day your mind will be quiet, your breath too is regulated and orderly, that very day the ney will automatically start playing the right notes. If you ever tell a neyzen (ney player) that he plays the instrument very well, he will touch his ears and say, "No! I just hold the ney – it plays on its own."

According to yoga there are seven chakras or vortices of energy in the human body: mooladhaar, swadhishthaan, manipurak, anahat, vishuddh, agya and sahasrar. Just as a human body has seven chakras, the ney has seven apertures. Where are these chakras located? If we see from the point of view of anatomy, they are located in the backbone; if we see the physiology, we will not find any such chakras!

If you dissect a dead body, you will not find any chakra in the backbone. The chakras are just subtle channels that are in close proximity of the nerves ida and pingla, present in the backbone. These nerves are said to be present in your subtle body. The entire content of the seven chakras is said to be contained in these two nerves; and the chakras are said to be located within these two nerves.

All the chakras are closed. The survival of the human body is managed at the level of the mooladhaar chakra. All the functions of your body are connected to this fundamental chakra. When a seeker manages to open the mooladhaar chakra with the help of yoga and pranayama, the life-power that awakens is called kundalini. When the kundalini awakens inside the mooladhaar chakra, it is like a coiled snake awakening! Once awake, the snake slowly raises its hood. The snake has a particular characteristic: when completely aroused, it can balance itself straight up on its tail, like a stick.

Similarly, inside the mooladhaar chakra the kundalini power lies dormant. A devotee awakens the kundalini by pranayama or by other means. In yoga we are taught about yama, niyama, asana and pranayama, and while practicing these we are asked to concentrate on the chakras. When the mooladhaar chakra is activated, one experiences very special sensations. The moment the kundalini stirs, the body starts experiencing various types of kriyas.

When this awakened power reaches the swadhishthaan chakra, it gives bliss of the highest order, somewhat like an electric current running through the body. Our whole being becomes absolutely calm. If the kundalini rises further and goes up to the manipurak chakra, then it is possible that it may even go back down; but if it once reaches the heart or the anahat chakra, then it does not ever revert to a lower level.

A person whose anahat chakra is open, reaches a state of complete composure and becomes resolute, calm and unperturbed. Nothing in the world can cause any change in his state of mind – it becomes completely resolute, firm and tranquil! If the seeker continues unfailingly in his practice even after the opening of the anahat chakra, then the kundalini reaches the throat or vishuddh chakra. The voice of one, who manages to open the vishuddh chakra, is astonishingly sweet and charming. His speech develops the power of manifestation – whatever he says comes true.

Moving up from the vishuddh chakra, the kundalini reaches the region of the forehead and there it opens the chakra located right in the centre – the agya chakra. The body, mind and senses of a person whose agya chakra is open, follow all his commands and he becomes the master of the senses.

And finally when this power reaches the sahasrar chakra in the head, then a state of Samadhi (pure consciousness, where mind and its modalities, cease to function) is achieved. Yogis and ascetics in India have talked about this journey of the seven charkas – from mooladhaar to sahasrar – and have also described the methods to undertake this journey.

In Turkey, I was surprised to see that the ney made by a Sufi is nothing more than a stick of reed! Just like a bamboo stick, they have a reed that is straight and long, and has a small part at the tip called bashper, which is usually made of ivory, but these days it is also made of plastic. I realised that the ney with an ivory bashper has a sound that is distinctly different from the one with a plastic one.

When I met the dervish who played the ney, I asked him about his instrument. I said, "What is ney." He started talking and I started smiling; remember he was talking in Turkish. He said, "This instrument – the ney – was invented sometime around the 11th century. The ney is like our body – there are seven chakras in our body and there are seven apertures in the ney. Man's chakras are closed; ney's are all open."

The sound of the ney is not called a 'sound'; it is called the ney's 'crying'. The ney cries! And why does it cry? It cries because someone cut it and separated it from its family. It was doubly pained when its insides were cleared with a hot iron. The first pain was of separation from its family; the second was when an hot iron was inserted into it. When these seven holes were made in its body, it was hurt for the third time. Then bashper was fixed on its mouth. The ney is open from both ends – it is not closed; there is no obstacle anywhere.

Once the ney was ready, it reached the hands of the player. Now here the Sufis changed the legend and said that the ney was placed on the lips of Prophet Mohammad. Here in India, we say on Krishna's lips; there they say the lips of the Prophet. When the Prophet said 'Hu..u u u' into it, the sound that emanated from the other end was the song of Allah's name. Whose lips were they? Those of Prophet Mohammad, the first Sufi of Islam. Now, we don't say that he blew into the ney, we say that he spoke the word 'Hu' into the ney.

'Hu' is not a word, but the sound created while exhaling – it is just the sound of the breath coming out of your mouth. When you exhale with your mouth slightly open, the sound that is produced is 'Hu'. That is why if you say 'Hu' from the throat, it won't be effective; we do not have to use the throat at all. Take a deep breath through the mouth, and exhale only from the mouth.

Remember that while breathing out the sound should come not from the throat but from the diaphragm. The singers in the cassette have been trained earlier. I have not brought this tape from Turkey; this entire recording has been done here in India itself. First they were taught and later the recording was done in a studio. The mike being extremely sensitive, it caught every little vibration of the throat, so we had to be very careful while recording. The mike was brought very close to the mouth and then the sound of 'Hu' was breathed; that is why the sound is absolutely pure and clear.

But again, they are not speaking the word 'Hu' into the mike; they are only exhaling and the sound of 'Hu' was produced on its own. The 'Hu' sound comes out on its own – there is no need to express it – it expresses by itself, automatically. You don't do it, it happens.

I will discuss 'Hu' again later, but before that let me tell you that you must take the maximum advantage of the opportunity, which has come your way. Don't analyse; whatever you are learning and whatever I am telling you, is something I have never told anyone before, so don't make the mistake of thinking that you already know all of this. If you accept this with innocence and an open mind, you will be able to adopt it like a true seeker; you will be able to understand it better. Here the purpose is not just to understand intellectually, but also to brighten your dampened hearts.

Ships stationed at the seashore are tied, they are anchored. The boat on the riverbank is not left loose, it is always tied so that if a storm arises the boat does not drift. Similarly, the boat of your life should not drift in the river of time. Therefore you are being taught how to tie the rope tightly and how to secure the vessel of your life.

Farid says:

Beda bandh na sakio bandhan ki bela
Bhar sarvar jab uchhale, tab taran duhela
Hath na laiyu kasumbhade, jal jasi dhola
Ik aapi ne patli, sah kere bola
Dudha dhani na aavai, phir hoi na mela
Kahe Farid saheliyo, sahu aala esi
Hansu chalsi dumda, ae tan dheri thisi

When it was time to tie the boat you left it open
When the sea would be choppy then swimming
would be difficult
You won't catch hold of anything
World is just like a wild flower –
here you touch here it crumbles
I am so weak and powerless how can I call thee
When you will get old will you attract then?
Thus says Farid now is the time beautiful lover is calling
Be a swan and know that your days in world are limited

In Sufism God is considered as divine lover or husband and Sufi is the longing loving wife who has to win his heart. Farid says: 'My friend! Look, your lover is coming. Your lover is coming and your preparations are not complete yet! If you walk unsteady on the path of love, then not only will your body shatter to pieces, your journey will also not be completed – that is why you must not stagger. Your lover is calling you and you are still not ready! Just look at your state – you have become a skeleton! How will you please your beloved husband – God? Look at yourself, you have not even completed your make-up.'

Make-up? What make-up? Sufis explain: To please the beloved husband, a woman puts on make-up. Ornaments of humility should be worn; apply the bindi (mark on the forehead) of selfless service and adorn your feet with the alta (traditional foot decoration) of altruism. Add the chuda (bangles) of virtue. If you don't have these accessories, you can't please your husband! Farid says in Punjabi language: 'Sahu aala esi'.

The word 'aala' means very good or wonderful. Here 'sahu' means 'beloved' or 'husband'. The beloved is wonderful, better than the best, unique and incomparable. So this incomparable man's woman cannot be a commoner. Farid says: 'O my dear friend! In order to stand unto that inimitable beloved God, you too need to possess incomparable qualities. So please put on your make-up.'

The Sufi way of remembering God is such, that sometimes it feels as though a lover is remembering his beloved, or a woman is trying to please and charm her husband. It seems like a romance. Remember, I said earlier that Sufism is romance – it is a love affair with the Almighty.

There are two different ways of expressing this love. In one tradition, we make God the lover and ourselves the beloved i.e., loving Him with female emotions, as in the case of Meera and Chaitanya. It is another matter that Meera also happened to be a female. But she loved God with feminine emotions and considered the Almighty to be her husband, a male.

Sufis adopted another tradition – their way is very beautiful. They say that God is the beloved and we are the suitors – we are male while God is female. The reason is that we are seeking Him and not the other way round.

There is a basic difference between the nature of men and women. Even if a woman loves someone, she will never express herself – she feels embarrassed, self-conscious and shy. And leave alone loving someone, if a man develops even a liking for someone, he does not hesitate to express it. So Sufis say that the Almighty is the timid beloved who is in hiding, and it is we who seek Him.

Sufis have a saying: A lover is seen, the beloved invisible. We can be seen but the one whom we are discussing is not visible. So here the Sufis change their stance – they say, 'She is not visible.'

Aashiq dikhta hai mashuk dikhe nahin
Dekhi kisi ne aisi aashiqui nahin

The lover is seen and the beloved is hidden
Has anyone witnessed such a love affair

Has anyone ever seen such a love where the lover is seen but the beloved is not seen anywhere? But the fact is that the one who is invisible is 'the reality' and what we are actually seeing – the visible self – is a fallacy. Were you there a hundred years ago? No! You will again be non-existent in about ten, twenty or thirty years. Whatever is visible today, will come to naught.

All that will be left of the body will be ash. Though you are visible right now, this visibility is a fallacy. The Almighty is not visible – but only He is true. You are visible but mortal; He is invisible yet true.

The one who will be obliterated feels that he can never be destroyed! Do you think that you will die? Nobody feels that! What one feels is: 'Ok, I too will die, but not now. There is a lot of time to go; after a long time – but not right now.'

The visible world is an illusion; one can't say when it will cease to be. When Hiroshima and Nagasaki were bombed by America, at around seven or eight in the morning, did anybody in the two cities know that in the next few moments more than one and a half lakh people would perish? And even the descendants of the survivors would be born with birth defects? What do you think? Did anyone know?

Mass destruction takes place by bombing and by floods. Floods are just nature's bombs! An earthquake takes place and thousands of people die. There is no forewarning; it happens suddenly and all the buildings collapse. Finished! There is no guarantee that those who are living today will be here tomorrow. Will the house, building, city, country or piece of land we are living on today be here later? There is no guarantee! It is strange that people roam around with such arrogance, as though they are never going to die, or that the place they are living in will never cease to exist.

Man is trading in copper coins; he is collecting and accumulating copper coins in his begging-bowl. There was a time when even these bowls were made of gold, silver or brass, but now they are made of paper. A gentleman came to meet me once and put money in my hand. As I said earlier, people are really strange – they are never happy without showing-off! Things have become better, for cash is given in envelopes now. Earlier they used to give money openly – they called it sagan. They gave it openly even if it was for their own personal gain.

So this gentleman came and straightaway put some money in my hand. Now that it had been kept on my hand, I just turned my palm upside down. The money fell down and he felt very bad. Well! He ought to feel bad; I had done it on purpose. He said, "This is Laxmi – the goddess of wealth. I said, "Maybe it is Laxmi for you, but not for me." He asked, "Then who is Laxmi for you?" I said, "For me Laxmi is wisdom, and this, as our elders say, is just the dirt of our hands – a means of purchase." A person buying mutton gave money to the butcher; the note from the butcher's hand came to you. He was chopping meat, there must have been blood on his hands that rubbed off on the note. It was passed around – how many germs came onto your hands? How many people touched that currency note? Do you know how many infections currency notes spread? In wedding ceremonies, people even dance with notes held between their teeth. Direct delivery of infection into the mouth! This money is just dirt on our hands!

That gentleman was a little stubborn, he said, "If I get a bundle of brand new notes from the bank, will you hold it in your hand?" Now if he was stubborn, I could be more so. I said, "No, I will still not hold it in my hand because the notes have chemicals that are harmful to the human body and I do not want to harm my body." So you see, money is just like filth on our hands!

Money is called the dirt of the hands. And see how dirty you make your mind just for the sake of this dirt – it is all filth. But it is for this that a brother quarrels with his own brother, father quarrels with his son, wife quarrels with her husband, children quarrel with their parents and friends with each other. For what? Only for this dirt! Look at your so called wisdom!

In Punjab there is a folk song, which goes thus: Two co-sisters were chewing sugarcane and spitting away the remains. As long as they were eating everything was fine; as long as they were sucking the cane juice, things were okay. While chewing they were talking and as the talk continued they started quarrelling. While fighting, they came down to verbal abuses. Then they started identifying their possessions; they started dividing the sugarcane peel amongst themselves, and on the issue of this division, they started hurling shoes and abuses at each other! So money or wealth is simply dirt, remember this always. Once someone wondered: 'What is this game? We slog the whole day, yet we do not earn enough money and always fall short. And look at these ascetics!'

Ascetics are of two kinds – genuine ones and hypocrites but neither is ever short of money. The hypocrite is never short of money because all his time is spent in planning ways and means of earning money. Isn't it true? All his schemes are to this end. That is why, whatever money you offer him is invested in the market on interest. He invests it in a safe market, i.e. on his followers.

The genuine sage, who does not want anything, who is pure and does not need money, he too has a lot of accumulated wealth. Why? Because he does not want money, so Laxmi decides to stay with him. Why? Because: "In your heart resides my Vishnu (God who preserves the world and is also Laxmi's consort)." Naturally Laxmi will stay there!

Bhagti phirti thi duniya jab talab karte the hum
Chod diya hai jo isko to bekaraar aane ko hai

The world always darted away when I sought it
Now that I have renounced it, it is anxious to come

Wealth is an illusion, it runs away even faster from one who runs after it. An ascetic says: "Ever since I spat on its face, it has been licking my feet." One needs courage to reject wealth; only a courageous person can do so! The one who sees wealth as grime on the hands abhors it. Don't you wash away all the dirt with soap? If your hand gets dirty, you clean it with soap or some other cleanser. So a person who considers it to be just grime will not find it difficult to reject it. Wealth doesn't oblige him who seeks it, but when one does not run after it, Laxmi is always around.

83

Once a boy who had come from Allahabad said, "I shall stay in your service." I also get cheated sometimes, so here I got cheated! I said, "Alright, come in." But later I came to know that he had some other motive. When someone offers money, I don't pick it up. I don't have a pocket in my robe and I keep a handbag only when I have to go somewhere far. I don't roam around in my ashram with a handbag. Devotees keep money here and there; some people are used to giving it in a concealed manner – they just hide it somewhere. They place it under the shoes or doormat. This is too much! They even place it under the shoes!

Once in winter I decided to wear my shoes. When I stepped into them, they felt strange. I wondered what was there in my shoes, then I found a 500-rupee note! I asked someone to take it out and started laughing at the choice of place. So money keeps lying here and there and those who are with me take care of it. Why do they take care? Well, frankly speaking, I also know that they will take care of it.

I have travelled a lot in public buses, which have no doors or windows. You have to buy a ticket even if the bus is in shambles. Now, I was not a beard-sporting sage that I would be allowed to travel free of cost; money was required for the ticket.

Just as the electricity department is not bothered about the quality of service – its job is to send the bill. There was a time when one could make a hut anywhere in the forest and stay there; not any more. Now the forest department will come and shoo you away: 'Come on, go away from here!' Earlier one could sit anywhere by the riverbank, but now with all these departments having come into existence, the Water department, Canal department, etc. all the officials keep roaming around. They too say: 'Come on, get going from here! This is government land and you can't make a hut on government land.'

Times have changed! There was a time when there were kings who donated acres and acres of land out of generosity. Swargashram in Rishikesh has such a huge area, the entire land was given by the Maharaja of Garhwal, it was not purchased. Here, in this ashram, even if a needle is required it is purchased.

Yes, it does happen sometimes that while travelling we halt at some place and purchase something, and if the shopkeeper sees me sitting in the vehicle he refuses to take money. They just insist on not taking money: "You just take whatever you want." But if I go to the electricity department with the electricity bill and say, "I will come on the first of every month and show my face to you…". They will say: "You are most welcome, but please pay the bill." Do you understand why we have to charge a registration fee in the ashram?

So talking about that boy, whatever money he saw lying around the ashram, he would put in his pocket. Whatever almonds or cashews he found; he would put them straight into his mouth, not even in his bag. One day I caught him picking up things, so I called him and said, "Son, you cannot live here anymore. Go back home." He asked me, why? I told him: "I have seen whatever you've done." He lowered his eyes, felt ashamed and asked for forgiveness. I said, "Don't ask for forgiveness. There is nothing wrong; you are in need of money right now, so it is okay. But then learn to earn money. If you eye the money kept with your guru, then you are not fit to stay with the guru. It is good to have a desire for money, but you must learn to make an effort to gain it. Why should you eye other people's money? Your intentions are not pure yet, hence you should go back home." I made him understand very affectionately, so he went back.

See how man sullies his mind for the sake of money? He sullies himself for the sake of dirt and nothing can be more unfortunate than this!

So, what is seen today will not be visible always, and what is invisible will always be there. Where is your sight? Is it on the visible or on the invisible? The one who eyes the visible is a worldly person, and the one who eyes the invisible is a Sufi. One who seeks the perishable is a worldly person!

What is amazing is that Sufis never taught sacrifice. The philosophy of sacrifice exists amongst Indian sages, but not in the least amongst Sufis. Only when they carry out rites called chilla, do they observe celibacy. The place where chilla is performed is like an ashram and is called Tekke in Turkish. Tekke has small rooms and one cannot just go and attend it.

85

If someone requests his sheikh that he wants to stay with him and practice worshiping, the sheikh says: "Alright son! Here is a mat, come and sit on it and don't move for the next three days. You may go to the toilet, that is the only permission granted. He is served only one meal there and that is lunch – the quantity is decided for him. For those three days he has to sit there, and if he passes this test, only then is he permitted to enter the Tekke.

Here, often people say that they came at two o' clock and were not allowed to enter. I say that you should be thankful you were not asked to sit outside for three days. If you sit outside for three days, only then will you be allowed to enter! Here we open the gate for 3-4 hours in the morning and again for 2 hours in the evening to let you in.

This test is for three days. Whoever manages to pass this three-day test is allowed inside and is then made to sit inside the chilla for 7, 11, 21 or 40 days at a stretch. Chilla means that he does not have to come out of the room he has been assigned; he will be given food there itself. He is only allowed to come out to attend to nature's call. He is supposed to complete his early morning ablutions before other people get up or go for the 'namaz-e-fajr' (prayers offered at the break of dawn)

The time that Sufis spend in a chilla is that of severe penance. But if they are not in a chilla or not undergoing the test required for entry to the Tekke, if they are not practicing those rules, then they lead a very ordinary life. They do not even have a distinctive dress and may be sitting amongst you and you will not even know who they are. Absolutely ordinary! They have a saying: 'The one who can be recognised cannot be a Sufi! He who cannot be recognised is a Sufi'. This means that there is no showing off, not even a specific type of clothing is allowed. Al Hillaj Mansoor was finally recognised at the time of his death.

And what do I see here in the ashram? If anyone is given yellow or white clothes to wear, he becomes arrogant; he starts feeling superior to others. And if someone wears saffron, he starts saying: "Now I will sit on the high chair and you sit down there. Who can be greater than me? I have renounced everything."

Sufis have renounced the idea of renunciation. They say: "There is no need to renounce the world. What should I abandon? What is there that is mine? I can renounce something that belongs to me, but how can I abandon things that don't belong to me and which belong to the Almighty.

An ascetic says: 'I have abandoned my wife and children.' Why? What is your wife's fault? You don't have to give up anything. A Sufi only lives in this world – he does not belong to the world. He lives in this world amongst its people; he lives like an ordinary man and does not show-off in any way. The one who does not try to maintain a separate or distinct identity is a Sufi.

But look at the Shankaracharyas of today – they cannot even sit, if they are not offered a silver throne! Try to tell a Shankaracharya: 'Come, let us sit on the floor today. Let us get the feel of Mother Earth.' The revered Adi Shankaracharya was different – I am not talking of him here – he was a son of the soil.

Just tell some Mahamandaleshwar – head of ashram: 'Sir! Leave this throne and come let us sit on the floor today.' And just see the consequences! One follower always walks behind him with his mat – you never know when his lordship might want to sit down! So first his mat is rolled out and then he settles down; he always roams around with his mat! Then if someone becomes a mandaleshwar – head of small ashram, a silver parasol appears above his head and a flywhisk behind him. So if a fly sits on his face he will not brush it away himself! A follower fans the fly away! Imagine what would happen if a wasp or a honeybee gets entangled in his beard! What will he do then!?

If a disciple washes his guru's hands and feet while serving him, it is understandable. But what if the guru himself starts expecting these services? What if he says: 'Someone come and wash my hands, get me a towel, wipe my hands, etc.?' You never know, the next day he may say: 'Put some bread in my mouth and make me chew it!' So lazy and useless!

But in Turkey and Iran you will not find any such worthless Sufis. Every Sufi there works perfectly. And the best thing is that he works during the day and does zikr at night. Someone asked, "Then when do you sleep?" And they say, "Don't be crazy! Sleep? Sleep is forbidden! Life is so short, why should I waste it in sleep?"

"But what about the rest that the body requires?"

"We recharge all our strength through zikr, and before that if we manage to get some time – about four hours for ourselves – that is enough."

One name famous among Sufis is that of Mullah Nasruddin; his birthplace has not been verified historically. The fact is that many people believe there never was a Sufi by the name of Mullah Nasruddin, and that Sufis invented his character. Then, instead of anecdotes to share wisdom, a number of jokes were attributed to him. But through these jokes, important messages have been given and wisdom imparted in the form of jokes. Someone asked, "Why this way? Why through jokes?" Sufis say: 'If wisdom is shared directly, one becomes proud; if important things are told in the form of jokes, then one learns easily.'

You get withdrawn when you are sad, unhappy or angry. But when you laugh you swell with joy. And when you laugh you get radiant, your mouth opens with joy and somewhere deep down your heart also opens up and you feel light. I am not talking of members of the laughter club; there can't be more fake laughter than that! They start laughing – 'ha ha ha' – and then suddenly shut up. Is this the National School of Drama where you start crying or laughing the moment the director says, 'Action?' And the moment he says, 'Cut', you stop?!

This is my opinion; those who like laughter clubs are free to attend them. I feel this is artificial laughter – not at all natural. Have we become so artificial now that we need to go to a club even to laugh? Gandhi said that one must laugh at least once a day. So one of his followers was standing somewhere by himself laughing. A passer-by asked, "Sir, what are you doing?" He replied, "Just following the rule!"

Now listen to this strange thing: No one knows where and when Mullah Nasruddin was born but his tomb exists. On it is engraved the figure 386. A Sufi said, "No, this is wrong – write 683".

Someone present there said, "Nasruddin was quite a muddled-up person, so write it in the reverse order". Therefore '386' was written! His date of birth and tomb are both fictitious.

Talking of Mullah Nasruddin, once, he was travelling from Syria to Damascus with his mule, carrying a sack of grass. The guard on the border called out, "Hey! Where to? Who are you?" He said, "I am Mullah Nasruddin and I am a smuggler." The guard asked, "What are you smuggling?" Mullah said, "You are a guard, it is your duty to search me. So find out for yourself." The guard opened the bag and found grass in it. He searched each and every straw in the sack but found nothing but grass. There was grass, the sack, the mule and Mullah. So what was he smuggling? The guard just could not understand! Finally he said, "Okay, go."

The third day Mullah came again. The guard said, "Mullah, you are here again!"

"Yes".

The guard asked, "Now how come?"

Mullah replied, "To smuggle."

Another guard said, "Just don't believe him, there can't be a bigger liar than him. I wasted a full six hours on him, just let him go."

And so Mullah went off shouting, "Don't say I didn't tell you that I am a smuggler."

Several months passed by. The interesting thing was that Mullah was getting richer by the day. He had openly declared that he was involved in smuggling, but whenever checked, there was nothing other than grass in his sack. He had no other business and yet he was becoming richer by the day.

One day the guards' commander came to Mullah's house and what does he see? A magnificent bungalow, servants and lots of good food. He asked, "Mullah how did you become rich?" Mullah said, "I have been saying everyday that I am a smuggler. I smuggle goods." The commander asked, "What did you smuggle?" Mullah said, "I used to smuggle the mules. You were so busy searching the grass; the mule was always before your eyes but you kept looking inside the sack and never saw the mule! And I declared everyday that I was smuggling. I am not such a fool that I would tell you that I was smuggling mules. You always think that a mule is a mule, but no, they are of different types! Every time I had a new mule with me. I took them from Syria and sold them in Damascus. Mules are very expensive there. That is how I became rich."

You are also in business but you are not making any profit because you leave the mule behind and carry only the grass on your head. The sack of grass is worthless, dry! What use is that? You are only bothered about things that are of no use and are completely ignorant about things that are useful. That is why, while Mullah kept getting richer, you became poorer by the day. The reason is that you are bothered only about the thing that is going to perish; the immortal and the eternal doesn't concern you!

Sufis say that one should bother about that which is there, but remember, that which exists is invisible. The Sufi says: 'One who is seen cannot be my beloved.' The lover is visible, the beloved is not. People say: 'You are mad! Who has ever seen God? Who do you keep searching for? Why do you waste your time? See, there is a beer bar and women; there is good food and money! If you want to bother, why not bother about these? If you want to enjoy, enjoy these!'

Deep down somewhere you too want to err. Though you shoot from another's shoulder, it is you who trips. Then you drink, enjoy the company of the opposite sex and say, 'I made a mistake.' You didn't make a mistake inadvertently – it happened because you wanted it to.

Sufis wear a white cloak at the time of zikr or when in sema – a long white cloak. Why white? Because the shroud that covers the dead is white. As long as man is alive, and howsoever worried he is about his shroud, he is always running after the visible world – but a dead man does not. A dead body just remains lying; it does not react even if someone shouts, cries, sings or does just about anything. This world's existence does not have any meaning for one who is already dead.

So, who is a mureed (disciple)? One who dies! That is the reason they wear a long white cloak at the time of zikr or Sema.

Among the Sufis are the Mevlavi Sufis; they follow Hazrat Jalaluddin Rumi Mevlana and practice his teachings. Along with the white cloak, Mevlavi Sufis wear a cap on the head which is known as sikke. It is like a tombstone on a Muslim's grave stating his name and the date of his birth and death. Sometimes a prayer is also engraved on it. So Mevlavi followers wear a white robe, which is like a shroud, rather it is a shroud, and on their head is the sikke – the tombstone that tells you who lies under the shroud. They sit for zikr with the feeling: 'I am dead'.

Zikr means remembering Allah; His remembrance! Remembering not with words but with the breath. Here God is remembered through the medium of the breath – the entire concentration is on the breath. And with the breath, 'Hu' is pronounced as a gentle, medium, but deep sound. The sound of 'Hu' has to come from the chest, lungs, stomach and diaphragm and not from the throat or tongue. Why not from the tongue? It is said that nothing can be more impure than the tongue – all lies and deceit come through the tongue. You discuss dirty politics with the tongue. You want to say God's name with the same tongue? Shame on you! Not with the tongue! But with your heart!

Zikr is done in a continuous flow like an oil-stream. When water flows there occurs a break in the stream, but when oil flows it is like an incessant stream and it is difficult to stop its flow. In the same way, a continuous flow of the sound of 'Hu' carries on like a stream of oil. Only a very minor break is at the junction of the in going and out coming breath. The sound produced while exhaling through the mouth is to be heard with the ears. When you exhale you must hear the sound with complete consciousness.

First practice the sound that is produced while breathing out. You have to understand how the breath is to be exhaled. Practice the deep sound of 'Hu' later on; first learn the correct sound of the breath.

CHAPTER 5

THE FIRE OF LOVE

Bahauddin-al-Veled was a Sufi, who, because of his knowledge, education, understanding and common sense, was a highly respected and revered personality of his time. To this Sufi, a child named Jalaluddin was born; he was lovingly called Jalal.

Little Jalaluddin used to attend zikr along with his father. One thing often repeated in zikr and is a favourite of the Sufis is: 'La Ilaha Illallah'. In Syria, Iran, Damascus, Afghanistan and even in India – wherever there is Sufism – or even if it is not there, they have managed to preserve at least this mantra: 'La Ilaha Illallah'.

Just as there are Hindus, Sikhs and Jains who believe in the letter and not the spirit of religious laws and scriptures, similarly there are Muslims who are caught up in deconstructing the scriptures. They do not go deep into the meaning of what is written, in fact they don't understand the meaning at all. All they do is memorise the scriptures and feel proud!

Memorising any text, any scripture, is only an exercise of the mind. Even a computer can do that with the help of the latest technology. If a man memorises and recites the entire Gita – all eighteen chapters – that is creditable, but if this is done on a tape recorder, CD or DVD recorder – and there are thousands of ways of doing this – then it has no meaning. If you put it on auto-play, it will go on repeat-mode and the cassette will keep on playing. The recording could be of any scripture, how does it make a difference? After all it is written on paper.

So Kabir says:

Tu kehta kaagaz ki lekhi, main kehta aakhan dekhi

> You talk about that which is written on paper
> I talk from what I have seen with my eyes

You talk of literary knowledge, there is nothing great about that. Guru Nanak made fun of it saying that it is like parrot learning by rote. He must have seen some celibate or learned Brahmin on the banks of the Ganges in Kashi, reciting the verses and grammar of the Vedas.

None other than Shankaracharya himself has told such Brahmins: "Why are you troubling your mind? Remember God, remember God, remember God! O foolish person, just remember God! O confused fellow! Why are you trying to thrust these scriptures on your poor mind? Have you forgotten your heart? If only you welcomed the Lord's name into your heart, all your time would be well utilised.

Sufis have also allowed only one name to reside in their hearts: 'La Ilaha Illallah'! Under some sects in Sufism, such is the understanding that the name of beloved God and God alone should be taken. Many a time, Sufis only recited the first line of the great verse and left out the second. It was done not out of disrespect, not out of ignorance but out of the understanding that God is the one who has made great people what they are. It is his love alone that triggered the process of acceptance, revelations, grace and mercy, upon which paths were laid down.

Sufis felt that it was of utmost importance, more than the person who was delivering the message, to follow the message. The message called for utmost attention. The actual work began when the message was understood and was brought to practice. So what was the message? "La Ilaha Illallah" There – is no God except for that God. Upon this knowing, that the supreme entity self exists even before great personalities were born and even after they leave the world and that the message holds the utmost value, many times, rest of the verses were left out.

He who gets entangled in words will suffer. Do not get caught up with words! We ought to understand the meaning and the connotation of words. Like I have told you earlier, the master will judge the receptivity of the disciple and accordingly will tell him about things that he can understand.

Let me once again remind you of the story of the king who went to a Sufi and said, "I too want to become a Sufi." The Sufi said, "A man who is not in his senses can never become a Sufi, and that too a person like you who is most unintelligent; you have no understanding of the things whatsoever." The king insisted that he did. The Sufi said, "Alright then, you have to fulfill my condition, I will test you. Whatever I say, your response has to be that you believe me."

So their conversation began and the Sufi said, "I was there even before Moses."

"I believe you."

"I was there even before Jesus."

"I believe you."

Here I am telling the story with gaps between, explaining it to you as we go along, but when the Sufi was talking to the king, there was no break. He kept on saying continuously… "I was there before Moses; I was there even before Jesus." The king kept saying, "I believe you."

Then the Sufi said, "I was there even before you."

"I believe you."

In the end he said, "Your father was a poor farmer."

Now the king retorted, "Now here you are lying. You will get thrashed as my father was not a farmer."

The king forgot that he just had to say 'I believe you'. Till the time the ascetic was talking about 'unimportant' things, the king replied as instructed. But actually they were not senseless things, for the Sufi was stating facts.

When the Jews asked Jesus, "Have you come to tarnish our religion? What on earth have you been saying?" Jesus also gave the same reply, "I was there even before Moses and today I have come to give a new interpretation to Moses' religion, not to tarnish it."

Man's situation and psychology change with time. With the changing psychology, masters have to change the tools of imparting wisdom. The Buddha's era was a totally different era. In the Vedic period, men were different from today's men. Twenty years hence, your next generation will not be like you, i.e. if the world survives and some mad politician spares the world a nuclear attack!! The generation gap between a father and son will always be there, so if the thinking of the two differs, then it is inevitable that thinking will change completely in several hundred years.

In order to cope with the changing times, several mystics have come to earth – and will keep coming in the future too – to present new interpretations. But Truth never changes! The means change but not the Truth! Customs change but not reality! 'La Ilaha Illallah' was as true at the time of Moses as at the time of the Prophet Mohammad, and is equally true even today. Even today, it is God that is Truth – nobody and nothing else! The facts are the same as they were then.

There has been another Sufi named Fariduddin. He said that Sufis have been here earlier too but were not called Sufis. Jesus was a Sufi, Moses was also a Sufi, and they both lived before Prophet Mohammad. There have always been Sufis and there always will be. As long as there is the darkness of ignorance, there have to be torchbearers. As long as night exists, the moon and stars have to be there.

All mystics carry the torch of wisdom- like watchmen. As long as there is darkness, the torch will keep giving out light. If one torch is put out, another one is lit. If one Sufi goes, another will come. One Sufi will not be sufficient for the whole wide world that is why Sufis have taken birth in every religion and in every country. Their language, dialect, faces and appearances have been different – but Truth is eternal. What is true for Sufis in India is true for Sufis living in Iran as well. It is the same for those attaining enlightenment in the future, just as it was in the time of Rishi Yagyavalk! Truth will remain the same.

'La Ilaha Illallah' – to sit in zikr with this mantra is an art, a specialised art; there is a style to it and there are certain rules to observe it. 'La Ilaha' can be chanted with the movement of the tongue, or from the depths of your being with your breath. It can also be chanted at a speed where the rhythm of the breath is controlled. In simple words, if the chant is synchronised with the breath, then it assumes an altogether different form.

The Sufis of India have talked about the verbal chant, the mental chant, and the un-vocalised or ajapa-jap. Sufis have described this in their language as alfaazi or vocalised zikr, dum or breathing zikr, dili or heartfelt zikr, and lastly, fikr or meditating zikr. Alfaazi means remembering God with the help of words and the use of the tongue. Dum zikr means that we recite the zikr along with our breath. And the third is the dili zikr, in which the tongue does not move and the breath is not controlled; without uttering a single word or using the vocal chords, the chant carries on incessantly in the heart.

As per Sufism, after transcending these three stages you reach a stage that is called fikr. What is fikr? In Hindi this translates as 'worry'. The word fikr used here is a Persian word and it means remembering Him effortlessly. When you do not utter the chants or even think of them; when you do not use the rhythm of the breath either, but His thought is present without any effort whatsoever, then you are said to be in fikr.

Kabir and Nanak have called this surati. Persian Sufis call it fikr; we have to go from zikr to fikr. Initially it is the alfaazi zikr where we use our voice, but by the time we reach the stage of fikr, the voice is not used and the mantra carries on involuntarily in this stage. The chant goes on deep down in the heart, and even though you are not uttering the chants aloud, their fragrance spreads in your heart.

Jalaluddin used to sit with his father to practice zikr. Using the breath to do dum zikr, he would remember the God Almighty by his various names. He would sit in the lap of his learned, knowledgeable and philosophic father, and listen to the philosophy and discourses that he taught his students. At a very young age he gained a great deal of knowledge, talent and skills. People would be surprised at his achievements, and Bahauddin too felt happy and thanked God for giving him a son, who even before reaching youth, was well versed in zikr. One night his mother went close to him and found him muttering 'La Ilaha Illallah' even in his sleep!

Jalal was a genius, he had an extremely sharp mind and was a very learned man. Soon he became a professor in the university, this was in the 12th century. There is a city in Turkey by the name of Konya where Bahauddin built a house, and Jalaluddin also lived there. Soon Jalaluddin earned great fame but not like Hitler or Mussolini! They too were famous and history is replete with their stories. Historians love to write about notorious people, they never write about Sufis and nobles; they only write about political leaders and what happened during the reign of Shahjahan, Aurangzeb, Hitler, Mussolini and Mao Tse Tung.

The world's history does not carry on because of religion, but because of cruel people who have caused much devastation the world over. But when I say Jalaluddin gained popularity, it was among the Sufis. There happened to be a Sufi in his time by the name of Fariduddin Attar. It is said that he was an alchemist and a very rich man. He kept the most expensive medicines in his clinic, and one day while attending to his patients and selling his medicines, he saw an ascetic standing before him in tattered and soiled clothes. He kept standing; Attar thought that he would go away after sometime, but he did not. So finally he asked, "What are you waiting for?" The ascetic said, "I am just wondering where you will take all this wealth and these possessions? I am tired of carrying just this cloak, and you own so many assets and riches!"

Attar replied jokingly, "I will also leave it behind the way you will."

"All right! I leave it right now." He lay down on the floor, took the name of Allah and left his body behind. This ascetic had learnt the yogic art of leaving the body at will. When an ascetic gets into the mood, he just burns his hut regardless of whether the hut is his physical body or a worldly dwelling. What difference does it make? When Attar saw this, he was shocked. He was just joking; rather, he was being sarcastic when he said that he too would leave everything behind! Having witnessed this scene,

Attar could not sit in his clinic any more. He distributed all his possessions amongst the poor, donned the same cloak that the ascetic was wearing and joined the Sufis.

It was the same Attar who sat with Jalaluddin's father, Bahauddin. They have a custom of drinking tea during discussions. This is not the usual tea made with milk but a special tea with different tea leaves. They just pour hot water on the leaves and their tea is ready – they don't even add sugar. So they just keep drinking tea and discussing the Quran Sharif for hours together.

One day Jalal was sitting and listening to the discussion of these two Sufis. When the assembly was over, Bahauddin started towards his house with Jalaluddin walking behind him. When Attar saw this, he said, "Just look at this scene! See this vision! An ocean is following the sea."

Bahauddin was leading and Jalaluddin was following. Jalaluddin being Bahauddin's son was younger in age and mental faculties, but Attar said, "It is the ocean that is following the sea. What can be seen here is the sea of knowledge and skill that is going ahead, but what is following is the wisdom of ocean."

Attar made the prophecy that Jalaluddin would turn many people towards God by the force of his vast wisdom. Jalaluddin was completely ignorant about this at that time. While children played with kites, Jalaluddin would sit and do zikr. Children would come to him and say, "Come let's fly kites." And Jalaluddin would answer, "I am worried about the kite of life which is flying off and which is going to be cut off by death." His elders would say, "Child, act according to your age. Enjoy yourself! Go and play." And Jalal would reply: "I enjoy remembering my God; my mouth is sweetened taking His name and thinking of Him. I don't require any other sweets; I don't want anything else."

Jalaluddin's popularity was such that he had hundreds of followers. When he went to the university to teach, his followers would make him ride a horse. Beautifully embroidered sheets were spread on the horse's back, and they would take their teacher in glorious splendour to the university where he would sit and philosophise. Jalaluddin was a great astrologer too. He could give a complete account of a person's life merely by seeing

the face. He was so popular that people with ailments would come to see him because just seeing him cured their illness. As a writer he became so famous that whatever he wrote became a precious treatise. He authored 'Masnavi' which became famous for its poetry and philosophy in the whole world. He was a great writer and wrote thousands of poems and stories through which he imparted knowledge.

Zikr is done in two ways; it can be done either in the sitting position or in the standing position. Whenever he practised zikr in the standing position, people would try to stand next to him because it was believed that when his cloak moved, a sweet fragrance would spread around. A devotee sometimes attains great mystical powers, but Jalaluddin had them constantly.

One day a strange incident occurred. Jalaluddin was going to the university, riding on his horse. As usual his students and followers were with him when suddenly an ascetic appeared in the centre of the road. His cloak was tattered and dirty and even his body was unclean. But his eyes shone with such brilliance that no one could muster enough courage to stop him, and he walked straight up to Jalaluddin. He caught hold of the horse's reins and posed a question: "Who is greater? Abu Yaseed Bastami or Prophet Mohammad? Tell me, who is greater?" The sharp gaze of the ascetic pierced Jalaluddin's heart! He began saying, "Certainly the Prophet is greater and not Yaseed." When Yaseed got a glimpse of God, he began proclaiming, "Who could be a greater king than me? Who could be more fortunate than me? Who could be luckier than me! Who could be more knowledgeable than me!" But when Prophet Mohammad witnessed God, he was not satisfied with just that much, for he remembered the verse of the Quran in which God says that He is the hidden treasure that lies within man. And remembering this, the Prophet said, "We have not been able to understand you the way we ought to. Our mind is not capable of knowing or recognising your persona, your reality!" Jalaluddin Rumi said, "Yaseed was content drinking just a handful of water, and the Prophet remained thirsty for God's love even after having drunk rivers-full. He still suffered the pangs for more, wanting to go deeper and deeper into His love."

It is believed that the moment the ascetic heard this answer, he was so charmed and ecstatic, that he became unconscious and fell down. Rumi got off his horse at the speed of lightning, took his hand, put his head against his own and embraced him. When the ascetic regained consciousness, Jalaluddin was holding his hands. They both got up together and steering clear of the crowd, walked away towards the desert. People started asking who this was, who was this person whose feet Jalaluddin was kissing? Someone from the crowd called out: "He is Shams Tabreez."

Shams and Rumi were so engrossed in their newfound friendship that they did not meet people for months together. They stayed in a desolate area and reached such a state of divine consciousness that they would either do zikr together or they would go into fikr. They would either talk or just be quiet. Shams taught Rumi to love God with his heart and not with his mind. "You have accumulated enough wealth in your mind but there is darkness in your heart – illumine your heart!"

People were unable to understand who was learning from whom – whether Jalaluddin was learning from Shams or the other way round. People would say: "Shams Tabreez is not even literate". Remember, the same thing was said about Prophet Mohammad. The same thing was said about Kabir and Ravidas. But where is the need to be educated, after 'knowing' the ultimate divine treasure?

Though it is said that Shams Tabreez was totally uneducated, one day a very strange thing happened. Jalaluddin was sleeping and had a dream. And in his dream he saw that he was teaching the nuances of the Quran Sharif to his followers. Suddenly he woke up and found that Shams was standing in front of him. Shams said, "I told you not to read any more books!" Jalaluddin got up with a jerk and said, "This was just a dream." Shams said, "Dreams are reflections of the mind and its thoughts. You have not yet been able to get over your professorship, even while you were sleeping, so no more books and no more scriptures!"

Just keep in mind that all that Jalaluddin had done in his life – from childhood to youth – was to read all the scriptures, understand them and learn them by heart, while living in close proximity of various Sufis. He became so learned that he started teaching all he had learnt to other people. And here was Shams, saying that he had to forget all the scriptures and leave everything he had learnt behind! "Leave everything, enough of verse and dogma. Now let your heart be kindled with the fire of love! Now illumine your heart with the glow of love's fire. You have wasted enough time – no more!"

Strange things were happening. On one hand Shams seemed to be so well informed that he knew what was going on in Jalaluddin's dreams, and on the other, he would be seen kissing Jalaluddin's feet. Both seemed to live for each other; in this way months passed. Jalaluddin's followers were unable to understand what was going on; he was not teaching or coming to the university, nor was he going home. They began to wonder how their learned and well-informed teacher could come under the spell of a stranger. What magic had Shams cast on him? If at all Jalaluddin came back home, it was only for a short while in which he would take a bath, eat something, pack a few eatables and again go off to the deserted place where Shams lived!

When men lose their senses, the consequences are always the same – the followers of Jalaluddin began defaming him. They would blackmail Jalaluddin on account of his father, urge him to leave Shams' company and fraternise with them instead, and be a part of the madrasa that was running like a school. "Why have you taken up the company of this mad man?" They couldn't directly tell their sheikh that he had gone mad, but that is what they felt and implied. Sometimes I laugh and thank God that both Shams and Jalaluddin were men! Had one of them been a woman….!

Finally the scheme worked and Shams was thrown out of Konya. Now Jalaluddin suffered the pain of separation and longed for his friend's company; he yearned for the nights he had spent with the friend who had brightened his gloomy heart, but was not there with him anymore. Jalaluddin would go around asking everybody if they had seen Shams. Once a passer-by said, "Yes! I have seen him in Damascus." Immediately Jalaluddin took off his expensive cloak and turban and presented it to him. He then told his followers, "Come and get the horses ready for the journey to Damascus – Shams is there. We will go and bring him back to Konya."

One of his followers who loved him a lot said, "That man was lying." Rumi said, "As he lied about my Shams, I gave him my cloak and turban, had he told me the truth, I would have given him my life. I knew he was telling a lie, but I want to believe him. If he says that Shams is in Damascus, then he definitely will be there."

Somehow Jalaluddin managed to get Shams back. And the moment he came back, the classes that had begun in Shams' absence stopped again. Rumi and Shams got back together again, and everyone wondered what these two did because they never had anyone else with them! People wondered what it was that they did!

The jealous followers of Rumi could not take this friendship anymore, and so finally, one night they surrounded Shams and attacking him with a sword, they killed him. It is said that a few drops of blood fell to the ground, and legend has it that those few drops of blood were all the evidence that was found! His body just vanished!

Rumi went mad searching for his friend. The great blow suffered by his heart fanned the fire of mysticism in him. He would call Shams his Sun and himself the Earth. He would say: "He is my Sun. If I don't find the Sun, this world will not exist. He is my Sun." Remembering God and pining for Shams, Rumi started whirling – going around in circles – the way the Earth revolves on its axis and rotates around the Sun. He would keep going round and round doing zikr in that movement.

From here started a new sect of Mevlevi dervishes who came to be known as 'the whirling dervishes'. They wear a white shroud-like cloak and a conical tombstone-like cap on their heads! Remembering Allah in their hearts and with His name on their lips, they go whirling around in His memory!

Later Jalaluddin Rumi wrote 'Diwan-e-Shams', an epic in commemoration of his friend. In this masterpiece, he described the deepest secrets of spiritualism. The special style of zikr mentioned therein is meant only for some special people.

There is a very popular way of doing zikr, which I have mentioned earlier:

'La Ilaha Illallah'. This means that there is no God but God. There is no one but God! It is like analysing Om in a thousand words, but it loses its charm and the beauty of its sound if you get into a detailed analysis. Similarly, 'La Ilaha Illallah' has a lengthy and deep meaning. But we don't have to go into the depth of the meaning because we have to go into zikr.

There are two ways of doing zikr: In the first, we produce the sound from the tongue, and in the second we utter the sound with the breath. The emphasis here is on pronunciation, so for some time first, you must concentrate on pronouncing it correctly; later on you can do it with the breath. I want to forewarn you that this is not simple, you will not be able to grasp it in one go. Even if you wish to try it, you must speak very softly so that you can understand properly.

In the second style, it is important to breathe out in the right way; you must not speak from your throat – you have to bring the sound from your navel. Exhaling is of utmost importance here.

First you must listen to the notes and follow the rhythm. Later, if you have grasped it properly, you may start saying it softly along with the tape. As long as you are unable to understand it correctly, don't try it – just listen. Now all of you sit with your eyes closed.

Ya Allah Ya Allah Ya Allah!

O God of Gods!
I love thee, I seek thee
I wish to be bound in your serenity
Your name on my lips
And with you in my heart
I'll burn in the fire of your love
As from this world I depart

CHAPTER 6

PURIFY THYSELF

When we do the zikr of 'La Ilaha Illallah', the thundering sound of the breath should be evident – it should be audible. If it is not, it means that the zikr was not done as it should have been. Just as 'Truth needs no proof' – the power of the chant of zikr is such that it can be felt immediately – if done properly.

While repeating the chant of 'Hu', the breath has to be inhaled and exhaled only through the mouth. Remain quiet for some time and concentrate on listening to the tape. You may join in when you understand the right pronunciation and are able to catch the right note – when you understand how to inhale and exhale properly – it will be better if you do not start before that. To sit quietly and listen with devotion is also an art; it is a wonder in itself.

'Hu', as I said, means: 'He is the one. There is neither 'I' nor 'you'. It has not even been said that God is omnipresent, and that I as His servant worship Him. When the distinction between 'I' and 'you' is dissolved, then 'Hu' comes into play. When your false 'self' is vanquished and there is no 'self' left, then who will worship Allah? When there is no 'I', then in relation to whom will God be referred to as 'you'? The state of total dissolution of 'you' and 'I' is called 'Hu'.

I told you about the assassination of Shams Tabreez. All his life Shams kept repeating 'La Ilaha Illallah', but when his murderers killed him, his last words were, 'La Ilaha Ill Annah'. While 'La Ilaha Illallah' means God is the only one, 'La Ilaha Ill Annah' means that there is no God, there is only me. This truth, buried deep in the heart, came to the fore at the hour of death; it came to the lips of the dying Shams Tabreez in its own unique way.

Once, Jalaluddin Rumi said, that if the truth lying in his heart rose to his lips, he too would meet the fate of Al Hillaj Mansoor, who was killed by his contemporary religious leaders. You will be surprised to know that Mansoor's own followers cut his body to pieces because he said An-al-haq, which means 'I alone am God!' His own disciples performed this deplorable act because they felt it was blasphemy. How did he dare to say An-al-haq?

A person, who is caught up with the literal meaning of words and has not understood their reality, will never reach the actual depths of the subject. That is the reason why a person who just reads the Quran – without understanding its essence – will not be able to find the truth hidden therein.

Rumi said, "Mansoor's followers cut his body into pieces, but he had a small following. I have a very large following – if such a truth comes to my lips – my body will be cut into thousands of pieces!"

The fact is that all Sufis meet the same fate, whether it is Mansoor or Shams. Every true and pure master, every true and pure Sufi does not find equally true and pure disciples. The people, who gather around gurus, are often there on a personal agenda. Some are attracted to the guru's popularity; others are drawn by the presence of high-class and influential people who come to attend the satsangs. Many people visit gurus not because they have love for them, but because other people go there. "If others appreciate them, we must do the same. If others worship them, we must also worship them." They don't have any real emotions; they are not true disciples, they are just followers.

There is another incident that I would like to narrate. One of Rumi's followers came up to Shams and said, "Do tell me at least some of what you tell my master." Shams said, "Alright! But you will have to fulfill my condition." Remember one thing, Sufis never give lectures or discourses. They do not give of their wealth openly or freely. Whoever reaches them has to pass various tests, it is only then that the Sufi reveals the secret. So Shams said, "Fine! You go and sell all your wealth and property and bring the returns to me." So the follower went back and sold off his house, shop, horses and whatever else was there, collected all the gold and put it at Shams' feet. "Now," he said, "Whatever mystical wisdom you have been giving to my Mevlana – my guru – tell them to me too."

Shams said, "One who wears tattered clothes does not require your wealth. Whatever gold you have brought, weigh it, find out its price and then take four times that wealth from me." And Shams gave him four times the price of his gold. He said, "Now go back." The follower's name was Husum. Husum said, "I have kept my promise, now you should keep yours. This wealth, which is worthless to you, is worthless to me too. Whether it is what I brought or what you have made of it, they both have no value for me now."

Remember, those who go through these tests are very astute, they are fairly seasoned people. Sometimes it seems that it is not always beneficial to be a part of the crowd, as it never has the understanding and the thirst to 'know', to 'seek'. Those who seek the Truth have to make a lot of sacrifices. Someone asked: "The same sacrifice that Abraham had to make?"

Historical saga says that Abraham had a dream in which God said, "Sacrifice the thing you love the most, for my sake." This dream seemed so true that Abraham got up with a jerk, perspiring profusely. Worried, his wife asked, "What happened?" He said, "O fortunate one! God has asked for something. The one who has always given has asked for something today."

"It does not matter what He has asked for. Whatever He has asked for, you must give." Abraham said, "Alright then, He has asked me to sacrifice the thing I love the most and it is my son I love the most. So go and bathe our son, make him wear fresh clothes and bring him here."

That woman trusted her husband so much, that she did not cry or scream, did not ask any questions, nor did she appeal for mercy. She went and bathed her only son – who they had been blessed with at a fairly old age – made him wear fresh clothes and sent him to his father.

Abraham went to the hill with his son. "Father, where are you taking me?"

"Son, I will tell you when we reach our destination. Right now you just come with me." He thought that if he told him now, the child might get scared and just run away, or create a ruckus or fight with him. Which father would kill his son? That too, just for a dream! After all, it was just a dream!

When they reached the top of the hill, he said, "Son, now put your neck on that stone." The child rested his neck on the stone; he too did not ask any question. It is said that at that moment, Abraham's hands started trembling. After all, he was a normal human being and a father. It is true that he had attained great heights in wisdom and love, but after all, he was a father. He had managed to come so far in order to obey God's command, but then it does take some time to pacify a father's feelings. So he picked up the sword, closed his eyes and took God's name. The moment he struck, the sword slipped from his hand and fell next to a sheep grazing nearby. A voice said: "You have passed the test."

As long as he had not picked up the sword, nothing happened. Only when the sword was raised and then lowered to strike, did some supernatural power pull it away and saved Ismail.

Sacrifice has been considered of utmost importance in Muslim world. To know what should be the real nature of sacrifice, one has to delve deep. Sacrifice translates to giving away of what is dear to you, giving away of what you love the most. Why it is important to give away, to sacrifice? Human beings have overgrown into the bond of love to the point that it has taken the form of fundamental obsessions and attachments; sacrifice means loosening the bond of this attachment. And compassion is a selfless act, through which we can achieve this.

The incident in Abraham's life was symbolic of one of the greatest forms of sacrifice. It was giving away of what was dearest to him. It was a test for him, a test of willingness, of surrender to the will of God, to do away with the bond of attachment. The story says as he was about to fulfill the ritual, his weapon fell far away from the place of sacrifice and landed in front of a sheep. I simply ask that as a follower of this great story, have people imbibed the same qualities of selflessness, willingness to surrender to the will of God and most importantly the virtue of detachment within themselves.

Practice of sacrifice is not important, an act of sacrifice is. What Abraham did was an act of sacrifice. It was more of an inward journey for him, learning for him and so it should be for all those who follow this story.

Out of many beautiful names of Allah, he is also called Rehman, the compassionate one. The one who is compassionate to all his creations, thus it is required for his people to show mercy to all his creations. If we go by the above story, the son of the prophet was not harmed in any way; everyone came out unscathed in the story.

There is another custom that I would like to mention here. Once, someone came to Rumi with the message, that a disciple of his was sick and suffering from high fever. Jalaluddin Rumi was writing something at that time, so he picked up a piece of paper and wrote: 'Allah hu Akbar – God is the greatest; He is supreme. Do not put meat in your mouth, do not drink blood. If you believe that the Prophet was loved by Allah, your temperature will come down'. "Go and give this message to him", he said.

When the disciple read the message, he dissolved the paper in water and drank it. The ink and the paper dissolved and he drank all of the water. Someone said, "What are you doing?" He said, "It is my master's message; it is not meant to be read. It is to be consumed and to be lived." It is said that his fever came down!

Here I am pointing a finger at the practices that are followed blindly by society. It has become a practice that whenever someone falls sick, people start looking for fakirs and Sufis to get them to write something on a piece of paper – usually a verse from the Quran – and then that piece of paper is dissolved in water and consumed.

You cannot generalize what transpired between Rumi and his disciple. All these historical facts are not to be emulated; if you feel that what happened between them will happen to you too, it amounts to aping. When Rumi sent the paper to his disciple, he did what he did because of the emotions that rose in his heart.

But this is a case that is specific only to the interaction between the two of them. How can you make a rule of it?

But today you see so many Muslim households where this custom is followed. Whenever someone falls sick in the house, they start looking for a Sufi. It is difficult to find a true Sufi these days, but it has become a business for some. They charge money, scribble on a piece of paper, and instruct the family to either dissolve it in water and feed it to the patient, or tie it around his arm or put it around his neck!

Rumi often stood and did zikr – he was the first one to introduce the system of standing and doing zikr. Islam does not permit music, but Rumi said, "You will not come to my tekke – the place where zikr is done – without a bendir in your hand." In Turkey, hand held, frame-drum is called a bendir. Rumi combined music and poetry with Allah's zikr. This achievement of Rumi is a milestone. He was the first one to incorporate music and poetry into Allah's service. He said that music is not only to give joy to our ears, but is also a means of connecting with Allah. Here music doesn't mean any worthless music – it has to be spiritual. Before Rumi, when 'La Ilaha Illallah' was recited, there was no music to it as music was banned. But Rumi changed the style of zikr – the duff (a hand drum, sometimes equipped with rings or small cymbals along the rim), ney (reed flute also known as Sufi flute) and kudum (small, hemispherical drums). There is another instrument known as baglama (plucked string instrument), all these are played in zikr.

So while doing zikr, Rumi would stand up and start dancing. The tenets of Islam prohibit singing and dancing. But whenever Rumi experienced the height of divine grace, he would suddenly stand up in a state of ecstasy and start dancing. When 'La Ilaha Illlallah' is said in dum zikr, the breath is brought out in a gush. It is said that the person on whom Rumi's breath fell would be cured of all diseases. Though the people who came there came for zikr and not for treatment, gradually they realised that the gush of his breath cured all diseases.

The alternative therapy of Reiki, which has come from China and Japan, is similar. In this form of treatment, the patient is healed through touch. The touch of the Reiki healer recharges the energy channels of the patient's body. It is a different matter that Reiki has been totally commercialised nowadays.

The act of healing, the power of blessing is borne out of the state of blessedness. The one who is in deep reverence, sometimes the mere presence of such an individual or a physical ritual done by any such individual can trigger healing. So the power does not lie in the act, now this act could be blowing over a patient's face with pre-meditated recitations or by following any other method. The power lies with the one who does it, again it is automated, something that happens on its own, not as a pre-planned ritual. With Rumi, such incidents would happen own their own.

To go deep into zikr, one needs a pure heart and trust. A verse in the Quran says: O God! Give us your trust! We do not have faith, give us faith. May we believe in you! We lack conviction, give us the conviction we need.

If someone attempts zikr without purity of heart and without conviction, it does not have effect; it is reduced to a mechanical act. You recite like a machine and the practice of dum is reduced to a breathing exercise. That is not zikr! Zikr begins with conviction, purity of heart and love. Practice both the methods of doing zikr, the one in which we say 'Hu' and the one in which we say 'La Ilaha Illallah'.

Ji chaahe to shisha ban ja, ji chahe paimaana ban ja
Sheesha paimana kya banna, mai ban ja, maikhana ban ja
Mai ban kar, maikhana ban kar, masti ka afsana ban ja
Masti ka afsana ban ker, hasti se begana ban ja
Hasti se begana hona, masti ka afsana ban ja
Is hone se, is banne se acchha hai, deewana ban ja
Deewana ban jane se, deewana hona acchha hai
Deewana hone se acchha, khaak-e-dar-e-janana ban ja
Khaak-e-dar-e-janana kya hai, ahdil dil ki aankh ka surma
Shama ke dil ki thandak ban ja, noor-e-dile parwana ban ja
Seekh Zaheen ke dil se jalna, kahe ko har shama pe jalna
Apni aag mein khud jal jaaye, tu aisa parwana ban ja

If one desires
He may become a glass or a goblet
But why become a goblet, if one
Can become the tavern, the wine inside
By becoming the tavern, the wine, become a saga of joy
Become a saga of joy
And lose yourself in emptiness
Become the one, who is lost in love forever
Why just become the one, who is lost in love
When you can be the one, who lives in love, all the time
Why just live in love, when you can be the dust
At the doorstep of beloved
The dust of the beloved's doorstep
Is merely an adornment of everyone's heart
Be the calmness
That lives in the heart of every flame
Become the light, that is in the heart of the moth
But why burn for every flame
Be the moth, the one who
Perishes in the flame of its own fire

Do not be a moth that is ready to burn in any flame. The Sufi poet says that the heart that is attracted to and falls in love with just about anyone, has not really learnt to be a lover in the real sense. If at all you want to be a lover, you must burn in the flame that is in your own heart. Light the flame in your heart, be a lover like the moth and immolate yourself in this self-lit fire of love.

'Shama and Parvana' is a common analogy for consummate love in Urdu poetry. The attraction of the parvana (moth) for the shama (flame) drives it to madness: first it keeps circling the flame, and then, knowing fully well the consequences, yet unable to keep away, it goes closer and closer, only to be totally destroyed.

The skilled one says: "Learn from me! Don't be mired in worry. If burn you must, then burn in the fire of love."

You can even become the glass of which the bottle is made! If you want to be something, it is sufficient to be glass. Remember, for making the final product, the glass is first heated to a very high temperature. Glass is made from sand which is baked for so long that it melts; this liquefied sand is then shaped into objects, and to mould this hot, melted glass, the craftsman immerses it in cold water, and then the liquid glass takes on a solid form.

The poet says: You too burn in the fire of love. To become as glass, you have to burn in the fire of love. Once you have become like glass, only then can you be moulded into a goblet or a bottle.

The Sufi says that you first need to burn in the fire of divine love, and like glass, convert from a gross state to a subtler one. It is easy to remain in the solid rock form, but it is not easy to become glass. Glass was a solid even before becoming glass, but heating it in a fire changed it to glass. After turning into glass, it was moulded into a goblet or a bottle, and finally wine was poured into it. The wine is in the goblet as well as in the bottle. The poet goes on to add:

Sheesha paimana kya banna
Mai ban ja, maikhana ban ja

Why just glass? Why even a goblet or a decanter? True intoxication lies in the substance that is inside. So if you want to be something of substance, why not be wine itself? And then, why just a jar of wine, why not be the whole tavern?

Remember that a seeker is like an empty goblet, and a Sufi is like a tavern where seekers come and fill the empty goblets of their hearts. They come empty handed and go back contented, having satiated themselves with the wine of divine love. But after travelling some distance, they again become empty and that is why they keep coming back again and again.

How long will you keep returning to the tavern? Till you yourself become a tavern! How long do you need to keep a Sufi's company? Till you yourself become a Sufi! How long do you need to seek a guru's patronage? Till you yourself become a guru!

The external guru is important and is required till he awakens the guru within. The actual guru resides within you, but the worldly guru is required to awaken and activate the guru within.

How long do we need to be in a master's company? There is a word popular among Sufis – silsila, a chain of events. A master teaches a disciple who then incorporates the teachings into his own life. Then one final day, he too gets established in the teachings and becomes solid like glass. From there he progresses to become as a goblet and then as wine. Finally one day, he becomes the source of intoxication – he becomes the tavern! So the disciple becomes a Sufi the day he becomes a tavern. And once he has become a Sufi himself, he has no need to go to any other Sufi.

I would like to narrate another incident from Rumi's life. One day the Mevlana was invited to another tekke where zikr was to be performed. In those days it was a custom for the sheikh to sit on a sheepskin, though later this was changed. Earlier it used to be just a sheepskin, but now in Turkey and Iran, when a sheepskin is laid out for any sheikh, red colour is sprinkled on it. As you know, sheepskin is white, but after the assassination of Shams, they started sprinkling red dye on it. When asked why, they say: "This is Shams' blood. We don't want to forget his assassination and martyrdom." So even today – at least in Turkey – whenever a sheikh is offered a seat, the sheepskin spread before him bears red spots that represent Shams' blood.

When Rumi reached the tekke, he saw the students and their sheikh sitting there. The sheikh's name was Kunnavi and he was on his seat. As he saw Rumi coming, he called out, "Come, we will both sit here." Both were sheikhs, so Kunnavi invited Rumi to sit with him. Rumi replied, "Two sheikhs can never sit together on one skin." Kunnavi, very respectfully, showing all his love for Rumi, slid the skin towards him and said, "If only one sheikh can sit on a skin, then you will sit and not I"

So the chain or silsila carries on from a Sufi master to his disciple, till the disciple is ready to become a master. But like I said earlier, there are very few seekers who come to the master for the right reason. The rest – this crowd of thousands – is a farce. I don't say that you too are farcical, but I would definitely like you to look inside and see what it is that you have come here for.

Do you know the reason why you are here? Is it purely for love? Are you reading this book to understand the nuances of this path or for some other reason? Are you interested because others are interested in zikr? Or because you heard that I talk about Sufism? Is your interest merely fleeting?

The chain of events that is called silsila moves from a guru to his disciples and never from a guru to his followers. The chain moves from the murshid to his mureed. As stated earlier, the one who manages to kill his mind, and the one whose desires are dead, is a mureed. If the chain moves in the right direction, then the disciple does not remain a disciple for long.

A stage of overflowing joy is reached, and then the world sees you as a container filled with joy and ecstasy; as though a living saga of joy is moving around. Step by step, the tradition is carried forward. First it is said that you become as glass. Then from glass you are asked to become a goblet, then from goblet to wine and then to a tavern! Then you are told that rather than becoming a tavern, you become a saga of joy. For becoming a tale of bliss and joy, you will have to cross one hurdle, you will have to become oblivious of your own existence. You will have to completely forget the sentiment: 'I too am something'.

Let me remind you of Abu Yaseed Bastami. The experiences he had in the initial stages of worship made him so content that he began shouting: "Who could be more fortunate than me? Who could be luckier than me? I have become a king!" That is why Abu Yaseed could not become a real Sufi, for he had become proud and vain!

Who can become a saga of joy? Only one who completely annihilates his very personality! I often quote this couplet; maybe you will understand it better now:

Mita de apni hasti ko gar kuchh martaba chahe
Ki dana khak mein mil kar gul-e-gulzar hota hai

We must sacrifice our existence
To achieve the ultimate power
Like a seed, when lost in the soil
turns into a blooming flower

Masti ka afsana ban ker, hasti se begana ban ja
Hasti se begana hona, masti ka afsana ban ja
Is hone se, is banne se acchha hai, deewana ban ja

> Be story of ecstasy, be oblivious of self
> Be oblivious of self and become story of bliss
> From being and dissolving self
> It is better to lose yourself in love

You became wine and then a tavern and then a saga of joy. All the while, the process of 'becoming' continues. After this, if you say that you have annihilated your 'self', you forget that the person saying it is still there – he still exists! Till such time as the person saying all this exists, he has not perished. The poet says that you have to completely erase your sense of 'self' and of being.

Now what can you do to achieve this state of total dissolution of the ego-self? You have to dissolve yourself in love. A 'deewana' (the one whose sense of 'self' is completely dissolved in love) never says that he has dissolved himself, that he is lost in love; it is the world that calls him so. A man who has given himself to love, never says that now he exists no more, he is gone; it is the world that says so. Similarly, if someone says that he has annihilated his ego, know that he is lying, for, had he done so, he wouldn't say it. But as he is saying it, it means that the 'I' in him is still there.

As long as the disciple tells his master that he loves him, his love for his master is false. If it were true, there would be no need to express it. When the need arises, love speaks for itself – it does not need words. No words or letters of the alphabet are required to express love. When words are spoken, it means that love has not reached its pinnacle, and that is why expression is required to convince the other. This poetic expression, becomes even more profound, when it adds:

Deewana ban jane se deewana hona acchha hai

If someone says that he has dissolved his 'self' completely, know that he has not reached his destination, for you are not to become anything – you have to break down and destroy your 'self'. You are not even to proclaim 'yourself' as a lover of God.

Do not be even a lover of God. Be if you must, the dust that lies at His doorstep.

Deewana hone se acchha, khaak-e-dar-e-janana ban ja

What will happen if someone becomes that dust? That dust will then become the balm that will soothe your heart – the heart that has been blinded.

Se ankhadiyan biyan jan dasidando ma piri

Farid says that man lacks the vision to see his God. The day you lay your ego at His feet, your own ashes will become a panacea for all your ailments.

Khaak-e-dar-e-janana kya hai
Ahale dil ki aankh ka surma
Shama ke dil ki thandak ban ja
Noor-e-dile parwana ban ja

The day the dust of humility adorns your being, your heart will light up like a candle and you will discover a light within you; the light you seek to illumine your path will be ignited in your own heart.

Let us start again: First you become a glass; why just a glass, when you can become a goblet and then even the wine itself. You can become the entire tavern; a saga of joy; and then even a deewana. But why stop there? Become dust at your beloved's feet. This very dust that is your false-self, lying at the feet of your beloved, will then become the balm, that will illumine your heart. And the day, this flame is lit in your heart, you will become radiance personified; and then you become the lover and the beloved, the seeker and the sought; you become man and his God.

The poem says this flame is within you, in your heart; the Truth is also within you – it is you! This fire cannot be bestowed upon you, as divine grace by any guru – no one can give it to you!

The poet Zaheen writes: Learn from me how to light the flame of love and do as I have done.

Seekh Zaheen ke dil se jalna
Kahe ko har shama pe jalna
Apni aag mein khud jal jaaye
Tu aisa parwana ban ja

Zaheen asks you, to walk the path of love and burn yourself in the fire of love. The way his heart burns in love, let your heart burn in the flame of love. "Do not destroy yourself for petty things," he says. "Don't burn worrying about worldly possessions; don't burn in jealousy."

Do you know that jealousy blinds the heart? Attachment to anything or anyone destroys the heart! If at all you want to burn, burn yourself in His love.

The fire which will purify your 'self' cannot be sourced from outside. Even your guru cannot provide it to you. I cannot give it to you; I cannot light it for you. You have to find the fire within and 'you' yourself have to burn in this fire – nobody else can do it for you. Understanding this intellectually may look simple but practicing it in reality is difficult!

Mullah Nasruddin was a man who lived in his own world, busy with his own thoughts. One day he was invited to deliver a lecture at a Muslim seminary. When Mullah reached there he saw a large crowd gathered to listen to him. The moment he reached the podium, he said, "All of you who have gathered here, are you aware of what I am going to speak on today?" All of them said, "No, we don't! How would we know what you are going to talk about?" So Mullah said, "If you don't know what I am going to speak about, then what's the use of telling you anything at all?" Saying this, he walked out of the hall!

Everyone was in a fix; what strange behaviour was this? They felt their answer was absolutely correct, but Mullah had not found it to be so. Together they went and requested the Mullah to come again after Friday's prayer. They assured him their mistake would not be repeated. Mullah reached the seminary and standing tall on the rostrum, he asked in a high voice, "Do you know what I am going to talk about today?" So, all those who had said 'No' earlier, shouted, "Yes, of course we do!" Mullah said, "When you

117

already know, then why should I speak? Why should I waste my time telling you what you already know?" Saying this, Mullah again walked out!

Now they were in a real dilemma. Mullah walked off every time, whether they said 'yes' or 'no'. Again a meeting was held and strategies were discussed. Mullah appeared to be a great Sufi, who was clearly avoiding, speaking with them. Again Mullah was approached: "You will have to come this Friday." Mullah Nasruddin said, "Have you forgotten the last incident?"

"No, we remember everything, yet we request you to please come again." So the Mullah agreed and said, "Alright! I will certainly come."

So now the Mullah reached the school for the third time. This time the crowd had multiplied manifold. Mullah again posed the same question, "Do you have any idea what I am going to talk about today?" Half of them stood up and said, "Yes, we do," and the other half said, "No, we don't." They thought this was a good strategy to adopt as he had walked away on two previous occasions regardless of whether they had said 'yes' or 'no'. Mullah then said, "So half of you know and half of you don't. Very well! Those who know may tell those who don't. Why should I speak? Those who know may speak and those who don't know may listen. Why do you want to waste my time?"

Do you understand what Mullah is trying to point out? It is so easy to develop the misconception that one knows everything. Nothing is further from the truth; nothing is more incorrect! Sometimes one feels that even if one lacks knowledge, what is the use of knowing everything? But Mullah has an answer for this dilemma.

Mullah Nasruddin was among those Sufis who did not believe in preaching their philosophy. They gave living examples through their own real life experiences. If you ask them a question, they will not reply in words. They create situations and circumstances, which reveal the answer in an indirect but effective manner.

One day Mullah Nasruddin asked his wife to make a semolina pudding. She put in a great deal of effort in preparing the dish for him, and pouring it in a serving dish, she placed it before him.

Mullah did not even bother to serve himself and began eating straight from the dish. He ate up most of it by himself! The wife, who was busy with other chores, did not realise it. Later, being tired, she went off to sleep. Mullah went and kept the dish in the kitchen, took his blanket and went off to sleep.

It was midnight when he woke up his wife and said, "I have a brilliant idea." Now the wife knew that her husband was a learned man and a philosopher, and that philosophers get ideas out of the blue. So she asked, "What is this brilliant idea?" He said, "First go and get the left-over pudding." The wife went to the kitchen, heated the pudding and promptly brought it to him. Mullah finished off the remaining pudding, his wife looking on expectantly, waiting to hear his brilliant idea. After polishing off the whole dish, and wiping his face and beard, he said, "O my pious wife! The idea is that one should not leave the pudding unfinished; one should not keep it for the next day. Whatever is cooked today, should be finished today!"

One should not leave anything half-done. Even worship should not be left half-done. The search for God should also not be incomplete. If you actually do not want to do it, then don't do it, but do not pretend. And if you genuinely want to do it, then do it wholeheartedly and completely – because God is complete. If God is complete, how can his worship be left halfway? Don't worship incompletely; don't remain incomplete.

If, while sitting for zikr you think of worldly issues, then neither zikr is complete nor are you able to complete your work properly. So it is better for you to leave the zikr, stop thinking about Him and get up and finish your chores.

So what does Mullah say? He says don't leave things half-done. If you keep thinking of the left-over pudding and dream of getting up tomorrow and eating it, you will not be able to sleep due to your unfulfilled desires; you will only dream of the pudding! So it is better to finish it off and then go to sleep.

Similarly, when you sit down to worship you must be completely involved in it. Do not bring the outside world into this arena. If you sit down to worship and continue to be involved with worldly problems, it amounts to blasphemy. There can't be a bigger sin than thinking of worldly issues while praying! What is sin? Dwelling on the material world while praying is sin – the only sin!

> **Seekh zaheen ke dil se jalna**
> **Kahe ko har shama pe jalna**
> **Apni aag mein khud jal jaaye**
> **Tu aisa parvana ban ja**

If your search and your longing is true, then it won't be difficult for you to complete this journey. Another thing to remember is that Sufism accepts sudden enlightenment – a person can reach a certain stage after years of worship and practice. This is one way; another is to receive God's grace. He can straightaway elevate a person to a stage that a Sufi may have reached after years of practice. This is known as a miracle, a marvel! We consider curing someone's illness, ridding someone of evil spirits or helping in financial gains a miracle. But for a Sufi, a miracle is when He showers His blessings on someone and opens all doors.

I would like to narrate another incident from Rumi's life. The main door of his tekke made a creaking sound whenever it was opened or closed. It gets very cold in Konya during winters; they have snowstorms and blizzards. Because of the severe cold, the door could not be left open, so each time people went in and out, the door had to be opened or closed, and every time it made an awful creaking sound.

One day a mureed said, "Sir, this door is creaking, it makes so much noise. What should we do? Shall we change it?" Rumi said, "Do not change the door that makes a sound each time it is opened. Let it be." The mureed asked, "Why? Why not change it?" Rumi said, "Every time the door opens, it gives a message that God has brought one more person closer to us; one more person is entering this tekke; one more person has set foot on the divine path. So every time the door creaks, it gives the divine message: 'See, I am not far from my beings!' There must be hundreds of thousands of travellers who just pass by this door without stopping, but the person who comes in must be a fortunate one.

The creaking sound is an announcement of his good fortune. Therefore we will not change the door; let it be as it is."

Well, we were talking of sudden enlightenment. Some people have to work hard to gain the status of a mureed (disciple), and after several long years of practice do they become a Sufi. But some are born Sufi; they do not have to make any effort to become a Sufi or even a mureed! When they open their eyes to this world, they do so with the divine light. Such enlightened people should not be asked where they gained all their wisdom from, for they do not attain wisdom – they are born with it.

In India, such people who are enlightened at birth are called avatars; in Persia they are called Sufis. That is the only difference – they are born Sufi; they do not become Sufi by any effort. This also conceals a secret – the message that whatever is made with an effort can always be undone.

Making and unmaking go together. There is always a fear of the effort made being spoilt or undone. But there is no fear for the one born with divine love – with God's affection. It is a different matter that even when one has an audience with such a great Sufi, one is not able to light up the inner self with that divine light. Such a person is the most unfortunate person in the world.

So Rumi asks his disciples to let the door with the creaking sound be, because it gives God's message that one more person is entering the tekke and joining in the worship to consume the wine of love; the message that God has been gracious to him, which is why he has been able to come here.

In this way, Sufis keep taking birth at different places in different times, whether we get to know of them or not. Till date, whenever I have held a satsang or given a discourse, I have talked about several great ascetics and yogis. You have heard of Meera, Kabir, Ravidas, Paltoo, Dadudayal, Sahajobai, Charandas, Guru Nanak, Shankaracharya and Buddha from me. Whenever we discuss them, people feel that there can be no country like India. Many people have even written to me asking what is so special about India that so many mystics are born here?

Now, with the discussion on Sufism, you have learnt that a

121

number of bright stars have been born in Turkey as well. Truly incomparable! The list is long: Sufi Fariduddin Attar, Shams Tabreez, Jalaluddin Rumi, Kunnavi, Humsuddin, Baizeed Bastami and even Rabiya-al-Basra.

Who says all mystics are born only in India? The fact is, all these stories of Sufis that I am telling you are not even two percent of the total. I don't know how many Sufis had been giving me a call, that I finally undertook this journey to Turkey. It is only after reaching there that the mysteries of Sufism started unraveling before me.

A dervish told me that as long as the Ottoman Empire existed, Sufism spread and developed well especially in places like Turkey and Syria. Ibn-al-Arabi and other Sufis showed the path with extreme love and affection. But after the disintegration of the Ottoman Empire, Sufism was banned and declared illegal, particularly in Turkey. All the tekkes were burnt and a ban was imposed on practicing zikr. Things came to such a pass that even today dervishes get together stealthily to practice zikr.

I happened to visit places in Istanbul that no ordinary person would ever be able to reach. Now, anyone can think that I went there as per my wish, but it is not so. I had gone there at the call of these Sufis, and their call was so emphatic that I just could not refuse. I just had to go and then things began to straighten out. One day a dervish said that it would probably be through me that their zikr and Sufi music would reach the people of India. He said that I had probably been selected because through me it would reach the hearts of all those who are associated with me.

Today they cannot practice zikr openly. Locks have been put on the doors and guards posted outside. By 1960 some people managed to convince the government to be allowed to do zikr on the condition that they would not do the whirling zikr; they would not dance. So by 1960 limited permission was granted, but even then government employees would come and raid the place at random to see what was going on. And if they felt that Rumi's Sufism was coming back, they would lock up the place right then and arrest all those present.

Jalaluddin Rumi's wonderful epic poem, 'Masnavi' is called the Quran of the Persian language. His three amazing treatises, viz. Masnavi, Deewan-e-Shams and Fihi-Ma-Fihi reached Europe through Spain and Syria, and then by the 14th century, started being translated into other languages all over the world.

Several European countries including the USA became aware of Rumi and the whirling dervishes; people from all over the world began coming to Turkey to see the tekkes and the whirling dervishes and to listen to Sufi music. When the government realised that they could earn through Sufi tourism, they began giving limited permission for exhibiting Sufism.

When I went in the November of 2003, it was not actually the best time to go to Turkey. There had been a bomb blast in the British embassy just four days earlier. I was in London then and everybody tried to dissuade me from going. There was a rumor that all flights had been suspended; but I insisted on going. A British Airways official told me that the service to Turkey may be withdrawn. But I said to him that if it was withdrawn, there was nothing I could do, but if the plane for Turkey took off, I would surely be on it. Finally the plane took off. And so I went and found the city shut down for the day due to a bomb scare.

By chance I spoke to my friend in Singapore. He had some business contacts in Istanbul, and so he made arrangements for our stay. He also deputed a local person to look after me and take care of all our requirements during the visit. By chance we were in a hotel that was just a few yards away from the British embassy. The police had cordoned off the entire area and everything was closed. We seemed to have arrived at an inopportune moment. We could neither buy a ney as shops were closed, nor could we hear Sufi music as it was Haj time. We could not even meet a dervish as they had all gone for Haj, our escort informed us.

For three days it felt like a wasted trip. I defied everyone to come here, and here everything was closed and we could meet no one. Not knowing the language was a problem and our escort was most unhelpful. He knew little English and his standard response to all our queries was: 'It is closed.' One day, he finally took us to see a famous mosque, which was extremely beautiful. The

123

next day, leaving him behind, we went out on our own to find a music shop so that we could buy a ney. It was difficult because I did not speak Turkish and the locals – for the most part – did not understand English. So asking for directions to a music shop was a tedious job. Later when I learnt that they say 'moojic', I too started asking for 'moojic' shop! Finally someone responded with 'toonell'. I immediately concluded that he meant 'tunnel'. Off we went looking for a tunnel! Finally we found someone who spoke some English. He told us that toonell did not mean tunnel but was the name of a street – the one we had walked up and down several times looking for a tunnel! So finally when we found Toonell Street, we realised that all the 'moojic' shops were there! There were so many instruments that I had not seen earlier. We tried some of the instruments and bought some. We even bought a ney – without knowing how to play it!

So now we needed to find a teacher. The shopkeeper offered to help and took the address of our hotel. In the afternoon we received a phone call asking if we wanted to learn the ney and if the caller could come and teach us. What more could we ask for!

In a half hour, two people arrived – a young man of about 25 years of age, named Goronay, and his friend, a young girl named Dolonay. They started their classes with a theoretical lesson on paper, followed by a practical demonstration. They taught us how to keep the ney near the lips, how to hold it and how to blow into it to get the sound of 'Hu'. Then they gave it to Kanchman who had come with me from India, and asked him to try it.

The moment Kanchman put the ney to his lips, Goronay said, "It took me two years to learn this. You must at least try to learn how to hold it. I will teach you how to blow 'Hu' into it." Kanchman just held the ney and said 'Hu' into it, and lo and behold! The ney started playing! Goronay was absolutely amazed. He said, "This is impossible! How did you do it?" Kanchman said, "Even I don't know how it happened." After this both of them went away but promised to come back the next day. I asked them to introduce us to their teacher so that we could learn to play the instrument properly. They said their teacher didn't have time, and that is why he had sent them. Then they told us that the shopkeeper from whom we had bought the ney, was a great friend of their teacher.

Here let me tell you that there were at least thirty shops in that lane. It just so happened that we had gone to the shop whose owner was a very good friend of the best ney teacher in Istanbul! The next day Kanchman insisted that we go out. Though I was not too keen as it was very cold, eventually I relented. Just five minutes into the open, a man passed by. Kanchman immediately said, "Gurumaa, this man seems to be a ney player." I asked how he could tell. He said, "Look at the long box in his hand, it may hold a ney."

"If that is what you think, then go and ask him."

"I feel embarrassed talking to a stranger out of the blue."

"Alright, you stay here and I will go and speak to him."

But Kanchman refused to let me speak to the man and walked up to him.

"Do you play any musical instrument?"

"Yes, I play the ney."

"May I know your good name?"

"I am Yavuz Yekte."

And then I remembered Goronay had told me that his teacher's name was Yavuz Yekte!

"How come you are here?"

He said the previous evening his student told him on the phone that a Sufi had come from India…!!!

A lady Sufi! He was quite amazed! He said his student told him she is a woman but she is a Sufi. "Another thing that he told me was that there is a person with her who just keeps the ney on his lips and it starts playing on its own. So I came to see who this person is."

We went to the hotel room and for two hours we sat and discussed various things. Then he made Kanchman play the ney and was thrilled to hear him. He said, "I am seventy-five years of age and have been playing the ney for sixty years; I have taught hundreds of people, but if I had found a student like you, I would die content in the knowledge that my skill would not end with me. Now please come and settle down here and I will teach you. And if you can't come then I will come to India!"

This was our first meeting and we were completely unknown to each other. While we were talking, Kanchman said in my ear, "Gurumaa, I understand that he is a very good teacher, but he is not a very good player." Remember, a teacher is not a player. The characteristic of a good teacher is that he can teach very well, but it is not necessary that he is able to play as well too.

I said, "So what? He who has sent him here, will show us the way further ahead too."

The moment I said this, Yavuz's phone rang. He talked for a while in Turkish and then said, "There is someone who wants to meet me. May I call him here?" I told him to go ahead saying that I had no problem at all. When the person arrived and we were introduced to him, we learnt that his name was Ali, and he was the second most famous ney player in Turkey!

Do you understand what was happening? Kanchman almost started crying in amazement! When the city was shut down we were not able to meet anyone – and now all avenues were opening up. We were getting everything we looked for! First we got a teacher, and then a player who was willing to come and play for us. On our request he started playing – Oh! It was wonderful! He is an amazing person. Initially he could not comprehend the concept of a lady Sufi, but later on when we explained he understood. "If ever you need any help, do remember me," he said before leaving.

Four things had been achieved and only one was left now – that of seeing the whirling dervishes. I was upset at the thought of going back without seeing them, but the Bombay program was fixed and we had to leave in time for it. Out of the blue I got a call from Yavuz Yekte. "Would you be interested in visiting a tekke where whirling dervishes do the Sema?" I said, "Most definitely! Why not?"

When we reached the place and were surprised to see that it was the same area where we had bought all the musical instruments. This place was right opposite the music street. Nothing comes to one before the allotted time! We were looking for one dervish and here we found thirteen!

Then we saw the sema of the thirteen whirling dervishes. And we met not one, but ten accomplished musicians who played Jalaluddin Rumi's music. Who says Sufis are born only in India? As we watched the whirling dervishes, I realised that there were many hidden messages being conveyed by the events that were unfolding before us; I had not been summoned here as a mere witness. Whatever was happening, was happening by the will of unseen, mystical Sufis. The task of giving a new direction, form and colour to their unfinished job – that too in a new land – was being assigned to me. I often wonder why of all the mytics and gurus in this world, was I chosen for this job?

People there eat non-vegetarian food, so we faced a problem looking for vegetarian fare. By God's grace, on the third day we met a Pakistani national who owned 'Noor', a restaurant displaying a huge board saying: Pure Vegetarian food. He used to serve us food with great affection. One day I said, "Your restaurant is far from the place we are staying in. Is it somehow possible to send the food there?" He said, "Yes, that can be arranged. Is there anything else?"

I said, "We have been eating this rich food for so long; it will be nice if you send us some simple food."

He laughed and said, "Alright, that too will be done."

The dervish who I met at the tekke said, "Today, in our country, where all the traditions of Sufism have taken birth, we don't have the freedom to practice it. Maybe through you, the flame of Mevlavi Sufism will be revived."

You are very fortunate to get an opportunity to learn these secrets. Fortunate are you, to read the first ever discourse on this subject in India; fortunate to be listening to the names of those people who's every fiber is drenched in spiritual love.

Your destination has been shown to you, but you have to make a beginning. And the starting point is to destroy all vices, desires and worldly values of the mind, in order to become as refined as glass. Then your heart will sing with love, affection and faith.

CHAPTER 7

ILLUMINE YOUR HEART

There is a saying among Sufis: One who seeks will never find, and one who does not look for Him will never meet Him. An aspirant asked, "Then how do we meet Him? If we seek we won't find Him, and if we don't seek then there is no question of finding Him! How will we ever meet the master of our universe?"

This is known as unconsciousness! Earlier I explained what sin is. Moses says there are ten types of sins. If one does not commit any of these ten sins, he becomes virtuous. Stealing, lying, cheating, infidelity, etc. are the violations of the religious code; Moses listed the Ten Commandments and instructed all Jews to follow them.

But morality took a turn for the worse around Prophet Mohammad's time. Man's mentality is such that he finds ways of breaking rules even before they are made. While people stopped committing these ten sins, they got entangled with hundreds of others. When Prophet Mohammad was asked what sin is, he said, "There is only one sin, and that is ghaflat."

Ghaflat means unconsciousness, indolence or ignorance. It is said that there is no greater sin than this. Because of ghaflat, man does not even set out in search of God. Every day he sees death around him, but due to lack of awareness, he is unable to realise the meaning of it. Every day he sees a funeral and feels it is an alien bier. This is what ignorance really is! It is because of this that man is distant from his God. And if he is away from Him, how will he look for Him? And how will he find Him if he does not even look for Him?

If you will not find Him by looking for Him, then what is the clue, the secret to finding Him? The seeker asks, "If seeking comes to naught, then what should we do? Should we stop seeking? Should we look no further?" But the fakir says, "The secret is not to give up the search. Because if you do not seek, how will he reveal Himself to you? So it is necessary to seek; the search must go on."

"For how long?"

Anyone who asks this question will never find Him! The search has to be unconditional! That is the condition!

I will again go back to Jalaluddin Rumi and Shams Tabreez. One day Shams said, "Jalaluddin! Give up the scriptures." Jalaluddin was a great scholar and a professor in the university; he was always immersed in his books. All the fakirs and Sufis respected even his father, Bahauddin, a learned and famous personality, for his knowledge and learning. But Shams asked Jalaluddin to give up the scriptures.

I told you about Rumi's dream in which he was teaching in a seminary. Suddenly he woke up to find Shams standing in front of him.

"Why won't you not leave these books? I stopped you from teaching in the daytime, and now you are teaching at night! Leave all of this now! He cannot be found in cerebral texts; He can only be found in the depths of the heart."

All that the mind possesses is irrelevant. It is the mind that bears all worldly attachments; it is the mind that is full of words and letters!

There is a very beautiful verse in the Vedanta:

Jahn bol tehn akshar aawa
Jahn abol tehn mann na rahawa
Bol abol madhya hai joi
Jas wah hai tas lakhei na koi

To understand letters you need to use the mind. Kshar means mortal and akshar means immortal. The mind is unable to reach the inner self that is immortal. So what should we do? When we speak we use words; when we talk, our mind is involved, and the mind does not have access to God.

Speech involves the use of the mind and of the alphabet. It brings the external world into our inner universe. But the Supreme Power is ineffable and beyond the grasp of the intellect – imagination cannot reach that power.

The question now is: How then do we reach out to Him? We cannot reach through words, and our mind cannot reach that which is beyond words. So then how do we ever reach there? The mind will not be able to reach there; it has a very narrow horizon and will consider the scriptures the way it does the world.

Shams says, "Now you have to come out of this rigmarole of words and reading. Just discard them." It is said that the day the incident of the dream took place, Shams picked up all of Rumi's scriptures – all of them, and they were not a few – and threw them into the water! He took him along and said, "See, I am drowning them before you. If you think you can achieve something from these books, you may retrieve them. Those books were not printed in a printing press – they were all hand written. The moment they were put in the water, the ink was completely washed off! "

It was then that Rumi said that he did not want to gain any more knowledge. "The knowledge that is taking me away from my God deserves to be discarded. I do not desire it any more. It is this knowledge that has become an obstacle between me and my God, so let it burn. This philosophy, these words and these scriptures are preventing me from reaching my God."

Rumi taught a new way of performing zikr – the one done in the standing position; the zikr in which, for the first time music was used within the constraints of Islam. Religious leaders did not grant permission for this; they opposed it then as they oppose it today.

Here I would like to tell you about another silsila that is in vogue in Turkey. Just as there is the Mevlavi silsila of Jalaluddin Rumi, there is another silsila called Halveti. It is a unique practice that is followed even by some Indian yogis. And that is to sit in zikr after consuming alcohol! Why? Because the mind loses its sharpness and becomes less active!

If a troubled and distressed person consumes liquor, he feels better. Who doesn't have sorrows and troubles? No matter how you try to console your mind that this is a passing phase, it remains concentrated on worldly troubles.

So these people found a new way. While Rumi adopted music and poetry, these people adopted the practice of drinking alcohol before zikr. When told that drinking alcohol is forbidden in Islam, they retort that even music is forbidden; if music is used in a unique way, why not this?

Various such traditions and customs are followed in the practice of meditation. In Rumi's style of zikr, one stands and performs the rite with dum. The way they say 'La Ilaha…' with force, similarly, the Halveti style of zikr is done with dum, using 'Al Hai', which is one of Allah's ninety-nine names. There are two meanings of this word – the first is: 'the one who exists' and the second is: 'the seeker faces or presents himself to the Lord'.

A Persian Sufi said to Kabir, "I have heard that there is no Sufi in India as accomplished as you. I have come to ask you a question. Do you know Allah?

"Allah knows me," replied Kabir.

That we know Allah is of little import. That he knows and recognises our being is of consequence.

Some Muslims from Karnataka and Hyderabad had come for the camp. They came to me in the morning and I said, "You are Muslim by birth…" I am saying this because in my view, and I repeat, 'in my view', it is incorrect to determine religion by birth; it is not necessary that you agree with me. Man should be free to make his own choice on a subject as profound as religion. So it is not necessary for a person born in a Hindu family to be attracted to Krishna. It is quite possible that he prefers calling out to Allah. And it is equally possible for a person born in a Muslim family to find the sound of Onkar dear.

In the social structure set up by the mullahs, bhais, popes and pandits, one does not have permission to move even an inch from the prescribed norms? They call it 'religious conversion'. Always remember that there is only one religion – that of Truth. All others are sects – various paths that lead you to the Truth. There is only one religion – it is unique, universal, eternal and omnipresent! There is no question of any choice in it; if at all, we can make a choice between Truth and non-Truth. You can choose the path you wish to tread, but how can anybody choose or reject Truth? Truth is eternal!

So I asked our Muslim friends to recite a few of the ninety-nine names of Allah. But neither Riyaz-ul-Rehman nor his friend Ahmed spoke up. I did not get an opportunity to ask the few others who were there. Allah has ninety-nine names! I personally feel it is not necessary for every Muslim to know all the ninety-nine names – one name is sufficient; if one grasps the gist of that one name correctly, then even one will suffice!

Sufis keep reciting 'La Ilaha Illallah'. Somebody asked, "Why don't you complete it by saying 'Mohammad Rasool Allah'?" Sufis say: 'No, this alone is the whole Truth. Mohammad Sahib conveyed His message to us. For this we worship, revere and praise him and are forever grateful to him. But the real message is just this much, and it is sufficient for us.'

Another Sufi said, "Where is the need to utter such a long name? It is sufficient to say 'Allah Allah Allah'! Our life is short, breath is limited and this mantra is too long. So it is enough to just say 'Allah'." In this type of zikr, the name that has been used is 'Hai'. The mantra 'Hai' is recited in a standing position and not in a sitting one.

I respect tradition and do not wish to change it. So you too must learn the right way of doing zikr. The method is really nice: Eight to ten people stand in a closed circle, keeping one hand on the other, placing it loosely near the stomach. Why in a circle? I have told you that the ney is tubular and so is our backbone. So they stand in a circle and recite the mantra. When all ten recite with deep breaths, their energy is concentrated at one point.

Let me use the example of a torch to explain this. If the energy discharged when the mantra 'Hai' is uttered is a torchlight coming from the heart, imagine the beam from all ten collecting at one place without scattering!

I have told you several times that when you sit in meditation, your body emits a bioelectric magnetic force, which is normally present in every body. The other thing is the rising of the kundalini from the mooladhar chakra at the base of the spinal cord. This upsurge of energy produced by the rising kundalini has to be stored. How do you store it? By sitting on the mat.

A jute mat or a blanket is necessary so that the energy produced in the body is not discharged into the ground and does not get earthed. So you place the mat on the ground and then sit on it. Whenever you sit in meditation you should form the gyan mudra where the thumb and first finger are joined, keeping the rest of the fingers straight, while resting the wrist on the knee. Alternatively, you can form the mudra the Buddha taught us, where the right hand is placed on top of the left with both thumbs joined together. In this way, the energy emitted from one thumb goes to the other, from one hand to the other and from the legs it flows to the thighs, thus completing the energy circle. This circle should not be broken.

Another outer circle is made in the zikr of 'Hai'. All stand in a circle and then recite the mantra with force and a deep breath; the sound comes from deep within the gut and not from the throat.

During the recording of 'Hu' and 'La Ilaha Illallah' we had no problem even though the recording was done in my absence. But when we came to 'Hai', the recording could not be done for more than one minute! The musicians would sit down saying their heads were reeling.

"We will not be able to do it!" They said.

When I was informed I went to meet them. I explained everything to them very patiently as they had no idea at all about this subject. They play the instruments and are knowledgeable about them, but they have never sat in meditation. It is one thing to play a musical instrument for meditation, but sitting in meditation yourself is an altogether different experience.

Those who proofread the Guru Granth Saheb before its printing cannot be called learned. Am I not right? The Gita is printed in Gorakhpur – the proofreaders, writers and typists are not scholars or intellectuals.

So I sat and discussed the matter with them. I asked one of them, "Do you ever drink?" He said, "Yes I do, sometimes."

"How do you feel when you drink?"

"I feel good. My mind feels light and I feel wonderful."

"What happens if you drink in excess?"

He said, "Then I get a heavy head."

"That's it!" I exclaimed. When you did this for one minute, the intoxication within was uncorked. You are not familiar with the taste of this divine liquor that is why your head was spinning. Your head was not really spinning; you were experiencing the intoxication of spiritual liquor."

They seemed to understand, so I asked, "Shall we continue now?"

"Yes, now let us continue."

Then we did a trial and they really enjoyed it. During the rehearsal some new people joined in, and when the first take was done, some of the new entrants sat down with their heads in their hands! They said, "What is this thing, it's so powerful! In fact it is dangerous! What is it?" So once again I had to explain to them. In my experience, when the zikr of 'Hai' is performed with dum, it has a unique effect; it takes you to an indescribable state of intoxication.

A good teacher is not one who reads something and then goes and preaches to others. Professors in colleges and universities first read the syllabus and then go and rattle it off to the students. Whatever we share with you is first tried out by us. We conduct extensive research before presenting the results to anyone. It is almost like we have plucked the best flowers from the Sufi gardens of Turkey, and are now garlanding you with them.

When I went to the centre in Turkey, it was extremely cold there. I wore four sweaters – one on top of the other – and an overcoat, and still I was cold. The person who accompanied me was called Rifet; he too is a ney player. I noticed something unusual in Turkey – once you are introduced to people, if you mention that you want to see a particular place or meet a particular person, they are extremely forthcoming. All they would say is, "Alright!" And then they would come, pick you up, treat you to good food and tea, and even drop you back to your hotel!

This is pure affection. Sufis have said that a seeker should possess three qualities: Sijjat or purity of heart and thought; karamat or offering, distributing and sharing; khushu or humility and affection. Often I feel that if you want to meet a true Muslim, if you want to see what a true Muslim should be like, you should go to Turkey.

At the centre I was taken to see their sheikh. He met me in the manner of the Sufi tradition, with his right hand on his heart and head slightly bowed. When a mureed wishes his sheikh, the sheikh too bows as low as the mureed. By custom the sheikh should not bow his head, but he does. He bows to indicate that God is present equally in your heart as well. When you bow your head, it is not to the sheikh but to the light that is within him. So his obeisance too is for the radiance that is within you.

Refet introduced me as a Sufi from India. We had several rounds of tea – of course sweets were served – and then we started the process of zikr. They sang Ilahis – hymns on mystical texts – for a long time. When the Ilahis were over, the sheikh called out to indicate that the zikr was about to start. As this is their daily ritual, no explanation was required. Suddenly they all got up and started the zikr.

They were all sitting, and all of a sudden, from that very position, they started with 'Hai'. Then, one by one they got up and formed a circle in which they started calling 'Hai' with heavy breaths. So much energy was produced by this collective zikr that the whole room was filled with vibrations. That energy generated so much heat, that despite the severe cold, I felt like taking off all my woollens!

Please remember that I was not participating on that day – I was just a spectator. I had gone there as a guest and was watching the entire spectacle of zikr as a witness; I had gone to learn and complete my research.

The most beautiful part was when the sheikh picked up his bendir and went into the centre of the circle. He kept playing the bendir and the chant of 'Hai' carried on with it. So when the sheikh played his tambourine along with the sound of Hai, and when he himself sang 'Hai-Hai', it seemed as though a million crackers and sparklers exploded. The sound and brilliance were spectacular!

Wherever we went we had cameras and other equipment with us; we intended recording everything. But wherever we reached, we found things were not upto the mark. There were some nice places, but they were done-up by the government for the sake of tourism; such places lacked authenticity.

One must have the sensitivity to differentiate between an original and an imitation. For this, special radar is required in one's brain. Unfortunately, whenever we went to the right place we did not have our cameras with us; when we did have the cameras, the place turned out to be inappropriate! I wish I could have recorded that day's zikr – it would have helped me understand it better on later viewing.

You have not seen your faces while meditating – they look very beautiful. Why! The most beautiful faces in this world are of meditators. When even the most ugly and foolish person meditates, the beauty of Truth is reflected on his face. That is why it is said that if you want to become beautiful, you should start loving and practicing meditation. One who meditates is always beautiful. People in Turkey are, as it is, fair complexioned. Most of them seem to have white skin like the Americans. And when they do zikr, their faces are flushed and red!

That day, by the time the zikr got over it was about two in the morning. I signaled to Refet, "Shall we go? It is two o'clock."

We usually don't keep awake till very late; we consider two in the morning to be the witching hour! But for them, night is a time for zikr. They say, "The night is not for sleeping. It is for doing zikr." What a beautiful thought!

One night Shams and Rumi were sitting on the terrace. The moon was shining in the sky. The entire village of Konya was asleep. Looking at the bright full-moon Shams said, "Jalaluddin, look at the beauty of this shining moon, and look at all the people sleeping in ignorance!" Rumi said, "They are sleeping. We should not wake them up." Shams reprimanded him affectionately, and said, "Rumi, you are a sea of benevolence! Your job is to awaken people, whether they are of Konya, Istanbul or Damascus. Today you have said this, but never say it again. It is your duty to wake up those lost in slumber."

Later, after Shams disappeared, Rumi wrote a poem that is in the 'Masnavi': 'I remember the moon that paled in front of my moon'. He used to call Shams his 'moon'. 'I remember the moon that paled in front of my moon, because my moon is not a moon, it is a sun. O Shams! I suffer in memory of the moments when we went around doing zikr and whirling in the moonlight'.

Rumi used to say: "I am the earth and Shams is my sun." In the same poem Rumi writes: 'Let me describe that night, the night when the earth and the sun danced and the stars in the sky witnessed their dance. I orbited my sun and my sun revolved around its own self.'

So far I have explained just a few aspects of zikr. We haven't discussed the whirling part yet and how they used to go round. Whirling has a specific style; it is an art.

The mantra is 'Hai', and once again, it is not pronounced from the throat! Rumi's words are: 'Empty yourself from within like a ney just as the Prophet placed his lips on one end of the ney and the Almighty's song emanated from the other, similarly, the ney of your mind should be emptied of vanity, and then His song will begin to echo. There is pain, suffering and appeal, as in a sigh, in this zikr.

Once more I remind you that 'Hai' is not to be uttered from the throat. You have to inhale twice through your mouth – not once, but twice. And then, the way the breath is sucked in while sobbing, that is the way 'Hai' is to be enunciated – as though somebody is sighing in the pain of separation. This sighing is not done deliberately; it just happens.

Sufism is the -ism of love, of pain and of devotion. Do not use your tongue; it is a sin to do zikr with the tongue alone. The pain should rise in the heart and then the heart will need to sigh and call out. Somehow, somewhere, when this lament, this appeal comes from the heart, the love lying dormant in your heart awakens.

CHAPTER 8

THE MASTER IS AN EMBODIMENT OF LOVE

There is a popular Sufi story that goes like this: A Sufi went to sleep after his night prayers and had a dream. In his dream he heard God's voice, and the divine voice said, "Sinners have started living in your city, so it should be razed to the ground. Now my fury will ruin this city. As you are my loved one, I am telling you to leave this city and go elsewhere."

The Sufi asked the divine voice, "O Lord! Is it true that there are very few Sufis on this earth who love you and whom you love in return? Is it true?"

"Yes, that is absolutely true."

"Can you ever hurt the person whom you love?"

"Never! Such a one is my favourite."

"If a hundred Sufis lived in one city and the rest were all sinners, then what would you do?"

The divine voice replied, "I would be generous to that city where a hundred Sufis living together!"

The Sufi again asked, "What if only 50 Sufis lived in that city, then what would you do?" "Even if there were only fifty, I would still be generous."

"And if only 10 Sufis lived there, and the rest were all sinners, then?"

"I would forgive all the sinners for the sake of the 10 Sufis, since my loved ones, my dervishes live in that city. Even though they are just ten in number, it is enough for me."

Finally the Sufi said, "And now my last question. Suppose only one Sufi lived in that city, then what would you do?"

The voice replied, "For that one devotee, I would forgive all the sinners."

"Well! Then forgive the people living in my city! You love me and want to see me alive, you don't want me to get hurt – this is your wish! You are warning me beforehand to leave the city as your fury is going to ruin it. But I reside here and you have promised to love a person who loves you a million times over." It is said the divine voice spoke for the last time, "True! Whatever you have said is true. For you – the one Sufi, the one dervish, I have forgiven this whole city."

Even one is enough. If one candle is lit, it lights up the whole room. If a big torch is switched on, it removes the darkness of a larger area. If these worldly torches have the power to eliminate darkness, won't a heart illumined with love have an impact in faraway places? Definitely it will! Its fragrance reaches far-flung areas. Just as when a king or an emperor enters a hall, all the people sitting stand up respectfully, similarly when a Sufi adorns a seat, all the divine powers present in that place are activated. There are innumerable proofs of this; people change completely on visiting such places.

In the third century there lived a Sufi by the name of Baizeed Bastami who was going to Mecca for pilgrimage. He would meet every Sufi and dervish in every city and village he passed through; he would go and meet those pillars of wisdom. Thus he carried on with his journey, meeting people along the way. The land of Mecca was just a little distance away when he met a fakir.

The fakir asked, "Bastami, where are you going?" Bastami replied, "I am going to Mecca for Haj." The fakir said, "Wait! First listen to me. All the apostles have loved, respected and revered the house you are going to see. But this house that you are seeing, he said, pointing to his own body... this house that you are seeing here has been made by none other than the Almighty himself. A human being, after all made the house you are going to see. A human being made that house while the one you are

God himself has made. Then why are you going to Mecca? Come and circumambulate around me. Why do you want to go there? It is not assured that you will meet the Almighty where you are going, or whether you will even be able to see his brilliant light. But the house that is in front of you right now – do you not see the divine light emanating from it? Are you really not able to see the radiance?"

Then the fakir added, "You will give alms and offerings and do the ritual circumambulation; you may do all that here itself while reciting the holy verses."

On hearing this, Baizeed Bastami gave all the offerings that he had brought with him to the fakir and began going around the holy structure that was his body. He started singing: 'La Ilaha Illallah, La Ilaha Illallah'. He completed the same number of rounds that he had planned to do at Mecca; he completed them right there, thinking to himself how true the mendicant's words were.

Yes, it is true! Certainly this body of yours is the house made by God himself!

In order to reach the state in which the fakir was; one has to make big sacrifices and what are these sacrifices, the real sacrifices are that of your own breath and of your false 'I'. You have to sacrifice your ignorance! You have to sacrifice your duality! You have to sacrifice your pride and ego! What wrong have these poor animals done you? Poor mute creatures!

I always preach vegetarianism, so one day when this Muslim-born girl came to be initiated by me, as usual I told her to become a vegetarian. In this girl's house, everybody is non-vegetarian and she had been eating meat since childhood, but when her parents came to my camp they handed me a letter. She had written two things in it. First: 'I have become a vegetarian now.' And second was a beautiful couplet:

Tere naalem ka bosa sau sajdon pe bhaari hai
Teri yaad mein ro lena sau namaaz pe bhaari hai

Kissing your feet is higher than hundreds of bows
Crying in your love is higher than hundreds of prayers

Naalem means 'shoe' and bosa means 'kiss'. Kissing your shoe is a hundred times more valuable than bowing my head in prayer or reverence.

We have to sacrifice, but what? Our vanity! Our beastliness! This body of ours with which we associate the word 'mine' – that is the sacrifice we have to make. In other words, Sufism is the path of self-destruction. All that one has to do is obliterate oneself.

A Sufi never questions the rewards of his effort. "What will I achieve if I sit in meditation for so long? What will we get for singing 'La Ilaha…' for this much time?" A Sufi doesn't talk this language; this is the language of the householder! One who expects something in return cannot profess divine love. The one who actually loves does not seek anything in return. God can keep trying to give something, but each time the Sufi will say, "No, I don't want anything."

Someone asked, "If you love God and He asks you what you would like to have, then what is the problem in taking? One must take something."

But I say that he who loves God is not a Sufi. A Sufi has no love for God's reality; he just does not love God! But there is love! The Sufi does love! In fact he is love personified!

Maybe initially a mureed (disciple) loves his murshid (master). The second step is when he begins to love that Almighty about whom his murshid talks. And the third and final stage is when his love is only for the feeling of being in love. Now he is not in love with anyone or anything. Now he is only in love with love! Then he becomes a true picture of love, a true idol of love. Who is he in love with? With no one! Now love is only for the sake of love.

Someone asked a Sufi, "Why do you cry? Don't you know that the Almighty is everywhere? Don't you know he lives inside your heart? Then why do you cry?" The lover replied, "I cry because I find crying joyous. I cry because it gives me a chance to wash out the dirt from my heart. Every tear that comes out of my eyes, rolls on to my cheeks and falls on my bosom, clears some of the dirt from my heart." If a cloth is dirty, it can be washed with soap;

but if the heart is dirty, how does one clean it? They say that if we remember Him and cry, the heart is cleansed.

The first stage is when a mureed loves his murshid; in the second stage he loves God, and in the third stage he just loves 'love'. One who falls in love with love becomes a reflection of love himself. But by the time one gets there, the concept of 'me' and 'mine' does not remain. When neither the ego nor attachment is left, what is the object of attachment? What can one be tied to? Then one is totally free!

In Sufism, after bowing in front of his sheikh, the mureed seeks permission for whirling. Please remember that nothing is done without taking permission. The mureed bows in front of his sheikh and the sheikh kisses his forehead and wishes him good luck saying, "Go, you may go now." After that the mureed unfolds his hands slowly and it appears as though a bird is fluttering its wings and is about to fly away.

The dervish has to open up and spread his wings! If a bird has to fly, it opens its wings and flutters them. A dervish who does the whirling zikr spreads both his arms and says: "I am free! I am not attached to anything now, not even to this perishable body!" That is the reason why a whirling dervish wears a white cloak symbolic of a shroud. He has covered his own body with a shroud! There is no 'I' left, nor is there any 'mine'. All that is left is fikr – and it carries on incessantly within!

The nature and temper of a whirling dervish who goes deep into zikr holds no room for 'I' or 'mine'. Once zikr is over, if someone asks the Sufi what he has achieved, his answer is that when there is no 'I', then the question of achievement does not arise. Had 'I' existed, maybe I would have tried to calculate my achievements. I did not drown in zikr for any kind of achievement; I am just in love.

One can never say who will fall in love, and where and how! But whenever it happens, know that there is no greater blessing. No divine mercy or gift is bigger than this. A small spark burns down a whole house and even the goods inside. Similarly, a small spark of divine love, burns down the house of your mind, with all its desires, abnormalities and lust.

Sometimes Sufis say: "Don't count how many times you have uttered His name! Don't count how many times you have prayed or how many times you have read the Holy Scriptures! Just wait for the moment when divine love will arise in your heart. Whatever one goes through to reach that stage of love is insignificant. Nobody can claim that considering the amount of practice he has done, he deserves liberation. This is not correct. Nobody can claim to have done so much meditation, that he is entitled to a state of Samadhi – pure consciousness, where mind and its modalities cease to work.

Where it is entirely up to you how much you meditate, reaching a state of samadhi is not in your hands. It is unto you to meditate; you are free to do so. But if you meditate with a purpose, then you are not a true meditator. One, who meditates with only meditation as its purpose, actually meditates in the right sense of the word.

If you ask a singer why he sings and he says that he sings for money and fame, then his music loses all significance. One, who takes money for his music, can't be true at heart. In Turkey they have music centres in every corner of every lane where musicians gather. The place is open to all and nobody has to seek permission to enter and nobody is issued an invitation. If an acquaintance takes you along, you are welcomed with affection. Some food – like soup and bread – is served. So you eat and drink tea till others join in.

Once everyone has eaten and gathered, it is time for a meeting where people work with musical notes. They do not have any verbal training; they all have notation books in front of them and they are all given pages from those books. Singers as well as instrumentalists sit together and then they begin. One needs to know how to read those notations. They have three consecutive nights of meetings like this, from Thursday to Saturday.

One gentleman was playing very well so I asked him, "Will you come tomorrow morning? I would love to discuss a few things with you." He said, "Tomorrow morning I have to go to office."

"Office?"

"I am an electrical engineer."

He then told me that music was not a profession there. Someone works in an office, someone owns a shop, someone is an exporter, someone sells medicines, and someone else might be a government officer.

So I asked, "And what about music?"

"Music is worship for us. It is like a prayer. We don't earn money from it." I asked him why that was so.

"The day you start earning money from your music, that day your music will lose its essence."

What a beautiful sentiment!

One day it was pouring heavily and Refet had fixed a visit to a very famous mosque. He had asked me to meet him in front of it, and from there we were to go elsewhere. So we were waiting there for Refet as he was a little late. When he came he said, "Today I will not take you in a tram. Because of me we are late, so today I will take you in a taxi." I said that a tram was cheaper and moved faster as well, then where was the need for a taxi? But Refet insisted, "No, I kept you waiting so this is my punishment." He called a taxi and off we went. One thing about the people there is that they really love Indians. They are filled with joy on learning that a person is from India. They suddenly start calling, "Hindistan, Hindistan!"

So at this place they handed a paper with the notations to me too. I said, "I am not well versed in notations and that too in Turkish! So it will not make sense to me any way. What will I do with this?" But they said "No, you keep it in front of you and just listen. Don't read, just listen. Though the language is Turkish, the script is English." They started in such a pleasant manner and with so much love, affection and respect, that this Gurumaa who did not even know their language, started singing along with them!

145

Tere naam pe hoon main fana
Tere naam ka hai sila
Ya Allah, Ya Allah Hu Hai Hai Ya Allah
Tere naam ka mein deewana
Teri mohabbat ka main mastana
Ya Allah Ya Allah Hu Hai Hai Ya Allah

Oh Allah! Oh Allah!
You are my love and my desire
I seek thee for eternity
And will perish in thy fire

I could not understand most of the song, but what I did understand was the bit about 'Hai Hai Ya Allah, Hai Hai Ya Allah'. Till then I was not aware of the meaning of the word 'Hai'. When asked, I was told that it is a word of the Arabic language and is used in Persian too. It means: He is omnipresent.

If you ask any Sufi, "Why do you sing? Why do you play music?", he will say, "I am in love and that is why I drown myself in the oceanic bliss of music. That is why I sing." I asked some whirling dervishes, "Why do you whirl?" They said, "We are in love. We don't wish to achieve anything from this!" Seeking something is akin to poverty; seeking a little is kingship; seeking nothing at all is divinity! One who asks for just anything at all is poorer than the poor. No one can be poorer than him who loves with a purpose and remembers God for personal gain.

You often come to me and say, "I have been meditating for four years, what next? Nothing has happened till now." Till the time you wait for 'something' to happen, nothing will. Whenever someone says, "I have been meditating for four years, I have been coming to the camp for four years, how will I move ahead?" I feel that after four years, his mind should already have stopped thinking in this direction.

Meditation takes you beyond the mind. How will one who has transcended the mind calculate achievements and failures? This thought is an act of the mind. This person has not really meditated in the true sense. If you practice meditation with the aim of reaching a certain state, you will never be able to concentrate because your mind will always be occupied with the purpose of reaching that level. It means that you are sitting here, but your attention is elsewhere. If someone walks on the earth with his gaze fixed on the moon and the sky, won't he fall?

Why do we meditate? We meditate so that we fall in love with meditation. If you practice meditation without fully understanding it, you know what you end up doing? You simply turn it into an exercise! A person, who turns meditation into an exercise, and brings mental calculations into it, is not really meditating. A person who has a correct understanding of meditation, will, in fact, convert even physical exercise into meditation. Here you are converting your meditation into an exercise!

School children sing the national anthem or their school prayer every day, but while singing there is no emotion whatsoever on their faces. They just sing it in a routine manner as it is a must for them to stand and sing. But if some day the principal announces in the assembly, "Today we will not sing our daily prayer, instead we will sing the most popular film song."

How do you think the children would react? After all they were singing the prayer too! The prayer: 'Aye maalik tere bande hum, aise hon hamare karam', is a beautiful prayer. But children don't enjoy it; for them it is a mere exercise.

Just notice their faces when they sing the national anthem; tired, troubled and bored! They wait for it to get over, tired from standing for so long. "After this someone will read the news, the principal will give his speech… don't know how long we have to stand like this!"

They are uncomfortable even standing there. But in the same assembly if the principal were to say: "Today we will not sing the prayer, there will be no news-reading and even I will not give a speech; today a pop singer will come and perform."

What will happen then? The same children will get all happy and excited to the point, they may just keep shouting, 'Once more, once more!' and keep making requests for their favourite songs. They may also sing along! See how they open up and feel exhilarated? Because they enjoy it.

147

We must meditate because it gives us highest degree of joy. Those who do not enjoying meditation should not try to do it, because they are spoiling something as beautiful as meditation. Search deep within yourself and find where the trouble lies! Why are you not able to immerse yourself in this? What is the obstruction? What ails the mind that your concentration is diverted towards problems and worries?

Why do we need to meditate? Only for joy! There are three stages: in the first we fall in love with our murshid or a master. When this love deepens, only then is one able to get involved with divine love. Otherwise how can one fall in love with someone who has never been seen or heard; who one has never touched and who is invisible?

The murshid is visible; it is easy to love him. His word, his glance, his speech, his way of sitting, walking – everything leaves an impact. If love for the murshid is true, then one falls in love with God easily. When the love for God deepens, only then is the process of destroying one's self and one's ego completed. When the ritual started by the guru – of destroying the disciple's ego – is completed, then that day the love for the murshid or even for God ceases to be. Then love is only for the sake of love.

Benoor tha aashiyana ab ja ke raushan hua hai
Mujhe ishq se ishq hua hai, jaane kaise, kab se hua hai
Mera ishq salaamat rahe, ishq se yahi dua hai
Bus ishq se ishq hua hai, jaane kaise kab se hua hai
Kaanch se ho gayi kanchan jab se usne chhua hai
Bus ishq se ishq hua hai, jaane kaise kab se hua hai
Benoor tha aashiyana, ab ja ke raushan hua hai
Bus ishq se ishq hua hai, jaane kaise kab se hua hai

My life was devoid of colour itself
Now it has been illumined
I'm now in love with love itself
How and when
I cannot be sure
I'm in love with love

And I pray to love
To multiply ten fold
For the Lord himself
Has touched me and
I've turned from glass to gold

Glass is breakable and has no real value. But if it comes in contact with His love, it becomes gold. It becomes refined and valuable like gold. It becomes priceless!

Without His love, man's body is like a toy made of glass, ready to break at any moment. Just waiting to be broken – that is its reality! But, if in this fragile body, the infinite, eternal and immortal love is ignited and the flame of His love is lit, the body ceases to be a breakable toy and becomes as pure and sacred as a temple. It becomes fit for worship. But before that it is only fit to be buried in the ground.

If you keep looking outside, you will not find anything but deceit. Unless and until you look within and set out on the inner voyage, nothing is of worth. But this inner voyage has to be undertaken with great patience – always remember that! You have to have patience. One who does not have patience can never be a lover? A person with complete patience and complete love is a true lover, a true meditator and a truly learned man.

You must have heard the story of the hare and the tortoise, where both of them are running a race. The hare thinks, 'I know where my destination is. I already know it and I also run very fast, so I will reach there very soon. How can a tortoise match my speed? It is simply impossible!' So he starts running. On looking back he finds the tortoise far behind. He runs again and then stops one more time to see where the tortoise is and finds that he is not even visible. He feels he has already won the race. He is almost sure of that! Then suddenly he wonders why he is running so fast when he knows the tortoise cannot out-run him in a thousand lives! If he is already so far behind that he cannot be seen, then why not rest? He sits down to relax but goes off to sleep. After sometime, still in that relaxed state, he turns back and sees that the tortoise is still not visible, so he goes off to sleep again.

149

The tortoise is aware of the speed of the hare and he also knows that he is very, very slow, but he has one special quality, and that is of patience. So he walks and walks and keeps walking. And slowly he overtakes the hare and reaches his destination. And the hare, getting irritated with the slowness of the tortoise, decided to reach the destination and then rest, completely unaware of the fact that the tortoise had already reached the finish point.

So he began running. Imagine his surprise when he reached the finish point to see not a single person there. No judges, no trophy, nothing! He couldn't understand where all the people had gone. So he asked someone, "Where have all the people gone?" The person said, "What do you mean? The race was over long back! The tortoise has won, you have lost; he was given the trophy. They have even had the photography session." The hare was surprised and asked, "How is this possible?" "It has become possible today. Today patience has won; persistence has won!"

You have to understand two things today. First, don't meditate with any purpose. Meditate only for the sake of meditation. Second, be patient. A person who doesn't have patience cannot be an adept, a devotee. Talking of Shiva and his wife Parvati, when someone asked, "Why do you do all this when you are not even sure if Shiva will agree to your proposal; whether he will come out of his state of profound meditation?"

"It may take a thousand births and re-births, but in all of them I will have only one desire – that if at all I marry, it will be to Shiva, else I will remain unmarried. I am in no hurry; it may take a thousand births, but if and when I get married, it will be to Shiva."

One more thing: Before you come and ask me when you will achieve that privileged stage, ask yourself whether you are meditating for the sake of meditation? How many of you meditate regularly? If I need to tell you that you have to meditate, then it loses its value! After all this, if I have to remind you like children to finish your homework first, then…. Well, you must have some self-respect! What is the point of having to be asked whether or not you have done your meditation? Must you have such a casual approach to meditation? You do it if you are in the mood, and if you are not in the mood then you don't do it! There are always a thousand excuses ready for not doing it!

Once, a young boy worked at a goldsmith's shop. He would slog the whole day. If he worked the whole day he got money; and if he got money, only then would food be cooked in his house. One day he heard a Sufi singing: 'Remember God wherever you are. There is no need to go to any mosque or to a Sufi's tomb, or even to any dervish! Your God is where you are. So turn towards God residing within you. Worship Him wherever you be!'

The fakir was just passing by singing this verse, but it had a great impact on the young boy, whose job was to hammer molten gold, before it cooled down. So now, with every strike of the hammer, the name of Allah got attached. Every time he fanned the fire, he would utter the sound of 'Hu, Hu, Hu'.

When this child grew up, not only did he grow big physically, but his mental faculties also grew remarkably. He turned out to be a great Sufi himself. He weaved the name of the Almighty into his daily chores. He was not able to take time out specially for God, so what could he do? He made it a point to worship God wherever he was, no matter what he was doing or what state he was in.

What is the need to sit specifically for the practice of dum? Wherever you may be, whatever the body may be doing – whether walking, sitting or working – just keep your mind fixed on dum, on your synchronised breath. Who says it is necessary to sit specially for that? Forget the mantra; where is the need to take time out separately to watch your breath? If you can just be aware of your breathing rhythm, the ray of this awareness will engulf you and take you into a state where ascetics reach after years of practice and renunciation.

The question is not of what you do but of how you do it. For example, when you are driving a vehicle from home to office, your mind can either get involved in senseless things or it can be diverted towards the rhythm of your breath. Anybody who drives with this awareness will never miss a red light or cross the speed limit because he will be driving consciously and with awareness.

It is possible to weave meditation into your everyday life; it is even possible to convert meditation into an arduous task. My message is that you convert even your chores into meditation. Don't let meditation become a job. Meditation is not work; it should be done effortlessly. But in order to make it effortless, what is required is a clear and in-depth understanding of the whole concept. Without proper understanding nothing can be achieved.

Sometimes I feel there is something amiss! Either you do not understand properly, or I am not able to put it across effectively. I don't want you to get an incomplete understanding of zikr. So I would again like to explain the right way of practicing 'Hai' zikr. Though the tapes are available and you can buy them, but right now you must try to understand the basics.

Oh Allah!
I surrender my fate in your hands
I leave you to distinguish between wrong and right
And your love is such, it stays with me
Morning, evening and night
Whether I live or die
Your name will live on for good
But as I perish, I leave behind
These feeble bonds of brotherhood

All the practice that you do in the meditation camp is helpful to you for further practice. I have explained the three incorrect ways of doing 'Hai'. Though many people try to do it the right way, by the time they come to the third stage, they just give up. Others, while trying to get the 'Hai' right, forget how to breathe correctly. But don't worry, things become easier with practice.

One gets to know the depth of this practice only if one does it with patience. It is possible for people to understand their mistakes only through regular practice. And when we look at these shortcomings conscientiously, only then can we develop an understanding of how to get rid of them.

Some people have asked if the meditation CDs can be given to others for viewing. I would not suggest it. The reason is that when you are sitting here and learning things practically, even then you find it difficult to follow everything; how then would other people understand by just listening to recorded words? Who would correct your mistakes? Indeed, how would you even identify your mistakes?

I feel I need to conduct Sufi camps off and on – maybe once or twice a year. It would give you an opportunity to learn things practically. Zikr is only a part of Sufism. This is step No. 2 of Sufi practice. There are four salutations, four circles and four cycles! All in all, it takes an hour and a quarter for a whirling to be completed. There is a six-month training period for this. Those who are able to do the zikr properly and are interested in learning whirling, are then taught that as well.

I sincerely wish I could call some whirling dervishes to our ashram so that you could see them perform in person. The energy generated during their whirling is really divine! Seeing them perform the whirling zikr is an experience in itself. A practice in itself!

Whatever is written comes to pass. You have to decide for yourself what you would like to do with all that you have read and learnt. I have done my job of introducing you to zikr, and as it is, I am like Mullah Nasruddin! Remember he had asked in the madrasa, "Do you know what I am going to speak on today?" The people said, "We don't know." Mullah said, "If you don't know then what is the use of telling you anything?"

It is very difficult for any Sufi to decide what to speak on and what not to speak on. If he does decide, then arises the question of how much to speak? Who to speak for? This needs great contemplation. Talking of Mullah, one day he asked his wife, "Tell me one thing, why don't camels have wings?"

"How would I know why they don't have wings?"

"If they had wings they would have flown down to our terrace. And if such hefty camels came down on our roof, would it not cave in under their weight? That is why camels don't have wings."

153

What I mean to ask is, "Why aren't there true devotees? Why don't devotees have wings? Devotees with wings… It seems to be an impossible proposition – a devotee, that too truthful! Well, it is difficult! It is very difficult to become a Sufi, very difficult indeed. But one who crosses all the hurdles and keeps serving the Sufi, will one day himself become a Sufi.

CHAPTER 9

THE SEARCH

One whose intrinsic nature is love is a Sufi. One who is a natural worshipper is a Sufi. From the earth to the sky, wherever he looks, he who sees only God, is a Sufi.

The body is the outer veil of our inner true self; the mind is the second, and lack of consciousness the third veil. All three cover our true 'self'. The true 'self' is hidden! It is like a person wearing a veil remains hidden unless he pulls back the veil and reveals his true identity. If someone passes by wearing a burqa, no one can make out who it is; you cannot see the person's face. The burqa is made of cloth – so it is just a piece of cloth that works as a wall between the eye of the beholder and the face of the person behind the veil. A mere piece of cloth works as a screen between the two! It hides the identity of the wearer.

Similarly, the true 'self' is hidden behind these three veils; how then can it be seen? The true 'self' is the one behind the working of the body, the working of the mind, the action of breathing, and the actions of the heart and the mind. When the body moves, one can feel that there is something because of which the body is moving. The mind visualizes because there is some power behind it. The mind thinks because there is something that gives it the power to think.

What is behind this body, heart and mind is our true 'self'; it is known as 'atma' in Hindi and Sanskrit, and 'rooh' in Arabic, Persian and Urdu. Like a woman, the true 'self' wears the veil of the body, heart and mind. The face of the wearer remains hidden till the veil is lifted. Till the time you lift the veils from your mind, you will not know your true 'self'. So who is a Sufi? One who lifts the veils from his mind; one who is in the process of lifting the veils is known as a Sufi.

Sufi is a representation of an individual's inner divine state, it is intrinsic thus many a time, outer dress codes and external events are not given that much of an attention. When we say who is a Sufi? Well, Sufi is the one who cannot be defined by any particular religion. Sufi is one's own true self, the ever pervading truth. Thus its essence is universal. Just as truth is universal and wears the garb of many religions, similarly a Sufi is truth in all its glory and purity and can take up any outer appearance or may not do so, it is immaterial.

So let us not get caught up in the argument of what an outer appearance of Sufi should be? What should be the dress code of a Sufi? Because by doing so we may miss the point. All this is being stated, just to create an understanding that we have to move beyond outer peripheral appearances. This subject calls for direct understanding, as a listener or as a reader, you all do know of rituals, ceremonies and outer appearances, I am not here to share with you of what you already know; nor I want to contradict it. I am here to share with you, of what you do not know and of what you think, you have an idea of. Since having an idea of something is not enough, definitely not enough to know who a Sufi is!

So what is Sufism? Sufism is love! Prophet Mohammad was in love with his God. It was this love of the Prophet for his God that took him to the cave where he sat for years and prayed and called out to his God, "Where are you? Who are you? What do you look like? There are so many idols in the temple – which one is actually your face? Which face resembles yours? How will I know? How will I understand?"

There have been several apostles from Adam to Abraham to Moses, and many after them as well. All of them have worshipped God dwelling in the house that is in the form of the body – that is why this house is priceless. But what did they actually do in this house? Nobody was able to see that, nobody was able to understand that. The common man tends to misunderstand because of his limited knowledge, and due to this misunderstanding, things are defined in a manner such that they lose their meaning. The meaning simply changes! Whatever is experienced by Sufis is something only they know, the outside world has no idea whatsoever.

There was a Sufi by the name of Baizeed Bastami. He was so particular about his namaaz, that the Sun could forget to rise but he would never forget his morning prayers; the sun could forget to set but he would never forget his evening prayers! But one day something unusual happened – everybody reached the mosque to offer prayers but Baizeed was not there. People wondered if he had fallen ill. Then someone said, "Who says illness can stop him? Even when ill, he reaches the mosque on time, whether coughing or in a state of high fever. God forbid he has passed away!"

Everybody thought that he had died, or else he would never miss namaaz. People finished their prayers and then rushed to his house but there was no wailing or crying sound coming from inside the house. Now they wondered why he had not come to the mosque if he was alive! What could have happened to him?

His house had no doors – only walls. Doors are made when there is a fear of someone stealing the goods kept within. A person who feels the whole world is his own, who has no enmity or attachment with anything, does not care if someone takes away his possessions. Whether somebody keeps something or takes something, it does not bother him at all. No doors! No locks! Nothing!

There was no door in his house, so they all went in and found Baizeed sitting on the bed, alive and well. They heaved a sigh of relief and thanked God that he was alive. But then, why hadn't he come?

"What happened Baizeed? Why didn't you come?"

Baizeed smiled and said, "If God himself comes to your place, why would you go to him? Why should I go for prayers when I have already found Him, who I have been seeking all these years? When I have already found Him, there is no need for me to go to the mosque – now my own body has become a mosque. The mosque made of stones and cement was also holy and sacred for me – I used to go and bow my head at its doorstep. But today when I have had the awakening, I realise that my body has been made by the Almighty with His very own hands."

This form made by His own hands is more precious and holy than the house made of bricks and mortar – it is man who makes all the places of worship.

Baizeed says: "Man's mind and hands are both tainted! But the God who made this body, He himself and His hands are pure, so nothing is purer than this body. Now you will never find Baizeed in the mosque – forget it!"

The crowd could not understand Baizeed. All that they could say was that he had gone crazy! What could anyone say to him now?

People began saying all sorts of things about Baizeed: 'Probably he has lost his mind; he used to recite mantras for forty days at a stretch. He would even keep awake the whole night and recite the verses of the Quran – probably that is why he has gone mad. He says he has become one with his God ! Who can ever be one with God? This is blasphemy! He has become a kafir! He has become impious!'

So many Sufis have had to pay with their lives for speaking the truth. People can never understand a Sufi; people cannot be convinced either.

I would now like to complete what had I started saying: Is it necessary to be a Muslim to talk on Sufism or to be a Sufi? The answer is a clear 'No'. To be a Sufi you don't have to be a Muslim; you just have to be in love.

There have been Sufis before and after Prophet Mohammad; there still are Sufis in the present, and they will continue to be there in the future too. This land will never be devoid of Sufis, nor has it ever been. Some will be known and some will remain anonymous – that is the only difference. Some will be recognised by the world and people will revere and worship them; some will remain unknown and will complete their worldly journey alone, living in the solitude of their own beautiful world.

When a Sufi is born, society finds it difficult to accept him, yet when he dies, people are not ashamed to throng his tomb. As long as a Sufi is alive, he appears dangerous; people feel secure in his death. Therefore, people keep waiting for the death of a Sufi. The moment he dies, those who pretend to be his disciples get a free hand; they get the freedom to interpret his sayings to suit their own convenience. They say whatever they want to; they do whatever they wish.

When I visited the tomb of Khwaja Garibnawaz in Ajmer, I was surprised. Though I shouldn't have been surprised but I still was. Well, one can't really help it. When I went to that land of Sufis, I thought there would be a large assembly of followers there. I expected to find people singing and dancing, completely drenched in the love of God Almighty. But what I saw there was shocking! The crowd there consisted of people who had come to ask for His blessings, or to thank Him for having showered His blessings on them, or even to complain because their wishes had not yet been fulfilled. There were no ecstatic love-drenched worshippers! They were all beggars begging for His blessings!

It was quite like the crowd of beggars in your temples and gurudwaras. Someone wants his shop to profit while another wants to get married! Someone wants his child to get married soon while another wants to get rid of an illness! All bonded like slaves to their desires and lust! The crowds in the gurudwaras are not of the true Sikhs of the guru; they are of seekers of worldly profits.

But for me it was a nice experience, a very lovely experience. It felt like homecoming. I felt the contentment and the joy that one feels on coming back to one's home. The reason is that it is a place where a great mystic, a Sufi had once stayed for quite some time. Even after his departure, his vibrations, his energy, his aura and his splendour continue to make that place fragrant. But you have to have the nose that can smell it and the heart that can feel it.

People don't have the heart to feel or the eyes to see the right thing, which is why when they go there, they just look at the outer walls and appreciate them and come back. But they are unable to touch or feel that energy, the aura that is present there.

Who is a Sufi? One who loves unconditionally! Who is a Sufi? One who does not ask for anything from God. Who is a Sufi? One who performs miracles? Don't be under this false impression.

Once, the popular sheikh, Hasan, came to meet Rabiya-al-Advaiya. While talking he said, "Come Rabiya! Pick up your mat. There is a river there, we will go and sit on the water. Hasan wanted to show-off his ability to sit on the surface of water. He knew he would not drown in the water, so he said, "We will sit on water today, not on land." Rabiya said, "You often sit on water. Come, we will sit in the air today. We will talk, while sitting in the air and will also remember our beloved God. If water is His creation, air too is His creation. You have been sitting on water, come today we will sit in the air." But Hasan said, "Rabiya, I don't have any such powers. I cannot perform the miracle of sitting in the air."

Then Rabiya said, "Fish live in water. That they live there and do not drown is no miracle! Birds fly in the air. They flutter their wings and fly but do not fall. That birds fly in the air is also no miracle. If we humans try to imitate what fishes and birds do, then we are actually regressing. We are not achieving anything. Man is superior to birds and animals. So, is this your superiority that you go and sit on water like fish? Hasan! You are a man. Try to be a man! You are a man of the land, so remain on the land! Your body is made of this soil, so sit on it and feel proud of the fact that you are still sitting on the soil and have not gone under it. Be proud of the fact – if at all you want to be proud of anything – that you are not yet buried in the soil. What will be left of you once you are buried in the soil? God has been kind and has given this life to us. Don't waste your life imitating the powers that nature has given to these creatures!"

What a coincidence! Sometimes one fails to understand how this incident in the life of Rabiya-al-Advaiya of Basra in Iraq, could be so similar to an incident that took place in India. Rabiya was born before Ramakrishna, but Ramakrishna once said a similar thing to an ascetic, though in a slightly different manner.

After twenty years of spiritual practice, an ascetic achieved the power to walk on water without drowning. He returned to his village after twenty years. As soon as the village folk got to know that a child of their village had become such a great ascetic, they began making arrangements to welcome him. Auspicious leaves were tied on doors, flags and buntings were put up and a dinner was planned. There was an atmosphere of joy all over, as though some big festival was being celebrated. When he arrived, he was made to ride an elephant to enter the village. Everyone was shouting slogans praising him. Wonderful arrangements were made in order to ensure that his stay there was comfortable.

Four days passed; the whole village came to meet him. The only person who didn't come was his younger brother. The ascetic was keen on meeting him since he had come home after a long time. He began wondering: 'Everybody has come to meet me, why hasn't he come?' Finally he sent a message home to his brother asking: 'Why haven't you come to meet me?' The messenger also said, "What kind of a brother are you? Your brother has become such a great, learned man. He has achieved powers, he can walk on water; the whole world is welcoming him, but you didn't come! You are a member of his family. You should have been the first one to go and meet him."

The brother replied, "It is all right that he is my elder brother and that people are welcoming him. I too am happy about it – very happy – but I doubt that he has achieved any special powers." The messenger went back and told the ascetic, "Your younger brother is a very rude and indecent person. He said that you have not achieved any special powers. If you had, then he would definitely have come to meet you."

The elder brother couldn't contain himself on hearing this, so he went over to meet him. Now that the achiever of special powers, the learned ascetic himself had come to his house, the younger brother took him inside affectionately and offered him some water. The ascetic said, "I have not come here to have water. I have just come to ask why you said that after twenty years of rigorous practice, I have not achieved any power?" The younger brother replied, "Yes, that's right. You have not achieved any power, instead you have just wasted twenty years."

"What does that mean?"

"Respected ascetic! Even we can cross the river for just two pennies. In these twenty years you have done a job worth merely two pennies. How can I accept this as any divine power? You walk on water and cross the river, while we pay two pennies to the boatman and cross the river by boat. So where is the divine power?"

So who is a Sufi? Not the one, who performs miracles, treats patients and helps people get jobs. You would have seen advertisements in the newspapers or hoardings: Come and meet the healer! The dervish! The Sufi! And their names are also quite interesting and funny. 'Miracle in two days! You can see the results. Not getting a job? Not getting married? Problems with love affair? Court case not getting solved?' You can gather a large crowd like this. But they are not Sufis.

In fact there is a very popular saying in Turkey: One who is recognised is not a Sufi. Somehow, somewhere he himself is responsible for it. Had he not been involved, nobody would have recognised him. If someone deliberately allows himself to be recognised, it means he wants the world to know him. And to achieve this, he would have somewhere or the other, impressed others with his powers, or he would have displayed his superiority to others.

Sufis have always lived in hibernation – they never surface. If you pass by a Sufi, you will feel he is just an ordinary man. But actually it may well be the Almighty in the form of that man! Just as Sufis live a mysterious life, similarly, if two Sufis come face to face, their conversation also takes place in a very mysterious manner. Nothing is evident! Nothing is obvious!

The one who still needs to know is a seeker, but the one who already knows everything is a Sufi. There are no questions and no answers left for him. What can anybody tell him or explain to him? He does not have any questions nor does he seek any answers.

Do you remember the poem I have sung in my album titled 'Shoonya'? The poem goes like this: Sawaal poochhoon nahin, jawaab chahoon nahin. There isn't any question left to ask. When there isn't any question left, then what answer should I wait for?

Sab kuch thera hua hai thande jal sa
Aaj shunya hai

Everything is tranquil and still as cold water
Nothingness alone is resonating

Everything is tranquil like cold water. Today there is only nothingness! For whom all is tranquil – in the stillness is the echo of 'Anhad naad' – the sound of silence – that person is a Sufi.

All the Sufis have led mysterious lives and if they happen to meet other Sufis, their conversation also takes place in a mysterious manner. Thousands may witness their conversation, but no one will be able to understand exactly what they say.

Mullah Nasruddin seems to be a character created by Sufis; an invention of Sufi minds. Sufis hold private meetings, and in one such meeting they must have come up with the name 'Mullah Nasruddin'. And to him they started attributing a whole lot of stories which are more like jokes than like stories! Every joke establishes the Mullah as a crazy and senseless character. So a common man's madness or senselessness is depicted in Mullah Nasruddin's character. Over a period of time, several new stories have been added to his name; after all he is just a fictitious character!

What is surprising is that not only has the character been devised, but to make him seem plausible, his date of birth and death has also been made up. As his death was concocted, it was felt he must have a grave too. So his grave was made – though there is nothing inside it! And as there is a grave, it was necessary to put a tombstone describing who was buried and when. So they wrote 'Mullah Nasruddin' on the gravestone! Then they had to write the date of his death. Now they didn't know what to write. Someone said, "Let's write 386 on it." So it was decided – three hundred and eighty six.

Then somebody said, "This Mullah Nasruddin was an upside-down character all his life…"

Someone else said, "Don't write '386', write it in the reverse order i.e. 683! He never did anything right all his life, so write the date in the reverse order."

Then some Sufi said, "Since you are deciding the date and year on your own, how can it be true?"

"How do we find which date would be the most suitable?"

The Sufi replied, "Catch hold of a spider, dip it in ink and set it on a piece of paper. We will decide on whatever date and year its footprints look like!"

Another of his famous stories goes like this: One day Mullah Nasruddin was walking in the marketplace. A fakir was coming from the opposite side. It is very difficult to recognise Sufis by their appearance. If somebody is wearing black or green coloured clothes, he may be a Sufi! One whose cloak has patchwork on it may be a Sufi! All this has been said as marks of recognition for those who sit in one place – but there is no apparent mark of recognition for someone who never stays in one place.

At the most, one Sufi can recognise another Sufi by the fire of love that may be smoldering within their hearts. They recognize each other by that fire. If someone suffers from a physical illness, there may be dark circles under his eyes or he may look pale. Just by looking at his face you tend to ask, "Are you sick?" Just as the signs of physical sickness become visible on a person's face, similarly, one whose heart is ailing with His love, also shows some signs of illness. And only a sufferer knows what the signs of a patient of love are. Thus they recognize each other by these symptoms.

Well, Mullah Nasruddin was walking in the marketplace and the fakir coming from the opposite direction was walking with one of his fingers pointing upwards. He kept coming closer to Mullah with his finger pointing to the sky. The people walking with Mullah said, "Oh, this man seems to be mad, he is walking with his finger pointing towards the sky!" Mullah said, "Never mind!" Then he opened his sling bag, took out a rope and showed it to the fakir. The dervish walked past with his finger pointing upwards and Mullah put his rope back in his bag and continued on.

Now what was this? See, there may be thousands of idols but God's creed is one; the essence is just one. Truth does not lie in thousands. Truth is just one! For a Hindu, God is Om, Brahman, Nirakaar, Satguru, Ram and Krishna. For a Sikh, He is Waheguru, Akaal Purush and Ek Onkar. For a Buddhist, God is Buddha or Padmasambhava.

Later a Sufi related this story as: The fakir raised one finger to indicate that God is one. He was saying: 'There may be any number of names for God but God's creed is just one.' At this Mullah took out the rope. Now what does that mean? It means that one cannot reach up to the sky with the help of a rope. Though there is only one God, the ways that man has discovered to reach up to that one Truth or God are like trying to reach the sky with this rope. However long the rope may be, how will you make it stand straight? How then can you reach the sky with the support of something that can't even stand straight? As it is, no rope has ever been made or ever will be, which is long enough to reach the sky.

So in this incident, though nobody spoke, they had a conversation. Later, a saying became famous in Persian: 'Rope in reply to sky'. If the question is a finger pointing upwards, then the answer is a 'rope'.

Now remember, you need a conscious mind to understand these mysteries and not a mechanical mind. The mind that you possess is usually full of worldly thoughts. This mechanism that you call 'the mind' only deals with desires and jealousies, worldly ups and downs, notions of possessiveness and nothing else. Your mind cannot be the source of reaching up to Him. They say it is the 'heart' and not the 'mind' that needs to be illumined.

Jiska dimag chale woh duniyadaar
Jiska dil jalega woh sufi

He who keeps his mind working at all times is a worldly being
He whose heart perishes in the fire of love is a Sufi

To convert milk into curd, all that is required is a little bit of curd. A spoonful of curd is enough to convert the whole milk

165

into curd. Your mind is already dark enough, I am sure you wouldn't want to add more. We have to remove this darkness from our minds. We have to clean it, almost vacuum clean it – sanitise it!

Your mind needs sanitisation. Or else you will not be able to understand what I am saying. Whatever I am telling you is absolutely new, whether it is the tales of Sufis, references from the Quran Sharif, or about traditions. It is all absolutely new.

Again, it is not necessary to be a Muslim to be a Sufi. We will now talk about the Mevlavi tradition which started with Hazrat Jalaluddin Rumi. We will talk about the styles and traditions of love and worship expounded by this 12th century Sufi.

I have often spoken about Indian and Pakistani fakirs like Bulleh Shah and Inayat Shah during my discourses. So I will be talking on a new topic and you will have to understand it from your heart and not from your mind.

Understand the secret: there is a hidden ego inside your apparent 'I'. What you call 'me' or 'mine' – that is your worldly 'self'. But that is not pure 'I'. That is not sacred. It is perishable! We are not going to talk about perishable things here. We have to understand the non-perishable, therefore we have to understand this secret. There is another Sufi saying: If you try to look for Him, you will never be able to find Him. But if you don't even set out to look for Him, how will He show Himself to you!

If you look for Him you will not be able to find Him, and if you don't go out looking for Him, He will not give an audience either. So it is necessary to carry on with the search. This search is a must and therefore it must carry on – no matter what! What exactly does search imply? It means introspection, dwelling on the mind's machinations and turning your consciousness inwards, diverting it from outside to inside. From the outside, move towards the core. Your sight needs to be turned inwards.

Remember, right now you feel that whatever is apparent and whatever is outside is what is important to you. Your house, your family, your wife, your husband, your children, your job, your business, your trade and even your body – everything is outside! If you start thinking about these external things, then your mind can think of only one thing at a time – either you can be conscious of this world or you can remain unconscious of it. Sufi poet Kabir has said:

> **Prem gali ati saankri**
> **Ja me do na samayee**
> **Aap hain to Hari nahi**
> **Hari to aap nahi**

> The lane of love is so narrow
> It can't fit two in it
> Either it will be self in it
> And if God – then never self

If your mind is preoccupied with worldly issues, then how will you 'know', how will you seek the 'Truth'. That is why it is said: 'Just discard whatever is external'. Whatever is outside needs to be left behind! Whoever masters the art of leaving behind all that is external, is a Sufi.

If you have come to hear about Sufism or even if you have come to discuss Sufism, then you must know that you have made a mistake. I do not talk about Sufism. I will only show you the way to become a Sufi yourself. There is no point talking about Sufism. What is the use of talking? You will listen and that will be the end of it! You will listen and then forget about it. If I ask you to tell me what you have heard so far in previous camps, I am sure you will not remember!

You listen and then forget – so what is the use? If you want to follow the traditions of becoming a Sufi, then you will have to leave behind all that is external. It is better you leave it yourself, at this very moment, because the world is good at getting things done with a kick. Before others leave you, why not leave yourself. So instead of being kicked out by others, it is better you leave yourself.

> Remember and worship God's name
> Renounce all friendship, fortune and fame
> One may treat these impostors

As just the same
The futile quest of materialism
Is devoid of all love
It separates the man
From his God above
Take no pride in possessions
For all is made of dust
From the surface to the core
To the mantle to the crust
And although we live
On a planet robust
The ultimate treasure Is being devoid of all lust
With the Name on our lips
In God we trust
In the sojourn of love
Travel we must

Remember and worship God's name. Tomorrow you may be required to give a detailed account of what you have experienced and what is yours. Why do you keep saying 'this is mine', 'that is mine', thus increasing your distance from Him? You should not feel proud of your huge house; in other words, do not be proud of your own self. Your house and your body are both made of mud, and so is your lofty station. What good is mud? Why be so proud of mud? Worship only God's name.

You must remember that you have to make an effort. 'Trying' is a meaningless word, because man either does something or he doesn't do it. It's like – you are either present here or not present here. Physically you are present, which means you are here for a purpose. So concentrate on your purpose! Since you are bodily present here, you will have to give the life-blood of your 'self' to achieve your purpose. So, your eyes should be fixed only on your target and nowhere else. Leave all – your home, shop and market, everything – alone. Nothing now!

If someone wants admission to a tekke, he is made to sit on a musalla – a mat spread on the floor – for three consecutive days. He has to sit there for three days! He is only provided with a mashq – a leather bag – full of drinking water. No sleeping, no eating! He has to just keep reciting the verse that the sheikh gives him. He is supposed to say it aloud so that he does cheat saying that he will do it silently in his mind, and then goes off to sleep. He may get sleepy or lazy, so he is told: "Speak loudly! Your words must be heard by us." So for three days he has to sit on that seat; he is only allowed to go out to ease himself. I have seen this sight with my very own eyes. Things are the same even now. A seeker has to sit for three days without movement – and if he is seen to be troubled and disturbed, he is sent back. "Go! Your time to go in hasn't come yet."

However, I do not put you to any such test; do not ask you to wait outside for three days saying that only those who pass the test will be allowed inside. But I must warn you: there is no scope for any kind of mistake. In fact, sometimes I want some of you to create mischief so that I can send you back right away; an undeserving person should not get admission here.

Just reaching the ashram is no big deal – anybody can come. There is nothing great in it and you are not going to get any scholarship for this. After all, you do go for outings or to meet relatives. For that too you take leave and go, leaving behind your home, shop, job, etc. So you cannot just come here – it is necessary that you qualify to get an entry to this place. So keep an eye on your mind. Just keep an eye! You have to keep an eye on your own mind and not on others'. You don't have to keep an eye on others, on what they do and on what they say, or even on the happenings at your own place. You just have to keep an eye on your mind.

The easiest way to do that is to keep an eye on your dum, your breathing. Keep an eye on your breath. Even though you have not taken the three-day test, you must prove yourself equal to it. If you can't make even this much effort, then it is not going to help. You may reach here physically, you may even get to hear all this with your ears, but your heart will remain empty. Now it is up to you to decide whether you want to fill your heart or leave it empty – the choice is yours. Once you have decided, move further, take one more step. Now you have to decide how best to utilise your time between the sittings. Certainly your

169

behaviour is different when you are in front of me; it is not the same outside!

But remember one thing always as it is the first step to becoming a Sufi: you must understand that if someone cheats his master, he is never pardoned in God's eyes; he is unworthy of receiving God's grace. Another thing is that the master is after all a human being, so he can be cheated easily. But how will you cheat the God Almighty? He sees everything! He is sitting inside your very heart and watching everything. So if you want to get closer to Him, then don't cheat Him at least!

This lesson is to keep an eye on your breath, on your dum, and to just tell your mind: 'You have worried a lot about the house made of mud and the body made of mud; you have worried a lot about the world. Now you have to be concerned about the master of the universe. O Heart! Now take me within, not outward anymore!'

Farida jo ten maaran mukiyan
Tina na mare ghum
Ghar tinare jayee ye
Pair tina de chum

Sheikh Farid says: If someone hits you, is jealous of you, harms you, causes pain to you or troubles you, being a Sufi your attitude cannot be one of revenge. If your thoughts encourage the feelings of revenge, then you must know that you are far from the path! You are still very far from the path of Truth! Your behaviour towards a person who hurts you, causes pain and trouble to you, or has a hostile attitude towards, should be one of love and affection because a Sufi is an embodiment of love. He is love personified! There is no place for revenge in his nature.

Baba Farid said that even if someone hurts you; take the hurt with love, as he is none other than Allah, who has come to you in this form. Farid even suggests that you go to his home to caress his feet as they may be hurting from kicking you!

Listening and not practicing is not Sufism. It is easy to listen to talks on Sufism; since you have ears, whatever is being said will naturally be heard. But actually it is not considered hearing where words just go in but are not internalised. Sufis have called such ears which listen without the heart being involved, and which are devoid of love, understanding and belief – 'snake holes'. The openings of these holes are small but poisonous snakes get inside and live in them.

Those who have not learned to listen properly, may hear the words of great Sufis and yet not receive the divine nectar. In fact, sublime words also become poisonous once they enter those ears not because there is something wrong with the words, but due to the reason that the person listening to them is not adopting the meaning of the words correctly.

Once Mullah Nasruddin was sitting next to a pond and pouring curd from a vessel into it. An observer asked, "Mullah, what are you doing?"

"When my wife sets curd at home, she puts a little bit of curd in the milk and by morning it sets as curd. So I am trying the same thing in the pond."

"Mullah! Talk sense! Make some sense of your actions. You are putting curd in water, not in milk! By putting a little bit of curd in water, the pond will not set as curd!"

Mullah contemplated; he thought and thought and then said, "For all you know, it might just become curd. It just might. Who knows?"

This incident may show Mullah to be a crazy or mad person. But the fact is that Mullah's senselessness is the common man's senselessness. And this stupidity manifests the belief some people hold that just listening to the words of the knowledgeable is enough. They are trying to do an equally impossible job – trying to set curd in a pond of water!

I would like to remind you that whenever I talk about Mullah, I am not just telling you a joke. Listen to these jokes with all sincerity, as the fountain of wisdom will spring from them. Mullah's greatness is that he takes other people's stupidities onto himself; he owns upto them. If you tell somebody, "You are a fool", he will be annoyed. Mullah doesn't believe in teaching lessons – he doesn't preach. He creates situations in his own life whereby people can learn and understand.

To become a learned person it is not sufficient to just listen to words; one needs to put them into practice, with all of one's heart! The Sufi word 'amal' means 'manan' or profound contemplation in Hindi. One needs to reflect upon the words. Words are meaningless if not thought over. Nothing happens by just listening to words. One needs to practice whatever one hears. Practice what you learn and understand the real meaning of the words! If you don't, it is exactly like a snake entering a hole and just staying there. The journey of understanding begins with words, it doesn't end there! If your journey begins and ends with words, you must know that you have not actually gained anything.

Isn't it strange that those who listen are unable to think like this? To date I have not met a person who comes to me and says, "I have been listening to you for the past so many years, but have not been able to follow your advice in my everyday life; probably there is something missing in my contemplation, my spiritual discipline is not perfect!" A common lament is: 'It has been so many years since I have been meditating, but there hasn't been any substantive transformation in my life.' As though I am responsible if you do not experience spiritual growth!

If you are not evolving for the better, will you hold me responsible for it? You have never accepted that though you have been listening to me, you lack dedication and discipline. Nobody has ever admitted that to me. I have been waiting all these years for someone to come up and say that, but no one ever has. I have been giving discourses for the past 17-18 years and have come in close contact with a lot of people. I have known many people for 10, 12 or even 14 years, but they have never admitted that there is a deficiency in their practice.

Albeit, people have said several times – not directly, but nevertheless – that there have been many camps, but there hasn't been any inner realization. How would you have realization? First, you feel that for you it is sufficient to listen. You seem to have simply forgotten who is supposed to put those words into practice! Well, I am helpless as far as that is concerned! You will have to make your own effort. I cannot help in that area!

Sometimes I have felt that if I came a little close to you, that would work. But when I gave that liberty, all that you learned was very personal – what I eat, how I drink tea, when I rest, etc. You just tried to understand these things about me. Moreover, you began to feel proud of the fact that you knew me personally! To tell you frankly, no one will ever be able to know me as an individual unless and until he gets to understand my personal experiences. No one can claim to be the owner of a treasure by merely having seen it.

The guard at the government treasury or the Reserve Bank of India, cannot claim that all the money, in it, is his. A bank manager or cashier cannot say: 'All the money that I counted today is mine.' They only look after the security arrangements of those treasures. That is it! Nothing more.

Even those who live close to me make the mistake of thinking that they know me. Had it been so easy to know a mystic, a Sufi – well, then there wouldn't have been any problem! It is only a small part of the Sufi's reality that becomes evident to some select people. But the part of the Sufi that remains hidden may be so powerful, that you will find it difficult to believe that even he himself may not be aware of it! The fakir himself is unaware of the treasure of his powers and his capacities! Sometimes he himself is not aware of his power to achieve a particular feat. That is the reason he is always reciting: 'Subbhan-Allah, Subbhan-Allah, Subbhan-Allah.' Even his mind is puzzled.

God keeps opening new doors of wisdom and experience for the one who has not shut the doors of his heart, and whose heart is always filled with love for the Almighty. Such a person keeps on learning – forever! There is never an end to his learning because he knows that God is infinite. And for that endless, boundless Almighty, one cannot claim: 'Now I have realised Him.' Till date nobody has been able to understand even an iota of Him. The day someone can claim that he has understood Him even peripherally, God will cease to be God!

A sheikh from Arabia once asked Kabir: "Kabir Sahib! Do you know God?" He replied, "It is sufficient for me that God knows me. His eyes remain on me and I remain in his sight, that is enough for me."

How dare a man claim: 'I have realised God'? Man can at most sacrifice himself in the name of God; he may merge himself completely in the Almighty's form. Being one with God is his complete surrender.

The birth of a flower implies the death of the seed. The seed cannot claim that it has gained a flower. Can it ever say that? When its very form has changed – the seed has turned into a flower – it can't say that it has gained a flower. The seed cannot say this because if it had remained in its original form, the flower wouldn't have been born. It is only when the seed ceases to be, that the flower is born! Similarly, no man can say: 'I have understood God.' But yes, he can say: 'Both God and I are of the same creed.' He can say this but he can't say that he has found God.

At some point of time some Sufis have said, "I have found Him," but that was probably in response to some silly follower's silly question. If you personally ask any mystic whether he has found God, he can smile, sing or dance in reply, but can never say in so many words that he has.

Somebody asked Rabiya-al-Advaiya, "What is the difference between truth and falsehood?" She replied, "Four inches." This Sufi lady from Basra was known to be among the leading scholars of her time. A single lady living within the confines of Islam! So Rabiya replied, "Four inches." The person asked, "How do you say that? How can you give the exact measurement?" Rabiya said, "After all, there is a distance of just four inches between the eyes and ears. Whatever the ears hear is false, but what the eyes see is the truth."

When someone hears with his ears that there is God, it is almost like a lie. But whoever has known the unknown, is one with the Truth, for him even hearing that is true. Is it enough to just hear words with one's ears? Mere listening to words does not convey the actual meaning of these words. That is why it is believed in Sufism: 'One should not utter a word! Don't speak anything because your tongue spoils the eternal Truth'. The moment Truth comes within the confines of words it turns into a lie. So it is said that Truth can be felt; it can't be described and that is why they started using sign language. So a Sufi is one who understands the sign language of the mysterious and the unknown.

It is amazing – though the Sufi's journey gets completed in one sense, it never ends in another. That is to say, he has realised the Truth and found his treasure, so in this sense his journey is complete. But now he has learnt and adopted a thousand ways of understanding, stating and delivering that Truth. Sometimes the Sufi himself is unable to know what his next day will be like, but the one thing he is sure of is that howsoever it may be, it will be good for him. Both his eyes and his heart remain open. So, the one whose eyes and heart remain open, and the one who takes things as they come is a Sufi.

Let me tell you a Sufi story: One day a Sufi dreamt that there was a bridge in the capital city thousands of miles away from his village, and close to that bridge, just next to it, a treasure was buried in the earth. When he woke up, he forgot about it thinking it to be a mere dream. But the next night, he had the same dream. On the third and fourth night as well, he dreamt the same dream – that there was a bridge and a treasure lay buried close to it. This time he even heard a voice directing him: 'Go! Go and dig. Go get the treasure.'

The whole day he kept thinking: 'I am a poor man. It is not easy for me to go that far. Had I that much money, I would have gotten rid of my poverty right here. I don't have that much money. I will have to borrow from other people.' Again the voice said, "Go!" But again he thought it was not possible for him to travel so far. Then on the fifth night, he had the same dream again. This time it was a very direct and commanding voice that said, "You will have to go – this is an order!"

Next morning he told some of his friends that he had to go to the capital city. Everybody asked why but he couldn't utter a word. What could he tell them? People would laugh at him thinking him mad. 'He is going to undertake such a long journey because of a silly dream!' Somehow he managed to collect money, complete the long journey and reach the place described in his dream. He was surprised to find the same river, the same bridge and similar-looking buildings that he had seen in his dreams. But one thing that he had not seen in his dreams was a government official – a guard standing on the bridge. He had not seen that guard! If the guard moved, he could start digging and find out if the treasure lay there or not. He wondered if he was mad doing all this! For a few days, he kept hovering around that place.

One day the soldier spotted him and asked, "What is the matter? Why have you been roaming around here?" The Sufi said, "In fact, I wanted to ask you what you are doing on this bridge? It is quite unusual to find a soldier on a bridge that is not even bordering any other country. This bridge is right in the middle of the city."

"I am here because a number of people have committed suicide from this bridge. People just jump from it into the river. Now our king has put us on duty here and we keep vigil day and night so that no one else commits suicide. Why? Have you too come here to commit suicide?"

"No, I have not come here to commit suicide."

"Then why have you come here?"

Now what could the poor Sufi tell him? He didn't know what to do. He just kept pacing up and down.

Then one day the soldier again stopped him, wondering why this man came here every day. He said, "You will have to tell me why you come here. Every day I see you, you keep roaming near the bridge. Why?"

"The reason is very simple. I can tell you if you don't laugh! Do you believe in God?"

"Yes of course I believe in God! There is no question of not believing."

"Then you will have to believe in my dream too. I dreamt on five consecutive nights about this bridge and a treasure hidden near it. I even heard God's voice which said, "Go there! The hidden treasure is for you; that treasure is for you so that you can get rid of your poverty."

The soldier laughed loudly. The Sufi was surprised and said, "Why are you laughing?"

"I am laughing because even I had a dream at least ten times, that there is a village in our country...." When he revealed the name of the village, it turned out to be the one from where the Sufi had come. He said his dream was that a certain Sufi lived in a particular village. When he told the name of the area and that of the Sufi in question, it turned out to be the same Sufi.

The Sufi was amazed since it was his own name. The soldier said, "Ten times I have had this dream that in a certain village, a particular Sufi lives in a particular colony and that there is a treasure hidden under his bed. But I am not mad to set out on a journey just on the basis of a dream, to find the Sufi only to ask him to dig up the floor under his bed and see if there is any treasure hidden under it!" The Sufi was shocked to hear that. The name that the soldier gave was his own, and the description of the room also matched. He immediately went back running, covering thousands of miles. On reaching home he removed the bed and began digging under it. Sure enough, he found the treasure there.

The gist of the story is that there is a treasure hidden inside every man's 'self'. His true 'self' is the treasure. But man doesn't try to find it in his house, within himself. He unnecessarily undertakes a thousand-mile journey to look for it. Somebody just gets up to go to Mecca; somebody goes to Kashi. Somebody goes to Rameshwaram or maybe to Badrinath, Kedarnath or even to Mansarovar. The only thing one never tries to do is to go inside one's 'self'. And after travelling thousands of miles, there is hardly a man who is lucky enough to find someone who can tell him that he has undertaken the journey unnecessarily, the one who would say: "Why have you come here? He who you seek is right within you."

Ghanshyam Das goes on a pilgrimage every year. He has been to every place of pilgrimage within the country – from north to south and from east to west. At the beginning of every year, he starts planning to which place of pilgrimage he will go next. But this year he had a problem: where to go now? He had been to all the places of pilgrimage – from the smallest temple in his own city to the largest temple in the country – he had seen them all.

Now where to go? He felt a little sad. Then he thought that if one does not understand something, one must go to some mystic and seek an answer. So in order to solve his problem he went to a mystic.

"O enlightened one! What do I do? It is a tradition — as is told in the scriptures — that every religious person should go on a pilgrimage at least once a year. I have already been to every religious place. Now where do I go?"

The Sufi said, "Ghanshyam, it is wonderful that you have been to every religious place. But there is one religious place you have missed. It is good that you have come to me. Now I will guide you."

Now Ghanshyam was very anxious. "Where do I have to go? How far is it? Is it in the hills or near the sea? Is it near the river or close to a stream? Where? At the banks of which holy river? Is it near the snow-clad mountain ranges, or inside a cave?"

"Wait! Let me finish first. Don't keep posing questions, one after the other! Listen to my reply patiently. There is one holy place that remains to be visited. You never visited your own 'self'. You have been everywhere else; now go inwards! One who doesn't travel inside has not been anywhere!"

One can't begin travelling inside by just hearing about it. It won't be sufficient to just hear. Man wants to bargain for everything. You always try to buy things at a cheaper rate. I heard of a woman who was very fond of bargaining at shops. Generally everybody does that. It is more satisfying and entertaining if you are able to bargain with the shopkeeper. It is most un-interesting to go to a fixed-rate shop — you just go there, buy things and come back! What is the fun? So this woman went to a shop and asked the shopkeeper, "I want this lipstick, how much is it for?" He said, "This is a new brand that has been introduced in the market. It's an expensive brand and one lipstick will cost a hundred rupees." She said, "One hundred rupees!!? That's too much! I will take it at a lower price. I only buy good, branded stuff, and as I have come to your shop for the first time, you must give me some discount."

"Alright, for your sake I will reduce the price. I can surrender my commission and give it to you for eighty rupees. I would have made twenty rupees on it but I will give it to you for eighty.

"Eighty is much too expensive; you must bring down the price further."

"Well then, how much would you like to pay for it?"

"I will give you forty."

The cost was a hundred and she brought it down to forty – less than half! The shopkeeper said, "That is not possible." But the woman kept arguing and carried on till the shopkeeper got a headache. He began wondering, for how long she was going to eat his head for a lipstick? Finally he got so fed up, he said, "Okay, madam! You may take it for only forty. Come on now, take it for forty and be done with it!"

"Now that you have agreed to give it for forty, I would rather take two – why should I take just one?"

One is never satisfied without bargaining; we keep looking for cheaper stuff. You can find stuff at lower prices, but you cannot get valuable things at a low price. And nothing can be more valuable than the Truth. So the price for this expensive purchase of 'Truth' is going to be high and mere 'listening' cannot be enough. Only listening is not enough. What is required is amal or profound contemplation. Guru Nanak says:

Amal je kitey duni se
Se darge hoye ugah

The one, who has watched upon his mind with spiritual discipline and awareness, the one, who not only listened to the words said by master, but actually lived by them, only such person will reach the destination. One, who doesn't follow what is being said, but merely listens, will not be able to go beyond the mind and its complexities. So don't get caught up with listening; reflect upon them, live by them!

One who does not have jealousy, passion or a feeling of revenge in his heart is a true seeker – you need to look within, after understanding what I am saying. If somebody misbehaves with you or speaks ill of you, what will you do? Maybe you will not react immediately. Though I doubt that because you never give credit – you pay off immediately! You do not believe in this kind of credit. In such matters, you make all deals in hard cash. Do you ever give any credit of this kind? All the fighting and quarrelling we see everyday – on the streets, in assemblies, in every city, on every road, and also in every household – is because no one wants to give credit. They all want to pay back immediately!

The moment someone says something to you, you immediately give a befitting reply. At that time you don't behave like a government office where it takes years to do something! At times they take something like 20 to 40 years to complete a job. But you work with utmost efficiency! Somebody says something to you and right then, you conclude the deal. Whenever a question is raised, you immediately give a reply; in this you never delay.

In other words, you are more like toys than human beings. Had you been human beings, you would think at least twice before saying or doing something. But you do not think or contemplate even for a moment. All you do is give a proper reply immediately. The only people who delay in giving a reply are politicians – they reply only at the appropriate time. They scheme and they plan! And then they hit the nail right on the head; they always give a good hammering – it is never mild. How much time man wastes on all these things!

If somebody hurts your foot or steps on it by mistake, just saying 'sorry' can sort it out. It is really a small thing. Like if your own child steps on you, what will you do? Will you shout at him? Though there are some cruel-hearted people who would do that too – they beat their children black and blue! But if you cut your tongue with your own teeth, then what would you do? Would you knock your teeth off? If by mistake you manage to cut your tongue with your teeth, at the most you will feel agitated or maybe laugh at your absent-mindedness. What else would you do?

I remember when I was small I saw a neighbour being rushed to the hospital in an emergency. I enquired, "What happened?"

"He was brushing his teeth and by mistake the brush slid inside."

Amazed, I asked how that was possible.

"He was actually cleaning his tongue and in the process pushed it in so hard that it went in and got stuck somewhere inside."

This was really amazing – a toothbrush got pushed in?! Poor fellow, it had to be surgically removed! The doctor was amazed how anyone could manage such an accident.

But if we hurt ourselves because of our own mistake or absent-mindedness, then what do we do? At the most we can laugh at ourselves.

Now I shall tell you an incident that happened with me. As you all know, it is my habit to keep the paper with the devotional songs written on it right in front of me – whether they have been written by me or any other Sufi. Whether it is a good habit or a bad one, I can't say. And I don't really mind because I will always do it. So once I was called to a place where the hall wasn't too big. These days people write the bhajan very beautifully on a card and then give it to me, but those days the songs were given to me on plain paper, like that from a notebook. So this thin light paper was kept on my keyboard. It was summer and the fans were on. I had sung just half the song when the paper flew off. It was so difficult! What was I to do? On my right was Harimilan and Yogini was sitting behind me. When we sing, I keep singing a particular piece of music for as long as I want. So I kept on playing and turned around and told her that my paper had flown off. I kept telling her again and again till she got nervous. She didn't even know towards which side the paper had flown off. It was a new bhajan and the last three lines were left. I could neither leave it midway nor complete it!

Some people were looking at me, though more than half of them were sitting with their eyes closed, enjoying the bhajan. I was getting worried – what to do? I scolded her loudly, "Can't you understand, my paper has flown off!" Poor thing! What could she do? Well once a bird has flown off, it is not going to come back! So I turned to my notebook and found other songs related to the same subject and that is how I completed the bhajan! After the bhajan was over, the rest of the satsang went off exactly as planned.

Even today we all remember that incident and laugh. What a funny incident! But after that day I make proper arrangements. I write the bhajans on cards instead of paper, so that even if the fan is switched on the cards don't fly off. I don't take any chances now!

But that paper was never found. It remained a mystery, a Sufi mystery! That paper just vanished in thin air or became invisible. Or is it that the Sufi who had written that poetry or kafi came and took it away – only God would know. But 'Allah Allah khair sallah' – All is well that ends well! Till date, those sitting in that assembly do not know that the bhajan was not completed.

I narrated Mullah Nasruddin's story earlier in which he was invited to speak at a madrasa. When he went there he asked if they knew what he was going to speak on and they replied in the negative. He got annoyed and came back. Next time when he was called he asked the same question and they replied in the affirmative. Again he got annoyed, and said, "If you know, why have you called me?" The third time when he asked the same question, half of them replied in the affirmative and half in the negative. So he told them to tell each other instead of wasting his time. The crux of the story is that these religious and philosophical discussions should carry on among those who know and those who do not – whether Mullah is present or not.

The biggest fall-out of that paper flying away was that I came to know about your inattentiveness. I laughed after the satsang and was expecting some of you to come the next day and ask why I hadn't completed the bhajan. I expected you to complain that I had not completed what I had started explaining through the song. Nobody asked me why I left the song midway! Probably that is why Kabir has said:

Ram padarath pai ke
Kabira gaanth na khol
Nahin pathan nahin parakhu
Nahin grahak nahin mol

The secrets of the deep
Should never be told

Something so invaluable
Has no takers
Can never be sold

Just enjoy your divine treasure! Don't talk to anybody about it. Because whatever is your possession, no one would either be able to pay its price or bear its cost; nor is there any deserving customer. Then why should I tell others about my possessions? Why should I display my product when there is no deserving buyer?

Without meditation and dedicated practice of what you have learnt, knowledge based on just hearing is incomplete! In fact, without amal (profound contemplation) 'Truth' is also like a lie, though Truth can never be a lie. There will always be a difference between the two. Just as Rabiya said – a difference of four inches! What the ears hear is false and whatever the eyes see is the Truth! Here is Rabiya – who lived in Basra in Iraq – saying that what the eyes see is the Truth and what the ears hear is all a lie, and on the other hand is Kabir – who lived in the city of Benares in India – giving us the same message, saying the same thing with the same gist and same effect! Only the language is different:

**Mein kahata aankhan ki dekhi
Tu kehta kaagaz ki lekhi**

I talk of things which I have seen
You speak from what is written in books

I talk of whatever I have seen with my own eyes and you are only repeating the words of scriptures. So reflect on this, Kabir is saying my words are words of experience, I am not just repeating theories.

People who are concerned with hate and revenge can never love God. You have to overcome your pettiness and keep your heart pure; don't allow any kind of jealousy to breed in your mind; don't bear grudges and do not lose precious time in fruitless endeavours. What do you understand from this? This may seem to be a trivial matter, or just a matter of conduct, but actually it is not. This is also spirituality. Behaviour and spirituality are two sides of the same coin – how you live shows what your principles are. Your conduct speaks the language of your views; your thoughts are reflected in your day-to-day life. It is not possible for your thoughts to not reflect in your behaviour. Even the simplest and smallest thing defines who you are. Every action – big and small – is reflected in your attitude and behaviour.

Once somebody was asked to go and get some flowers from the garden. He went and mercilessly pulled out the entire bush on which the flowers were growing. He destroyed so many flowers for the sake of just one. Though he did manage to get one good flower, in the process he uprooted so many. Maybe you think there is nothing significant in this, but actually it is of great importance. This man had no understanding of anything. If only he had some understanding, he would have carefully cut one flower with the help of a knife or a pair of scissors. Then the rest of the flowers wouldn't have been ruined in the process. But a man who can hurt ten flowers for the sake of one – just imagine how much he must be hurting people with his language, words and behaviour! He is a dangerous man!

I have noticed that some people follow the rule of the book to the letter. It is these foolish people who create problems for others. Fools! They just don't use their brain. For using your brain what you need is attentiveness. If a man is not attentive and alert he cannot do anything properly. Sometimes I have to deal with such people and I try to give them different kinds of tasks, but they manage to make mistakes everywhere. If a man cannot talk sweetly, what would he do except for hurting or causing pain to others? He just cannot do anything else!

The first condition for moving on the path of Sufism is that you should hurt no one. This is a pre-requisite. And here you are, deliberately hurting others! Hurting others deliberately is still not as dangerous as hurting others unknowingly – not even being aware of the fact that it is you who is causing pain to others. This is even more dangerous, as the person does not even know, that he is causing pain to so many people. So stupid, so obtuse and insensitive! Do not hurt anyone. But one who is himself suffering from unconsciousness, unawareness and injudiciousness – what else can be expected from him? One can't help calling him 'poor chap' and pitying him.

But one who sets out on this journey of Sufism has to make a conscious effort to see that no one is hurt by his behaviour, his words or his actions.

Let me tell you one of my working secrets. I keep roaming all over, keep travelling here and there. The thousands of people who meet me, all love me – that is why they come all the way to my camps. Why else would they come? Whenever they meet me they say, "Please come to our home." I also say, "Yes, I will." Why should I say no to anybody? I don't lose anything by saying yes. That person also gets a ray of hope. He will be hurt if I refuse him. So why should I cause hurt to anyone?

Then my program co-ordinator or secretary has a tough time dealing with these people, because they say that Gurumaa had promised. As they have no such orders from me about visiting a particular person's house that day, or to go to a particular person's home in a certain city, they are in a fix. Then they come and ask me, "Why do you keep doing this? Now tell us what to do. You say yes to them and we are answerable! People think that we don't let you go to their homes or that we stop them from meeting you!"

I say that anyone who thinks that someone can stop Gurumaa from doing what she wants to do is a fool. Who can stop the wind saying, "Don't blow this way"? It will just keep blowing. I tell them not to bother about such people. They say, "But you always say yes to them!" And I answer, "That is for me to decide." Poor chaps, what are they supposed to do? I tell them: "You do whatever you think is right. If you think it is possible with my schedule, give your consent. If you think Gurumaa is speaking in the morning and is busy somewhere else in the evening and it will not be possible for her to go anywhere, you explain and refuse politely. Simple, isn't it? It is your job to decide whether or not it will be possible for me to go. I feel it is my job to say 'yes' and you can't stop me from saying that."

Sometimes they get agitated and even show affectionate

185

annoyance and say, "You give them whatever reply you want to give. But we just don't know how to tackle them." I say, "That is exactly what I do! If someone invites me to their home, I am going to accept."

"But often people ask you and you just keep smiling; they take it as your consent."

"Now that is irrational! Who says a smile is an affirmation? It can be a very simple and polite refusal delivered with a smile!"

This is a big problem for people around me. They are always in a dilemma – what to do and what not to do! But why cause annoyance to anybody? Why hurt anybody? Make sure that you never cause annoyance to anyone, for you never know when and who might be of help to you. So don't cause displeasure to anyone.

One more thing: Do not talk ill of anybody behind his or her back; the reason is that word travels. Whatever words we utter, they circulate and finally reach the person against whom they were uttered and then that person becomes your enemy. Why make enemies? If possible, make as many friends as possible.

Why talk ill of anybody? If you don't feel comfortable with someone, just stop meeting that person. But why pick a fight or get into a negative emotion like jealousy? Why indulge in mud-slinging? Instead of wasting your time abusing each other, it is better to say goodbye and part! Just keep in mind that you don't have to meet him again, but don't annoy him. Let him be happy with his own understanding of things – how does it make a difference to you? I am telling you a very practical thing. If you tell an ill-mannered person on his face that he is ill mannered, what will you achieve? He will keep insulting you; he will keep talking ill of you and feeling jealous of you.

Why cause heartache to anyone? Why? Let him go happily! If you two don't click, get along with your life and don't meet! Even if he invites you, just tell him it won't be possible to accept. Tell him nicely that as your views don't match, it won't be possible for you to get together. There is no need to get into an argument.

Do not retaliate if someone hits you. Don't! Go to that person's house and kiss his feet and see that they are not hurting! But there is another meaning to this: feet are the base of our entire body and they bear the weight of our whole body. Similarly, there must be some basis for that person's anger. So go deep into his heart and see who lies at the root of his heart. As you search, you will find that it is the same Almighty who resides in your own heart. So go and love and kiss that very God – why get into arguments? God lives in that person's heart as well – the one who was quarrelling with you.

Where is the room for revenge? Remember that this is the basis of Sufism. We have neither to pollute our heart nor anyone else's. We have not to pollute our tongue, nor pour filth into someone's ears!

CHAPTER 10

SURRENDER

Hazrat Jalaluddin Rumi is a jewel in the crown of Sufism; he is like a full moon that lights up the Sufi world! But before he experienced the intoxication of divine love, he was just a renowned philosopher, a famous writer, a person well-versed in the Quran Sharif, and a highly learned man. His father Bahauddin was already popular as a highly respected, learned and knowledgeable person. Scholars from all over the world – Syria, Iraq, Afghanistan and Iran – came to meet him. Jalaluddin was born to this very Bahauddin! Like father like son!

At a very young age, when other children were flying kites, he would sit learning the verses of the Quran. When other children played, the way children normally do, Jalal would be either practicing zikr or sitting with his father listening to discussions on religion, the Quran and other scriptures. He was a very serious child indeed, hungry for knowledge and learning!

It is said that once Bahauddin was going to the madrasa holding Jalal's hand. People started spreading their majestic and expensive shawls and carpets on the road for them, so that their feet would not get dirty. All this was done without any preparation whatsoever. Such was the respect that Bahauddin commanded at that time!

It is believed that Jalaluddin has written so many treatises that even if they were loaded on seventy camels, there would be many left over. Now just imagine – seventy camels! Such a man would always be busy with his books – reading and teaching, understanding and explaining.

Bahauddin once got an inkling that the place they lived in was about to witness some historical change – an event that would devastate the whole town. So he gathered his whole family and some followers who agreed to go with him, and started moving towards Mecca. Everywhere en route, he was accorded a warm welcome. It is said that the moment he left the city, the Mongol king Ghengiz Khan attacked the city and destroyed it. All those who had stayed behind could not be saved; even children were not spared. Women were captured and sent to his harem. Women who were old or ugly were murdered, and those who were young were sent to his harem or distributed as slaves amongst his soldiers. All young men were killed. He used to go around with bodies of children hanging from spears, and whoever tried to take these bodies down was beheaded. He brought about such a terrible disaster to pass!

While he was still living there, Bahauddin had told the king of the city, "You must mend your ways. Seeing your sinful ways, I will not be able to live here for long."

"Who cares?" replied the king. "Whether you live here or not makes no difference. You may go if you wish!" But little did he know that his city was safe only as long as Bahauddin lived there.

There is another beautiful Sufi tale that I would like to relate. It is said that a Sufi was sitting in quiet contemplation after his namaaz, when a voice came from within: 'The city in which you live is a city of sinners. Leave this city and go as I am going to destroy it.' The Sufi said, "O my Lord! At your command you can make or break anything. Who can question you? But today this servant of yours wants to ask you one thing – if in a city of sinners there lived a hundred Sufis, won't you forgive the sinners for the sake of these hundred Sufis?"

"Yes of course! I will. I will definitely protect the city where my hundred Sufis live."

"If they are not a hundred but only ten?"

"Even if there are only ten Sufis, I would forgive the whole city for the sake of those ten.

The Sufi then asked one last question, "And what if there is only one Sufi living in that city?"

"Even then I will forgive the whole city for the sake of that one Sufi."

"Well, then please forgive my city! I live here. You would not have come to warn me if you didn't love me. You want to save me from this imminent disaster, and I request you to forgive all these people for my sake."

A normal worldly person will never be able to understand the power of a Sufi. This Sufi tale was just a tale till the time Bahauddin's incident took place. The moment Bahauddin left the city, the whole of it was devastated. Not only was the city devastated, even the king was killed – the one who had said to Bahauddin: "How am I bothered whether you stay or go!"

Jalaluddin inherited knowledge from his father. But don't forget that it was all bookish knowledge. He got deeply involved with his studies, and in the process of attaining more and more knowledge, he illumined his mind and started practicing zikr as well.

As I mentioned earlier, there are ninety-nine names of Allah, and Sufis invented a few more. Any one of these is chanted during zikr. One of these is 'La Ilaha Illallah'. This mantra has to be a part of every Sufi's worship. It means: There is nobody but God; it is only God that is.

Now, there are two things to be noted here. There is no God for a blind man, and a man with eyes sees God all around! God does not exist for the ignorant. And one whose eyes have opened, one who has achieved wisdom, he gave the name 'God' to the power that runs the whole world, the whole universe.

It could have been said: 'There is no one except you!' But in 'La Ilaha', the negative emotion or 'rejection' is taken up first; then we move onto the positive emotion or 'assertion'. 'La Ilaha' means: 'There is no God!' And 'Illallah' means 'except Him'. From obliteration starts the process of achievement! Nothing can be achieved without reducing it to nothingness. That is why they start with a negative assertion.

However, according to the Muslim religious law, this is just half the saying – it cannot be considered complete. According to religious leaders, unless and until the name of Prophet Mohammad's name is added to this line, it is considered incomplete. So the complete kalma is: 'La Ilaha Illallah, Mohammad Rasool Allah'.

But Sufis recite only half the kalma. As I told you earlier, it is because they claim that Sufis existed even before Prophet Mohammad. Maybe they were known by some other name then. But as Shakespeare says: 'What's in a name; a rose by any other name will smell as sweet.'

According to Islam, Prophet Mohammad was the first Sufi, but Sufism goes much beyond the confines of Islam. Don't you think Jesus Christ was a great Sufi too? There have been some wise men who both Christians and Muslims claim as their own – both fight for their legacy. Among them is Ibn-al-Arabi. Christians claim he is their saint and Muslims claim he is their Sufi. And if he had been asked, he would have said: 'I belong only to God! I don't belong to either of them.'

One who gets attached to any caste or religion ceases to be a Sufi. A Sufi does not belong to any religion. The only thing that matters to him is the Truth. One who believes only in the Truth knows no religious definitions. It is the same with Guru Nanak Sahib! Hindus and Muslims both claim that he belonged to their sect. In fact, Sikhs stake an absolute claim to his legacy. I remember when I was holding a discourse on Japji Sahib, some people raised objections saying, "You are not a Sikh, how can you speak in the gurudwara? Only a Sikh can hold discourses in a gurudwara."

People can argue with me that if I am not a Muslim, how can I speak on Sufism? But I say that I do not speak on Sufism, I only talk Sufi. And that is because I consider myself to be a Sufi! So being a Sufi myself, I have every right to speak about Sufi."

Christ was a Sufi; before him even Moses was a Sufi. It is a different matter if one doesn't want to believe it, but Kabir and Ravidas were also Sufis. Only their words and language differed.

Again let me tell you, I am serving the same liquor that I used to serve earlier. Only the bottle has changed. But this bottle is really adorable. This bottle is wonderful; it is amazing, it is sweet. It also looks very charming! Often the perfume bottle is nicer than the perfume – we don't feel like throwing it away even when the perfume is finished. We often preserve such bottles. You will find empty perfume bottles in many bathrooms or dressing rooms. If you ask they say, "The bottle was so pretty, I didn't feel like throwing it away!"

So remember, every religion, every community is like a bottle; the real thing is the substance within! The perfume is the real thing. Every religion has a separate bottle, but the substance that is found in every bottle is called Sufi.

You make a beautiful bottle and go to the market to sell it. It can cost ten, fifteen or twenty rupees – maybe a hundred! If it is made of crystal it may cost a thousand rupees! But an empty bottle is an empty bottle – it is of no use! The bottle gets its just value only once a perfume is filled in it. Would you feel good if someone were to present you with an empty bottle? And the person presenting it was to say, "Wow! What a beautiful bottle! Such intricate carving, what a design! I present this to you on your birthday." Would you like that? No! You will not like it because it is empty.

The perfume inside the bottle of Islam is Sufi. The fragrance inside the bottle of Christianity is Sufi. The 'love' in the bottle of the Hindu religion is Sufi. In this context, I can say that Meerabai and Sahajobai were also Sufis.

There has been a Sufi in Kashmir called Lalleshwari or Lalla. But if you ask any Muslim, he will say, "No, her name was Lal-Ded. Muslims believe she was a Muslim fakir, a Sufi! If you ask Hindus, they say she was a devout follower of Shiva, a scholar and an ascetic. She is a fakir to the Muslims, and a devoted follower of the formless, unqualified Shiva to Hindus. But if somebody were to go and ask Lalleshwari or Lalla, "Whom do you belong to?", the answer is written in her book, which is popular by the name of 'Lalwakh': 'To tell you the truth, I am only Truth. I belong neither to this nor to that.'

Truth does not belong to any one person, caste, religion or region. Truth cannot be bound within the four walls of any religion. All the differences, the partitions that you see have not been made by God. These walls have been erected by men with vested interests. And who could those selfish people be? Those who have turned religion into a business enterprise!

Try to understand it this way: Nobody ever saw what happened in Meera's heart with his own eyes. What did people see with their eyes? They saw her dancing, her singing, her crying and her writings! People around her only noticed her way of sitting, getting up, eating and her way of talking; they described all that in their writings. And after her death, they started saying: "Ecstatic Meera used to dance, lost in Krishna's love."

But if Meera danced because of her love for Krishna, that does not make her a Sufi at all, because a Sufi does not dance! Dance just happens to him! Meera used to write devotional songs – if this is the only truth, then Meera was not a Sufi. Any lyricist could have written those songs. These days you make one call and thousands of writers are available. Meera was not just a poetess – she was much more than that.

Often people send me poems and ask me to sing them. They say, "I have written this." I tell them that I can't sing their devotional songs because they have been written by an 'I'. I find your 'I' objectionable. Your ego is present in that 'I'. It is basically to satisfy your ego that you put together some impressive words, but the words of one, who aspires to do things, only to impress others, cannot reflect the Truth. And I only sing songs that bear honesty; I don't sing songs based on falsehood.

Guru Nanak says:

'Whatever my Lord makes me speak I say those words'

Not once did Nanak say: "'I' have written this." Not once did he take all his writings to a publisher and request him to publish his works.

No, Guru Nanak and Meera are not writers. Writing just happened to them – it happened – it was not attempted! Similarly, I can give the example of Prophet Mohammad's words where he

193

said, "Ilham happened!" Guru Nanak says, "Sayings or verses happened to me." He did not say, "I have written." He said, "Sayings occurred to me. I wrote them as they occurred – that is it. I was just a medium. I was like a flute into which wind was blown, and the music just happened. I was hollow like a flute. He blew air into me and these expressions just happened." The flute can't claim to have sung these songs! Guru Nanak or Meera never said: "I have written this."

Whatever happens within is beyond comprehension. Only someone who experiences it can feel it. People around them only notice their outward behaviour and record that. And then these things become the foundation for various sects and communities. As long as the Sufi is alive, things carry on smoothly due to his strong and powerful personality. But the moment he leaves his body, people gather around and take advantage of his reputation to serve their own ends.

All sorts of people gather when a Sufi dies. First the poets and writers come as they finally get a chance – they begin attributing stories and anecdotes to the Sufi; stories that never took place. And the common man, bereaved by the loss of the master, respectfully, honorably and gratefully accepts all that is proclaimed. Well, this happens with the common man as well. If someone dies, his neighbours start asking, "What happened?" And then incidents are related as though people were actually present when the poor man shut his eyes to the world. The way they talk, it seems they were with the dying man all the time!

On the death of a man, one such character said, "We always sat together, drank tea and roamed around together." He began narrating incidents that must never have happened. Someone standing nearby said, "But brother, I never saw you going for walks with him!" He knew this fellow never got up before 10 o'clock in the morning, so couldn't have walked with him? But this character said, "Be quiet! It is such fun to gossip like this!"

Exaggerated stories are written about Sufis who are no more; later generations take them to be true. It has been written about Kabir that when he died his body was not found anywhere. Another story that is popular is that after his death Kabir's shroud

194

was removed and instead of his body there was a lotus flower. Absolutely illogical!

Now consider other more dangerous types who associate themselves with the names of great Sufis after their death. These are the people who establish an entire institution in the name of these mystcs; they pen down all kinds of rules and regulations in his name. In fact they publish a whole treatise on 'rights and wrongs' in his name.

You can pick up scriptures of any religion or community – each one of them will have a big book of 'dos and don'ts'. The followers of Jainism don't eat anything after sunset – if someone does, they consider it a sin. Things were different in Lord Mahavir's time, there was no electricity. Certainly all kinds of creatures – flies, mosquitoes and small insects could get into your food and eating them would make you sick. That is why it was said that one should not eat after sunset.

Every religion has its own set of rules, regulations and principles. Once I met a person, head of a sect, who had just published a book. Though people called him a 'sant' (seer or a mystic) he was actually a 'mahant'. There is a lot of difference between a 'sant' and a 'mahant', but people use these two words interchangeably. A 'mahant' is actually a superior or head of a sect. Anyhow, people started calling him a 'sant'. There is a difference between a 'sant' and a 'mahant', as there is a difference between a manager and an owner of a firm.

When I met him, he showed me the book which he had had published; in it he had printed the photographs of all the sixteen devout whose work has been included in the Guru Granth Sahib by Guru Arjandev. There were pictures of great sages like Namdev, Dhanna Bhagat, Peepa, Ravidas, and also of all the six gurus whose writings are compiled in the scripture. I appreciated the book for its ingenuity as it would give an insight into the personalities of these great men.

"You will be surprised to know that some representatives of the Sikh community have raised an objection to my work."

I asked why. He said, "Because when you go to a gurudwara,

you always cover your head. If someone sings devotional songs there, he too covers his head." Their objection was that even the picture of mystic Ravidas must show him wearing a headgear. When I said that Ravidas never wore any turban, they said, "How could you print a picture of someone with a bare head? It is not correct to keep one's head uncovered like this. It is against our tradition."

Then he added, "Ravidas was still better off – at least he had hair on his head! Swami Ramanand had a tonsured head. And he was a mystic! I must make his picture the way he was. But they started objecting to this too: 'You will have to draw his hair and put a turban on his head as well!' I retorted, 'How can I put hair and a turban on the picture of a sage's head?' They said, 'Alright, then at least put a handkerchief on his head.'"

I said, "Yes! But I can't really comment on this. All I can do is appreciate your imagination that got together the pictures of all the sixteen devotees whose names and verses we get to read in the Guru Granth Sahib. I really appreciate your effort – the way you obtained the photographs from their birthplaces, had them painted and then published in book-form. As far as these people and their comments are concerned, I really can't say anything. After all, they are all your people; you should know how to deal with them. But it is certainly very strange!"

A fakir once questioned Lalleshwari: "Don't you feel ashamed roaming around naked like this?" To remind you, Muslims considered her their fakir; in fact even today they consider her to be their fakir. If someone has to say his prayers – the namaaz – he cannot do so with his head uncovered. But there was Lalleshwari who did not even wear clothes! So a fakir, who had come from a far-off place just to meet her, said on seeing her, "Don't you feel ashamed roaming around like this? You remain naked!" To this Lalleshwari replied, "There is only one man. And nothing is hidden from Him! Only those who have something to hide, cover themselves. But in Lalleshwari's heart there is no sin; she has not done any wrong. So Lalleshwari has no need to cover herself."

She never wore anything at all! It becomes difficult to play the game of instigation with a personality like Lalleshwari – games which have been played successfully with other personalities.

Sikhism has its own set of rules and principles; a Hindu temple has its own rules. In fact the rules of various temples too differ. You go to any temple in North India and you will find women with their heads covered. When the priest puts the saffron tilak on their forehead, even men cover their heads; if nothing else, they will at least place their hand on their head. But if you go to any temple in South India, you will find that there they consider covering the head inauspicious.

I remember travelling in South India quite a few years back; we went around all the temples and places of worship. When I went to Tirupati, I covered my head as is normally done here in the North. A woman asked me, "Why did you cover your head?" I said, "Why! Isn't this a temple?"

"It is a temple; that is why I am asking you why you covered your head."

In North India a bride covers her head whether she is Hindu or Sikh. She has to cover her head. But in the South even brides don't cover the head. So, traditions differ. It is the priests, pandits, mullahs and bhais who have made these traditions; they are the ones who erect all these dividers. And furthering their cause are people with perverted minds who we call 'political leaders' – they then put cement on these walls and make them permanent. To tell you the fact, there is only one Truth. But their rules, regulations and principles may be different. It is these differences in rules and regulations that political leaders take advantage of, and make Hindus fight with Muslims and Muslims with Christians. And as long as people are fighting, their own power keeps growing.

If you just cast a glance at the various wars and conflicts that have taken place in the world's history, it has always been religion and its associated politics that has been the basis of them all. It may be called a jihad or any other religious war. Even a case of water shortage for a farmer is given a religious twist by politicians to start a religious war! Whatever be the case, it is given a religious colour. And the common man does not understand these hidden motives – his mental faculties are not really conditioned to think that way. That is why politicians raise slogans, and all the foolish people follow the slogan and go around killing and harming each other. If you ask them the reason they say: 'In the name of Ram!' One should ask them when Ram give them permission to fight and kill!

In my view, the actual basis of all the chaos that is prevalent in society and of all the conflicts that are taking place – is just one. And if you want to get rid of all this, just do one thing. Anyone, please do just this much: collect all the so-called religious leaders and also all the politicians… put them in a space-shuttle and send them up. Just a one-way ticket! No return ticket! Just one-way!

Okay, tell me one thing. When I said 'collect all of them', did you not think that I was going to say 'just shoot them' or 'hang them'? Why on earth would I say that? I believe in non-violence. I do not believe in violence. No! But this will be a good experiment. And like this we can even monitor their activities. The moment they are out of here, they will start blaming each other, and in fact there won't be any need for anybody else to kill them; they will themselves finish each other off.

Sufism breaks all the external walls! In my view, if we want to bring about love and unity in this world, we need to spread Sufism; we need to spread love.

I was talking about Jalaluddin Rumi; he was a reservoir of knowledge – he wrote so many treatises. He even became a professor at the University of Konya at a very young age. Very soon the entire world started respecting him; his name and fame spread far and wide. Jalaluddin's popularity went far beyond his father Bahauddin's; he was an ocean of knowledge.

One day, an unknown, unkempt, cloak-donning fakir came into Jalaluddin's life and completely changed its course. What did he do? All he did was to look into Jalaluddin's eyes! And just by looking into his eyes he conveyed the message: 'When will you start searching for that Almighty about whom you keep reading and writing? For how long will you keep putting pen to paper, and for how long will you keep blackening your mind? The time has come to illumine your heart with His love.'

And the name of this fakir was Shams Tabreez! The entire city of Konya was a witness to the scene of Jalaluddin and Shams' first meeting. Jalaluddin, before whom the entire city bowed in reverence, had this day bowed his head in the service of Shams Tabreez! But Shams did not allow him to bow – he reached for him and embraced him. Both stood there embracing each other for hours together. The world was witnessing this unusual scene where a scholar, a learned man, astrologer and person as skilled as Jalaluddin stood embracing a total stranger for hours together, water running down his eyes!

It is said that that very day the spark of love travelled from Shams' heart to Jalaluddin's. Remember, a small spark can burn down a huge palace! One little spark is enough! Jalaluddin received such a spark from Shams. Their love, friendship and affection was mutual.

Shams had great respect for Jalaluddin – something the world could not understand. At times Shams would kiss Jalaluddin's feet; at times Jalaluddin would rub the dust from Shams' feet on his eyes! People were unable to understand who was greater and who was giving what to who?

Among Mevlavi Sufis, there is a specific terminology, for the person who has to go through a set of discipline, where his will and dedication is tested. The person is called a muhip. Who is a muhip? A muhip is a person who gets a hundred percent marks in the three-day test. I mentioned the three-day test earlier. Before he enters the tekke, a newcomer is made to sit on a sheepskin for three days. For these three days he just has to sit there and do zikr. This is checked physically; they do not trust the aspirant's word, instead they put him to the test. So much endurance! So much patience! So much tolerance! Whoever clears this three-day test is then called a muhip.

Only after he passes this test, that he gets an entry in a Tekke. Tekke as we know, is the shrine or tomb of a Sufi, where sheikhs live and share with their mureeds, ways and methods of this mystical path. Sufis do all their practices at night; they do not do it in the daytime. They get together around 7:00 in the evening. They address each other as brother or friend. They eat and drink tea together; their tea is called kehwa. They make light conversation or even laugh and play music together. After that they either sit for zikr or their whirling starts. This getting together or assembly is called sema and the in-charge of this sema is called semazen bashi

One learns from the semazen bashi how to do zikr – there is a specific way of doing it. Unless and until you follow the right method, you do not achieve Truth. The method primarily followed in Turkey, Iran and Europe is called zikr. Though zikr originated long ago, it got its present form and colour from Mevlana Jalaluddin Rumi who received it from Shams. What is its colour? Its colour is the colour of love! The love about which Rumi once said:

> The power of love can turn poison into nectar
> Base metal into gold
> The power of love
> Can bring alive the dead
> Can turn a prince into slave
> This is what is the power of love

Zikr means reciting any of God's names, not only with the tongue, but from the heart. Zikr means repeatedly remembering His name with love. Zikr, which starts at the tongue, is then brought onto one's breath. When it goes beyond the breath, it turns into fikr. Here fikr does not mean worry; in Persian and Arabic it is called fikr, but in Hindi it means manan.

Let us get closer to the meaning. In the beginning we start with any one name of God recited with the tongue. We begin with this one word, and while remembering it over and over again, we reach a stage where the name goes so deep down, that the tongue and mind both get quieted, and the fragrance of the name is felt within. That fragrance is called 'fikr'.

In order to reach the stage of fikr, one needs to start with zikr. And one who does fikr, is called a fakir. So who is a fakir? The one who wears a black or green cloak? No! One, whose mind is quiet to the world, but whose heart sings songs for the Almighty, and one who is aware of his consciousness – he is a fakir.

One who possesses only zikr is a muhip, but as his zikr gets deeper, he keeps getting closer to fikr, and as he gets closer to fikr, he will get closer to becoming a fakir. This is what Sufis call silsila! What we call the tradition of a master-disciple relationship is what Sufis call silsila.

The mantra that is used for zikr is 'Hu'. 'Hu' means: 'Is there'. Here we don't say: 'God is there' or 'Truth is there'. All we say is: 'Is there'. The smallest word that is closest to Truth is not Brahman, or Nirakaar; it is not Omkaar or Allah; it is not Waheguru! The closest that any mantra can come to the Truth is 'Hu'.

I would like to repeat: A Sufi starts with the chant of 'Allah Hu', but as he keeps progressing in his devotion, only 'Hu' is left. And as the zikr of 'Hu' goes deeper, even 'Hu' does not remain. All that is left is the fragrance of 'Hu'.

At first you should only listen to the pronunciation of 'Hu'; you should not repeat, only listen. First listen with all your attention; don't listen half-heartedly. Don't analyze, do not bring your mind in it. I will show you the way to do it, and if after ten minutes you feel, that you have understood the rhythm, only then should you join in, and that too in a very low voice – but not for the first ten minutes.

We do not breathe through our nose while doing zikr; we inhale as well as exhale only through the mouth. There will be only one string of the mantra – only one! Just as when making treacle, we say that it is ready when a single string is formed, similarly, there has to be only one string of the mantra. So the breath will be taken in through the mouth and while exhaling it through the mouth, 'Hu' will be pronounced.

While doing zikr any mantra can be used; there are many names that can be used. But whichever name you use, one thing that needs special attention is the rhythm and the beat. Not one more, not one less! One thing that is not permitted in zikr is difference in the length of the sounds produced i.e., one person uttering a sound of a lesser length and another making the same sound longer. This is just not allowed.

When you meditate on the sound of Om, some people say a

short Om, while others may drag it a little longer and someone else may stretch it even longer! That is why it lacks synchronization. But this is the specialty of Sufi zikr – if one man does it, he will utter the sound with the same duration as when ten people do it; if a thousand people were to sit and do zikr together, they would also do it for the same length of time. The duration of enunciation is never changed.

So the breath goes in and as it comes out, along with the breath we produce the sound of 'Hu'. 'Hu' means 'the one who is'. Here the mind may start thinking that if it is God who is, then he would be like this or like that! But zikr is never done with the mind; it is done from the heart.

Before we start with zikr, let me tell you how Sufis meet each other or how one fellow disciple meets another fellow disciple. Their way of meeting each other is very distinct. They keep the right hand on the heart – as the heart is on the left side, the right hand is placed on the left side of the chest, and then they bow the head down to the waist. They bow very gently and then rise equally gently; while straightening up they look into each other's eyes.

Someone said, "It is okay that brothers, friends or fellow disciples should greet each other like this, but a mureed (disciple) greets his sheikh in such a manner!"

Just look at this greeting. Your heart too bows down along with your head – it is not only the head that is bowing! The person who is paying respect says, "See, my heart is bowing to you!" That is why the hand is placed on the heart. Someone asked, "Why do they put their hand on the heart?" Sufis say, "Because Shams' hand always remained on his heart, in whose heart the pangs of love – the twinge of divine love was always present thus we remember Shams while placing our hand on the heart and while bowing down!"

Then it was asked, "Why does a sheikh greet his mureed in the same manner?" This is because while the mureed bows and greets with respect, love, honor and reverence, the sheikh returns the greeting in the same manner, implying that God is present

202

equally in me, as in you. If you show respect to the God that is present in me, then I also pay my respects to the same God, that is present in you. There is no difference between you and me!

So when the mureed bows down with his hand on his heart, his sheikh responds with the same affection, bowing his head and saying that you and I are the same. That you and I also become one – all this effort is being made to this end. Let there be no distance between the sheikh and his mureed; let there be no difference between a guru and his disciple. Whatever little apparent difference is there, let us do away with it. As long as this distinction is there, we need to put in a whole lot of effort. This difference must go!

While the sheikh ceases to see any difference between himself and his mureed, the difference can still be seen by the eyes of the mureed. That is why he bows down – but the sheikh too bows because he wants to convey that He, who resides within him, is there in the mureed too. He is there equally in both!

And the mantra that goes closest to this fact is the mantra of 'Hu'. To practice zikr, let your ears and hearts remain open, and through these open doors let the zikr of the Sufi go deep inside your hearts. At first you must only listen. It is only when you feel that you have understood its tone and pitch, then in a very, very low tone, you may join in. But not before I allow you to do so – till then you just have to listen.

You have to breathe through your mouth and not from your nose. A single string has to be formed and to bring your voice in consonance, you need to be alert and awake while listening to it.

This is a practical method; an unusual and wonderful way to bring awareness!

CHAPTER 11

DIVINE INTOXICATION
IS ESSENTIAL

Al Hillaj Mansoor says:
Agar hai shaunk milne ka, toh hardum lau lagata ja
Jala kar khud numai ko, bhasm tan pe lagata ja

Pakad kar ishq ka jhadu, safa kar dil ke hujre ko
Dui ki dhool ko lekar, musalle pe udata ja

Musalla phaad, tasbeeh tod, kitaban daal pani mein
Pakad kar dast maston ka, ghulam unka kahata ja

Na mar bhookha, na rakh roza
Na ja masjid, na kar sajda
Wazu ka tod de kuja, sharab-e-shauk peeta ja

Hamesha kha, hamesha pee, na ghaflat se raho hardum
Nashe mein sair hai apni, khudi apni jalata ja

Na ho Mullah, na ho Brahmin, dui ki chhod de pooja
Hukum hai Shah Kalander ka, An-al-haq tu gaata ja

Kahe Mansoor mastana, maine haq dil mein pehchana
Wahi maston ka maykhana, usi ke beech aata ja

If you wish to meet the God, light the flame of love,
Let it reside within you, constantly
Burn the false ego and smear yourself with its ashes

Clean doorway of your heart with broom of love
Blow away dust of duality from the prayer mat

Tear the mat, break the string beads, throw away your holy books
Hold hands of master and be his loyal servant

Don't die with hunger, don't keep fast
Don't go to masjid, and don't bow your head in reverence

Break the mud cup meant for washing
Drink the wine of divine love

Always eat, always drink, never live in unconscious slumber
Live life in divine intoxication, keep burning your ego

Don't be a Mullah or Brahmin
Leave the worship of duality

I have found 'The Truth' within my own 'self'
Come and join the tavern of people, drenched in divine love

What was, what is, and what will be…. What existed, what exists and what will exist tomorrow – is the supreme power, which came to be known as Allah! The rest is all a game being played – a link between man and his maker. The world exists, but is transient.

Something that comes into existence and then ceases to be is called faani – perishable or mortal. Fana means death or annihilation. And the one, who is prepared for death and has understood death, is not scared of it; such a person is a Sufi.

A Sufi story goes: An elderly Arab fakir, lived contentedly in the desert, immersed in the remembrance of his beloved God; he ate frugally and wore clothes sparingly. One evening death knocked on his door and said, "Come! Your time is over now." The aged man replied, "Now that you've come, you are welcome! But I live alone in this deserted area and there is no one around to even bury me. At least give me some time to change my gown, so that when someone finds my body, it is not lying here shamelessly naked! This gown that I am wearing is already in tatters; it is my

205

fault for I should have been prepared for you. Please grant me some time."

Death said, "You have been devout all your life, so I grant you time! Go and get a new cloak; I will come back for you in three days!" The elderly man went to a nearby city and bought a new cloak. He even bought some cloth which he folded and tied to his bare head. He then put on his new cloak and waited for death every passing minute. In his heart he was grateful that he had been able to complete all pending tasks – whatever few had been left undone. He waited for his death in complete peace.

Death came exactly three days later and took away his life leaving the body lying there. Because he stayed in such a deserted place, probably no one would find it for a long time. Several days passed; the strong winds of the desert tore his new cloak to shreds, but at least his body was covered. Then one day a passing caravan saw this old man whose face was covered with sand and whose cloak was in shreds. Though they realised that he was dead, they came closer, thinking of giving him a proper burial, as his body was lying in the open and wild animals could come and tear him up. Why should anybody be subjected to such terrible conditions they thought, dismounting from their camels!

They went closer and realised that they had no cloth for a shroud. When they looked closely they found a piece of cloth tied around his head. On removing the cloth they found it was three yards long – the exact length required for a shroud. It dawned on them that this man had arranged for his shroud before dying, so that if an unknown person found his body, he would not have to run around looking for one. He had died with his burial shroud tied on his head! They covered his body with that cloth, dug a grave, and in the desert where he had stayed all his life, they buried him.

It is not known who those people were or what the name of that old man was, but from then on it became a tradition for every Muslim, to have a piece of cloth tied on his head, as a constant reminder that death may strike at any time. That is the reason all men in Arab countries tie a piece of cloth on their head – that cloth symbolizes a shroud. It is because of this incident that they carry a shroud on their heads; a Sufi always carries his shroud on his head. An unknown Sufi has said:

Sar per baandhe kafan jo
Wohi kare aashiqui

One who carries his shroud on his head
Only such a person can be a true lover!

But anyone who is afraid of death can never be a lover. Hazrat Jalaluddin Rumi has written in one of his poems, which is a part of his collection called 'Masnavi':

Death has taken me
From being a stone to a plant
From a plant to an animal
And from an animal to a human

But now I renounce my mortality
As I dwell in the fire of love
And now I find myself
No further than the almighty above

When have I lost anything by dying? Every time I died, I was born again in a much higher form. First I was a rock; from a rock, I took birth as a plant. When the plant died, I was reborn an animal. And when the animal died, I was born as a human being. And now when I died in divine love, I have a new birth – I am born as 'Truth', An-al-haq (I am the Truth). Death has never given me a raw deal. Rumi's poem says that death always gives something; it never takes away anything from you! Man is at fault when he says: 'Death snatches away.' Death never snatches, it always gives.

Death says: 'Because you still have desires, you will again get a new body.' Even one who is not desirous of anything gets something from death. It gives him freedom from the cycle of birth and death – this too is a gift from death. For achieving a state of bodiless-ness, one has to come out of the body! One can attain freedom while still living, but for body-less freedom, one has to come out of the body – one has to die! So, Kabir says:

Kab maroon, kaise maroon
Kaise miloon Har raya

How do I die? When will I die?
When will I meet thee? What should I try?

When will I die? How will I die? I have the desire to die!
I wish to die! But after dying, man gets into a state which is
described by Rasool as: 'While worshipping I reach a stage where
no prophet or angel can attain. No angel can dare to come near
me at that time.' Even so, it is said that the first time Prophet
Mohammad experienced ilham, it was an angel that granted him
the experience – the angel's name was Gabriel. All the Sufis who
came before the Prophet had also attained great heights. Here
the Prophet says: 'The state in which I unite with God – nobody
can come near me in that state. Nobody has the power to reach
up to that state. No prophet and no angel has the permission to
come there.'

Whoever can understand the depth of the words of the
Prophet is a Sufi. Others just get caught up with words and say:
'Whatever happened to Prophet Mohammad can happen only to
him and not to anyone else.' Christ said: 'I am the son of God!'
Many Christians have understood this to mean that only Christ
is God's son and no one else can be the son of God.

The incident that took place in Prophet Mohammad's life
was initially beyond even his own comprehension. Floodgates of
divinity were opening up in Prophet's heart; it is but natural at
this time even for great prophets to feel a bit uneasy. No matter
how great God's people, sages, sufis or seers may be or let's say
great people in the making may be, ultimately the power of divine
is limitless, so sometimes it spills out, why question it, why fight
over it, such can be the power of grace, that it can overflow.

The same happened with great Prophet Mohammad, now
under many statements and stories, these incidents are described
in much more detailed ways, like his body burned with fever or
he said to his wife either he was turning into a poet or something
was happening to him. Many would present their doubt over this;
some would say no such things happened and others would say

that they did. These are ways to give you an insight, to help you become a more ardent seeker. The grace of divine is tremendous thus it can make anything possible.

Though 'understanding' has nothing to do with age, Prophet Mohammad's first wife, who was older than him, possessed a quality called 'understanding'. When he was going through the experiences, which were getting difficult for him to comprehend, she said, "You just relax! Take a blanket and lie down. Do not talk to anybody. All I can say with authority is that you are a God-loving being, so nothing bad can happen to you. Whatever is happening must be with God's blessings. That's it! You just stay with this blessing. We humans have never been able to understand divine favours. Don't say anything, just relax." And he covered himself with a blanket and lay down.

When the experience first happened to the Prophet, he too got confused. The reason is that it is different when this is explained in a silsila – that is, when a master explains this to a disciple, but when it happens suddenly, that is, without a guru's initiation, then it is beyond one's comprehension.

This is but natural! This perplexity, this intoxication, this anxiety and this surprise – wondering what is happening! Why is it happening? – This question comes to the mind much later! The question 'why' occurs to the mind after a long time; for quite some time it is impossible to understand what is happening. In Prophet Mohammad's case, all that people were able to say was that he would get up early in the morning, have a wash, get ready for namaaz and then sit down for namaaz. Then they noticed that he was sitting for namaaz five times a day. The fact is that the Prophet propounded the theory of the five-time namaaz keeping in mind the understanding of his followers.

He said, "If not more often, at least do it five times a day! At least remember your God five times. A day is divided into four separate sections, so if you do the namaaz just four times that won't be enough. After doing it four times at four different times of the day, you must do it once more so that you can do it everyday – remember Him the fifth time wishing for a propitious tomorrow."

But actually, does one need to perform the namaaz just five times a day? What about the rest of the time? When Prophet Mohammad looks at himself, he feels he is not detached from his God for even a single moment. But to others he has given the instruction that as long as one is not able to reach this stage, he must offer prayers at least five times a day, once before the day starts, in the afternoon and then before the evening sets in. The time between noon and evening becomes very long, so make use of that to offer namaaz once more. And the last is when the night sets in. Before the night sets in completely, you must be done with all the five namaaz.

The Prophet who could not bear the idea of being separated from his God for a moment, needed to tell people to remember Him at least five times a day. So that became the rule – offer namaaz five times a day – whether whole-heartedly or just for the sake of it, but do it. Whether your heart is in it or not you must do it. People who gather around a true fakir – a prophet – can understand only his outward behaviour. So people around Prophet Mohammad only took note of what he did, what he ate, how he behaved and taking these things as a basis, they wrote the complete shara-shariyat (Islamic personal law). A few things that Prophet Mohammad had said himself were added later.

Some things have become a part of this religious law because silsila, the word-of-mouth tradition has carried on. So whatever happened to Mohammad sahib came to be known to very few people while he was alive. As for the rest, well, it is like saluting the rising sun! One by one people joined him in his endeavours, but they had to face a lot of hardship initially. Those were the days when tribes were continuously at war with one another. Idols were worshipped ceremoniously; thousand of idols were worshipped every day. In this scenario, Mohammad sahib's message was that God is not in this idol; idols are made by man. Several thousand years ago, rishis in India had said the same thing, but when the Prophet said this, society did not take it lightly. Everybody became his enemy!

Whoever said, "I interact with Mohammad sahib, listen to him, understand what he tries to say," would incur the wrath of the people. He would be dragged out of his house and stoned; many died like this. Those days people were bought and sold as slaves. There was a slave whom Mohammad sahib taught 'La Ilaha Illallah'. He taught him the lesson of endurance; he taught him that all men are one; he taught him how to perform namaaz. But one day his enemies surrounded him: 'How can a slave say that all are His children and all men are equal?' They pelted him with stones and grievously injured him. But every time a stone hit the man, he would shout with increasing intensity: 'La Ilaha Illallah.' Even streams of blood could not deter him from his perseverance!

Those were very difficult times. Mohammad sahib even had to fight wars to save his own life and those of his followers. It is said that at one such difficult moment, Abu Bakr was with him. In thousands the enemy was at their heels and they had to take refuge in a cave. They kept hiding, waiting for the enemy to go away. After all, how many people could they fight? Abu Bakr said, "How long can the two of us stay here?" Mohammad replied, "No, we are not two. We are three." Abu Bakr started looking around, "Who is the third?"

"The third is my God! We are not just two of us here. We are three, you are forgetting the third and that is why you are afraid and trembling. Remember our third companion!"

"The third one, He who is omnipresent and whom you call 'God' and who you claim loves you, why does he put you through such difficult times? Why?"

"He puts His loved ones to the test. You can't test an unknown person. Because He loves me, He puts me through these tests. He tests me and at the same time He gives me enough strength to be successful. Just have faith."

Those who have faith, immense faith, are Sufis. In those days many wars took place and the Prophet himself participated in several. But you will be surprised to know that His sword bore the words: 'My Message is Peace'. And the real meaning of Islam is also peace.

The one, whose heart resounds with the name of Almighty,

cannot fight, cannot go to war. But then neither is he a coward to meekly have his throat slit. Man has been granted this body by God's grace; it is his responsibility to take care of its safety and security. So also, God has asked man to use his intellect. The basic understanding of survival is possessed even by animals; won't men have it? The Almighty that helps you in difficult times has been called by another name – Mushkilkushan, i.e. one who helps you in difficult times and tells you not to be afraid of rough weather.

Even in the Prophet's own time there were very few people around with whom he could discuss his innermost feelings.

You will be surprised to learn that one day someone asked me, "Why did he get married so many times?" I said, "First, an all-learned man can do anything! He is above the rules and laws of society. Second, every time he got married, it was actually an act of kindness." In those days, there were so many wars and as a result there were fewer men and more widows. That was the reason behind polygamy. But before suggesting it to others, he himself married several times. Practice before you preach! Those days women were bought and sold like slaves. Even today Muslim women do not enjoy as many rights as he had given to them.

Without a woman's consent she cannot be married off, no matter how powerful or influential the man may be. Unless and until the woman says, 'I accept', the marriage is to be considered invalid. She was given the highest right – of choosing her own life partner. Marrying more than once was allowed keeping in mind, the welfare of those women, who had lost their husbands in war, and not just for the sake of marrying.

The Prophet himself married nine times; he told others to marry at least three times. A man, who has brought home a woman in marriage, will bear her entire responsibility; will keep her with all dignity. At least that woman would not be sold off in the market place. In fact, in those times many of the wars were fought for the sake of women. If men found the women of a particular tribe to be beautiful, they would attack the tribe and take away their women.

History is replete with such incidents! A huge battle was fought for the sake of Rani Roopmati. When she saw her countrymen being killed, she thought, 'So much bloodshed for the sake of this body! I will not marry anyone under duress!' When she was unable to do anything to stop the war, she immolated herself. Who hasn't heard of Rani Roopmati!

Mohammad Sahib suggested meher (money given compulsorily by the groom's family to the bride's family) in order to save the woman from being disgraced, and so that she gets respect and her due rights. It is a different matter that later on people began wondering if the three-marriage rule was still relevant as times and conditions have changed. Social conditions today are not what they were at that time. I have discussed this with many Muslims and they are of the view that this rule is not required now. It is difficult to manage one wife and two children – who would be able to care for three wives? No one will be able to do justice to any of them. Even if one marries thrice in keeping with the tradition, will he be able to give respect, comfort and happiness to all three? No, he won't!

However, I have no intention of delving into this subject; I just wanted to make the point that what happened in the spiritual life of Prophet Mohammad is understood by very few people. As it is, a majority of people lack that kind of understanding. Does a multitude possess that understanding? Thousands of people read the Bhagwad Gita, have they all understood the philosophy of the Gita? Millions of people read the Gurbani everyday – does it mean they have understood the message of Guru Nanak? How many of them have understood?

The fact is that whosoever has reached the Truth – irrespective of cast and religion – is a Sufi. And one who has set out in search of the Truth is a seeker. But remember, the achievement of Truth is not easy! Man is a creature of laziness, of lust and of sensory pleasures – for these he is forever ready! But he never has the urge to know, to seek! Where do you find the urge to seek? For those who crave wisdom, Al Hillaj Mansoor says:

Agar hai shaunk milne ka
Toh hardum lau lagata ja

Lau means flame – the burning flame of a candle! Start lighting the flame of divine love within yourself.

Jala kar khud numai ko
Bhasm tan pe lagata ja

Ignite the fire of love within yourself and then burn your ego in that fire. First exterminate your pride and ego, then smear the ashes of this ego on your body.

Pakad kar ishq ka jhadu
Safa kar dil ke hujre ko

Using the broom of love, clean up the house that is your heart.

Dui ki dhool ko lekar
Musalle pe udata ja

Musalla is the piece of cloth that bears the picture of Kaba-e-Sharif and on which one sits for offering namaaz. Here Mansoor says, though you are sitting on a musalla your prayers are not truthful. Even today a majority of people sit on a piece of cloth and offer superficial prayers. But this fakir – Al Hillaj Mansoor – says it is not sufficient to just sit on a musalla and offer namaaz. The feeling of duality with which you are sitting on it – that you and God are separate entities – needs to be dusted off. Only someone who has been successful in removing this duality of nature, will understand the exact meaning of being a Sufi. One, who has been able to kill and destroy the duality of 'me and God' is a Sufi.

A Sufi does and says things with the sole intent to awaken your sleeping mind and intellect. He is always working in accordance with the God's message. His approach sometime can seem bit revolutionary. Mansoor was one such Sufi, who many a time, said things that sounded objectionable or out of context but they were never meant to be so. He said follow the rituals, do the prayers, why shouldn't you. But make sure while you are offering your prayers on the holy mat, while you are rotating the beads, your attention should not divert. Your attention should be solemnly entwined in that process, in that technique, in that method.

If you are reading a religious text then submerge yourself in it, do not merely understand the symbolism, but open your heart to understand its deep meaning. If you are not doing so then you are simply disobeying the whole process. Why these things are there in first place, to help you walk onto the path of divinity. If your mind is engrossed in worldly affairs while you remember him then it is the biggest sin you can commit. So don't take his name half-heartedly. Messages of Mansoor were misunderstood as his way of saying things were very blunt. Again a Sufi sometimes does things to shock you because he wants you to follow the path of God sincerely.

Rumi says, "There is no wall, no obstruction between my God and me – my knowledge itself is the obstruction! Now I have to remove this wall."

Pakad kar dast maston ka
Ghulam unka kahata ja

Hold the hand of someone who is overflowing with divine love. Become his slave so that you can learn something; so that what was experienced by Mohammed Sahib can happen to you as well. Only someone who has destroyed his ego will understand this!

Na mar bhookha, na rakh roza
Na ja masjid na kar sajda

What is the need for fasting? You know why this practice of roza (fasting) was started? Roza was started so that during the period of fasting, your heart is filled with only His name – from morning to night. And roza is kept for not one or two days but for a full forty days! It was said that these forty days in the year do not belong to you. All of these forty days belong to God Almighty. How many people devote all these forty days to God? Do you give your forty days to God?

When it was suggested that you observe roza, it did not mean starving your body; it meant starving your mind, so that the mind stops wandering and the senses do not demand food and drink. Get over all these things! They are worthless! Whatever little is required to sustain the body is all that you should eat. But when to eat? They said, "Keep a specific time. Don't waste your whole day in eating!" And whose roza would be accepted? Only of those, who will starve their minds, and will fill their hearts with his love? Your fasting won't be complete if you do not offer or donate something – karamat! Offering is necessary. If you use foul language or if you hurt somebody's feelings, your fast will be broken. It will not matter that you remained hungry the whole day or that you ate 'iftaari'- the meal to end the fast!

The worst thing is when these pious days of fasting are exploited by political parties for playing their dirty games. They keep hosting iftaar parties! Now iftaar has also become a party for them!

What is the use of fasting the whole day? Roza does not mean starving yourself! Roza actually means that the tongue should be sweet and the hands should serve others, giving alms to the needy! Remaining hungry is not what roza is all about. That is why Mansoor says, "Na mar bhookha, na rakh roza." Your fasting is just a sham.

No one who believes in the religious law will ever be able to say this; no Mullah will ever be able to endorse this – only a Sufi can say such a thing. And the Sufi is saying it without any hesitation! Without any fear! It is a different matter that Mansoor had to pay the price for all this with his life – he was decapitated! Mansoor was aware of the result of his utterances, but he could not desist from speaking the truth.

I have often narrated this story, but I shall repeat it today: Once a Sufi sees God in his dream and God asks him: "Shall I make an announcement tomorrow that you are a Sufi? I, God, will make it known to the whole world that you are a Sufi." The Sufi replied, "Well, certainly if you please! You can do whatever you want. Certainly if you want you can tell the whole world. But then I too will meet the fate of Mansoor. If you want me to meet that fate, you may definitely tell the world! Mansoor was beheaded – I, too, will be beheaded. But tell if you must!

Sufis like Junaid instructed their disciples: Whatever you may achieve, just keep your mouth shut after that. Don't speak a word! Because people around you are blind and deaf! They will never be able to understand what you have experienced. Either they will declare you insane or they will label you a non-believer.

The same advice had been given to Al Hillaj Mansoor: Keep quiet; don't speak! Don't say An-al-haq! And Mansoor would say, "Alright, I will not say An-al-haq."

But whenever he was in a deep state of meditation, involuntarily he would utter – 'An-al-haq!'

Then Mansoor was made to sit and very deliberately it was explained to him: "Look, don't say this! People have already complained against you. Some religious leaders have already told the king that you are becoming a non-believer and that is why you say this."

His guru tried to make him understand: "Your life is precious to me. And see, if the king sends a message to me, it is I who will have to answer whether you are a non-believer or a dervish. You are putting me in a tight spot."

Mansoor laughed and said, "You tell him that Mansoor is a non-believer. But as long as you are a fakir, how can you say I am a non-believer? For that you will have to become a mullah. Will you become a mullah?"

And that is exactly what happened. The king's messenger came to Mansoor's master. An elaborate search was carried out and he was questioned; "Now you give us the facts and give it in writing." Keep this in mind that if he gave it in writing that in spite of saying An-al-haq, Mansoor was a true Muslim, it would have been against the written religious laws. Then, in any case they would take the master captive. It was not the master but the disciple Mansoor who was saying An-al-haq, but if the disciple says something offensive, his master was held responsible!

So, Junaid sat with the paper in his hands, all troubled and concerned. What on earth was he to do? How could he, as a fakir, write that the biggest truth of the world was wrong? How could he write that? And then whatever Mansoor had predicted, happened.

This fakir had to take off his cloak of a dervish, a fakir, and put on the gown of a Mullah and then finally he wrote: 'Whatever he is saying is wrong as per the Holy Quran.' When the news reached Mansoor, he had a hearty laugh: "My master would always remember me as the disciple who went to the extent of getting his dervish's cloak taken off!"

He did not feel bad or complain about what his master did. There was no anger at all. He had nothing to complain about because he knew that the master had told him many times not to say it. He had said, "The society you are living in would not be able to digest this. Don't say, don't say, don't say!" But Mansoor was enjoying himself; he was not bothered. One who has the courage to say:

Wazu ka tod de kuja
Sharab-e-shauk peeta ja

The utensil that is used to have a wash is called kuja and the process of washing one's face, hands and feet, etc. is called wazu. So, Mansoor says, "Break the utensil that you use to wash your hands and face, etc., because mere washing of the body won't cleanse the mind."

Drink the liquor of love! If at all you must, then drink this liquor of love. Since Mansoor just said, "Sharab-e-shauk peeta ja," the common man finds it difficult to understand it. It is difficult for people to understand the language of Sufis. To date, die-hard drinkers consider Omer Khayyam to be their messiah. He was actually a Sufi, a dervish. And now here, Mansoor too is saying: "Sharab-e-shauk peeta ja."

Hamesha kha, hamesha pee
Na ghaflat se raho hardum

The only sin that exists is being 'unaware'. So what is sin? Is it stealing or infidelity or lying, cheating or duping others? Are these sins? He said, "No!" Unawareness is the biggest sin. If you want to stop sinning, then don't go into the details of the various kinds of sin. Just leave one thing, and that is your unconsciousness! Your unawareness! If you come out of this unconsciousness, you will automatically quit all sins. Just leave this one thing.

Na ho mullah, na ho brahmin

You don't need to become any of these, neither a Muslim priest nor a Hindu priest. You neither need to be Hindu nor Muslim. Cast aside duality! It preaches that 'I' am different from 'him'! He is an idol-worshiper and I, just God's man. 'They' are non-believers and 'I' am a Muslim. Again, you have got stuck with duality. It is the order of Shah Kalander that you keep on saying An-al-haq!

Kahe Mansoor mastana
Maine Haq dil mein pehchana

Haq means Truth. So, where did he find this Truth? Within his own 'self'!

One whose eyes are forever wandering all around the world; one whose ears are always running after worldly talks and one whose tongue never tires of talking about this world – how will Haq – the Truth – be known? Can you remain without talking? No! You can't even stay without commenting on issues that are of no relevance to you. Some people are so senseless that you keep telling them to talk less but they do not listen. You may tell them a thousand times to talk sweetly but they don't understand. How would they talk sweetly when their hearts bear so much bitterness?

Wahi maston ka maikhana
Wahin par tu aata ja

You come and join this tavern of people, whose hearts are brimming with divine love. Keep coming and going! Then, over a period of time, maybe some ray of love and wisdom will enter your inert heart. Maybe, someday! Till then, carry on with the 'satsang'. In the Hindu tradition of India, this is what is called 'keeping the company of enlightened and truthful people'.

Somebody asked: "How will that benefit us?" They said, "Even if you don't see any direct and immediate benefit, just breathing the air your guru breathes is beneficial for you. Maybe you will understand from the fragrance of his breath, the things that you are unable to grasp from his words." That is why it is

219

said that it will be good for you to just go and sit wherever zikr is being done.

My whole trip and stay in Turkey was something like this. As I had gone there in search of only this...when a message of love is sent your way, you have to respond with only love. I had received this message from the Sufis of Turkey asking me to come there, so I had to go. I just had to go! If you get a message that the Chief Minister is calling you, you will have to go. If one of your friends sends a word wishing to see you, then also you will have to go. How can you not go?

On my second visit to Turkey, one of my disciples asked, "We consider you to be a complete guru, then why travel to a distant land? What can you possible achieve there?" I told him that I was not in search of anything. I simply wished to re-discover myself so that I could fulfill the responsibilities that were given to me. In other words, I wanted to know their closely guarded secrets.

Neither am I a Muslim by birth nor have I lived amongst them. I have only dealt with Sufi poets like Bulleh Shah, Baba Sheikh Farid, Inayat Shah, Shah Kalander and other such poets. It is through them, through their words and through their poetry, that I have come to acknowledge and understand their language. Therefore I didn't take long to unravel the mysteries surrounding their lives. Eventually, I concluded that they are simply reciting tales indigenous to their native place with a touch of originality and style. What I mean to say is, how complicated can that get?

But Turkey was different. When I went there for the first time, I saw everything – their language, their tone, their style; everything was very different. But above all, it didn't have any governmental sanction. All the tekkes had been closed. There were no Mevlavi tekkes there anymore. That was because in 1925 Kamal Ataturk had declared all the tekkes illegal. So all the tekkes were either burnt or locked up. Now whatever happens there happens in secrecy.

Therefore, in these circumstances it is difficult to find dervishes. Remember the tales of Mullah Nasruddin? In a crowded market place, a dervish would come with his finger pointing upwards and the Mullah would take out a rope in reply. This is the way they would communicate with each other. And in such a scenario, if an Indian claims that she will try to understand them, then she will have to stay there solely for that purpose.

I barely knew their language; but the people were nice, and some went out of their way to help. Wherever we went, we got the address with the help of the telephone. But talking on the phone was more than just an uphill task, as I would talk in English while the person at the other end persisted with Turkish. The conversations were senseless if not ridiculous as the language barrier posed more problems than we had anticipated. It took me ages to realise that the Turkish language had no response for the English greeting 'Hello'. There is no letter that brings out the sound of 'h' in their dialect. Whenever they have to pronounce the letter 'h', they either say it with great emphasis or not at all. In other words, it was 'Hello' from my side and 'Aallo' from theirs!

If I said I wanted to talk to someone like Doloonay, they would reply in Turkish leaving me with no choice but to assume that Doloonay was either dead or not available! As I accidentally met Doloonay at her university, neither of the previous choices seemed plausible! Therefore we continued with our endeavours and decided to fix a time with Doloonay – a very loving and pleasant person. She informed us that we could talk to her only if we called at a specific time when she was home, as all the others in her family spoke only Turkish.

Her home was an hour and a half away from our place, but she would come whenever I called. At times we would me   at a common location and then proceed to our ultimate destination. But sometimes we had to go to places all by ourselves. In that case we kept the address written in Turkish and showed it to the taxi driver. At times we even felt as though the taxi driver was taking us for a ride, just like they do here in Delhi. For example, if you tell them at the railway station that you want to go a particular place, they deliberately take a longer route to keep the meter ticking. The taxi drivers in Turkey were no different. However, we would ultimately reach our destination without too much harm done to the meter!

However, on one particular day we went around in circles and never reached the place we had set out for. The following day we tried again and much to our satisfaction, we finally reached the place where all the Sufis would get together at night. The place was just ten minutes away from where we had gone the previous day! When we finally reached we learnt that their time of worship began at about 9 at night and continued till the wee hours of the morning. Interested to know more, we went there again the following day, despite facing the possibility of getting lost again.

The following day we arrived at the Sufi spot and saw them clothed in formal attire sipping hot tea. They all spoke the same language – Turkish. Since we had no English speaking person to help us, we kept waiting until somebody came and asked us if we were from Pakistan. We told them that we were 'Hindistanis'. He asked us to sit down. It was only when our interpreter came that we could begin talking to the sheikh. We were introduced to him and then in their traditional style, keeping his right hand on his heart, he said, "Khushamadeed! Hindistani Sufi!" After that their zikr started.

Before the zikr started, we realised that it was extremely cold, as it was the winter season. I was wearing four sweaters and an overcoat on top with a warm cap covering my head. Though we had taken our shoes off outside, we were sitting with our socks on and still feeling cold. In all, there were about fifteen-twenty of them. They made a circle and sat down. While their sheikh sat on the sheepskin, everybody else sat on the wooden floor, forming a circle. We, on the other hand, were made to sit on the sofa on one side.

After all this their zikr started and within ten minutes the temperature changed. No one was sitting on the musalla and nobody had a string of beads in their hand. Their breath itself had become the tasbeeh. They had laid their hearts down in place of the musalla.

And then they started their zikr with dum. The floor, the ceiling, in fact the whole of that tekke was made of wood. It was getting terribly cold; our hands were getting numb as we had taken off our gloves since we assumed that they would be of no use inside. But the heat that was generated by the zikr of their combined breath was so great that within ten minutes we had to take off our coats and shortly after, even our sweaters.

When we joined in, I felt a surge of energy and realised that a Sufi never really dies in spite of thousands of rules and laws made against them. Any number of 'Mansoors' may be beheaded but a Sufi never really dies. A Sufi lives forever. In fact, he keeps getting stronger day by day. The zikr that was held there that day was 'La Ilaha Illallah', which in literal translation means: There is no God, only God is there. There is nobody apart from him. Actually it is just Him.

They began the zikr with their tongue and then started saying it with dum, with their breath. This implied that it was not only the tongue but also the breath that helped produce the mantra. We first chanted the mantra, after which the sheikh showed us, how the mantra could be reproduced, in synchronization with our breath.

Next was the dum zikr. This method also required us to synchronise our breath with the deep notes of our voice. We would breathe in twice and then speak the phrase 'La Ilaha Illallah'. Amazingly, our breath would come out as though it were coming straight from the stomach – from somewhere deep inside. Verbal zikr is also done with depth, and in the dum zikr too, the articulation of the chant is so deep that our emotional and mental faculties go numb. In short, the purpose of the dum is to completely bind the wandering and restless mind.

The way I did this zikr with the Sufis was just like the day I had spent in the octagonal room where all the dervishes did the zikr together. That day it seemed as though the sound of 'La Ilaha Ilallha' had begun vibrating with the winds. Its fragrance, its vibrations and its energy were such that it felt as though someone had let loose an electric current in the air.

When one does it properly, when one learns it and does it on one's own, one will get that electrifying feeling right up to the fingertips. The greatest sign of the zikr is that within two minutes of doing it, the whole body gets full of energy and power – if done properly and with deep articulation. If one does not feel the energy within two to five minutes, you can be sure that there is something wrong somewhere. Such is the power of the zikr.

Now, I will first do the verbal zikr and then the dum zikr to which all of you shall only listen. First try and understand the methodology. It is imperative on the person performing the zikr to know exactly how each breath is synchronised with the tone of the voice. The result is almost heavenly, but to achieve that I must have your total attention.

CHAPTER 12

ALLAH! THE MOST BENEVOLENT

Oh Allah! Your love is in our hearts
You radiate the Earth with your light
I stand here to pay obeisance to you
In the garden blooming with your love
And the seed of this garden
Was sown by my Sun

For Rumi, Shams means Sun. All the greenery on this earth owes its existence to the sun alone. If there were no sun, the leaves wouldn't be green, the flowers would have no colour or fragrance, and there would be no juice in the fruits. The chlorophyll that plants get from the sun gives life to the entire flora. But Rumi says, "The greenery of my heart is due to another Sun – Shams."

People who claim to love God claim to be looking for him. Such claims are completely different from the Sufi way of thinking. Sufi thinking can never accommodate 'I' and 'Me' in its philosophy. A Sufi by the name of Khalil Gibran has said in his poetry:

Khuda ki jaat ek
Andhar bahar wahi ek
Sari kayanat mein wahi ek
Haq, hakiqat wahi ek

God is one
He is the only one, inside or outside
The only one, in the entire universe
He is the Truth, the only reality

Khalil Gibran says: "He dwells within us all and if he is inside Gibran, then this name of 'Gibran' is His name. The almighty does not have ninety nine names." As per the Quran Sharif, God has ninety-nine names. They are Al Zamin, Al Samad, Al Wahad, Al Gaffur, Malik-ul-Mulk, Al Haq, Al Noor. I had described the names earlier as well. Khalil Gibran also says: "How can there be ninety-nine names? There are a hundred, and not ninety-nine names of God." When asked "How? Which is the hundredth name? We have never read about it; it is not mentioned in the Quran Sharif. Which is the hundredth name?" he said, "If you want to know the hundredth name of God, say Khalil Gibran."

In return they said: "This is your name." Gibran replied, "The wave that you are calling 'You' is a part of that ocean and there is no distinction between a wave and the ocean. So my name is His name too. Or I can say that those ninety-nine names mentioned in the Quran Sharif are all mine. It can be said both ways: "Khalil Gibran is God's hundredth name, or all those ninety-nine names mentioned in the Quran Sharif are mine." In addition, Gibran used to say: "Either you say Al Samad, Al Wahad, Al Noor, Al Gaffur, all these are my names, or you say Khalil Gibran is his name; which eventually translates into the same thing. If it is God who is running this whole system, then I, Khalil Gibran, am a part of that very system of God."

Banda bhi tu hai, Khuda bhi tu hai
Dhoondhe bhi tu hai, milta bhi tu hai
Sheikh bhi tu hai, mureed bhi tu hai
Ye bhi tu hai, tu bhi tu hai

You are the man, and his God
You are the seeker, and you are the sought
You are the master and the disciple
You are this, you are that
You are everything

This is what the Sufis called the ramaz, which means 'a mystery'. Whoever unravels this mystery does not then remain just a man; instead, he and 'The Truth' are now one and the same, thus the expression An-al-haq (I am The Truth, I am the one). He doesn't remain God's servant any more. That person would then, not even be able to say that he has found God. To simply put it, when 'he' ceases to exist, it is then 'The Truth' unveils.

Sheikh Hasan once asked Rabiya al Basra, "Rabiya, when does one find God? Rabiya replied, "Man never finds God." The sheikh asked again, "If man never finds God then what is the use of worshipping him? If one can never reach up to his master, what is the use of idolizing him? What joy is there in loving beauty that always remains veiled?

But there is a famous saying among Sufis:

Aashiq dikhta hai, maashook dikhe nahin
Dekhi kisi ne aisi aashiqi nahin

The lover is seen and the beloved is hidden
Has anyone witnessed such a love affair

In all classical tales of love, both the male and the female were seen and known. Hence, their love can be understood. But what kind of love is the one shared between God and his lover? The lover is seen but the beloved – God is not seen, and yet man is willing to go to any extent to appease his beloved. Hasan asked Rabiya, "Why should a man worship God if he can neither be seen nor be found? A God who always remains obscure from his people; one who never comes near his subjects; one who never reveals himself…. why worship him?" In reply Rabiya said, "Hasan, close your mind and listen to me with your heart."

It is only when one listens with his heart that he truly undersatnds. The wall that forms an obstruction between the man and his God is his mind. It is me, this is my name, this is my religion, this is my house and this is my family – all these obstructions have been raised by our own mind.

In continuation, Rabiya said, "Hasan. Don't bring your mind in it; listen to me with your heart. Try to understand with your heart." Hasan calmed down, took a deep breath and with renewed attention tried to listen to Rabiya's reply wholeheartedly. Rabiya said, "Man never finds God. That is because the day he finds God, he does not live to see another day. He does not remain a human being any longer."

Almost everyone claims to be in search of the Almighty. One always says, "I wish to find God", but in reality, one can never find God. However, all else is possible: it is still possible that the sun rises from the west; that all the oceans dry up, that the stars and the moon become visible during daytime and shine brightly. But the prospect of finding God isn't possible. Which is why it is said: 'Idhar fana, udhar baqa.' As you cease to exist. He will instantaneously become a reality. And since man cannot renounce his entity, finding God remains an impossible feat.

Khalil Gibran says, "Can anybody ever find 'You'? Only the person who tries to find himself rather than God can truly reach the Almighty. It is when 'You' (my beloved God) who decide to appear in someone's heart, that his heart gets ignited with the sparks of love. And not before that, it is 'You' who decide to illumine someone's heart that his heart gets illumined"

Love is a fire that can neither be ignited nor extinguished at will. Even Ghalib – a renowned Urdu poet knew this. What is it? What happens when one falls in love?

Let's move on to a Chinese story. I am now talking of Zen fakirs along with Sufis. They are also Sufis, though they may differ in certain ways. There once was a Zen master who lived in a monastery for several years with many of his disciples. One fine day, a young man came along and said, "I want to be your disciple. Will you accept me?" When a common man goes to a guru, you know what he says? "I want to make you my guru." I often receive letters with the same question. However, the question itself is wrong and there can never be a right answer to a wrong question.

The right question should be: "I want to become your disciple. Would you give me a chance to become your disciple?" Disciples don't make gurus; gurus already exist. And a guru will always be a guru even if he didn't have a single disciple. But what happens if a person does not have a guru? In that case he should say, "I am a follower." When asked, "Whose?" you say, "I don't know." There can't be a disciple without a guru. But the guru is still there, regardless of whether or not he has any disciples. Even if a guru has no disciple whatsoever, he still remains a guru.

There is a sequence of events that is coming to my mind. There is a particular gentleman who has known me for the past twenty years. He knew me when nobody knew me, and he knows me even today when the whole world recognizes me. One day he asked me, "Do you feel the difference between the times when nobody knew you and now, when literally everybody knows who you are?"

The question seemed to be an interesting one, and I decided to answer it on two different levels. The first level was: Before one starts expecting a vast difference by becoming famous, one should know that nothing of the sort actually happens. This is evident from the fact that from the inside, I was the same person as I am now. When I went out alone there were no cars or taxis; no sleeper or AC coach; I would travel on a third class ticket. I wouldn't use a bus even if my destination was twenty kilometers away. Money was limited and needed to be preserved for matters of greater importance. Hence, believe it or not, we would walk the entire stretch of twenty kilometers in order to preserve money with no fuss whatsoever. Today when I look at myself I feel that I am the same person; I would still walk twenty kilometers to save money. This is the first level.

The second level is: Now there are more worldly problems. At that time personal issues were of greater importance. I could simply lay my mat anywhere and sit down. I would sleep wherever I got a room. I once went to a temple in Solan, Haryana. However, when I reached there I realised that there was no place to stay. It was extremely warm and I enjoyed staying in the hills. Luckily, I had carried foldable bedding with me. I only carried two pairs of clothes, slippers, books to read and a small mat. It was all in one; bedding as well as suitcase.

When I reached I asked the locals, "If I stay on the rooftop of your temple, would that cause any problem to you?" In reply they said, "That won't be a problem for us at all." They seemed surprised to meet a woman keen on sleeping on the rooftop. I for one enjoyed the sight of the stars and would often gaze at them till the wee hours of the morning. I was always happy with the facilities available, regardless of the inconvenience they might cause.

The poor priest showed his concern for me after realising that no bathing facility was available. I told him, "There is a small pond of water down in the valley where the villagers go for their bath. I too will go there." This seemed convenient enough for me. Then there was this community kitchen where I too would go and have my meals. I had no desire whatsoever to have a separate seat in a separate place, with a special plate to eat from.

Despite all the problems and shortages, I enjoyed my stay to the fullest, as if it were perfect. I sang even then. In the modern world we use machines to produce an echo effect but my voice in the valley seemed to echo on its own accord. Even the trees seemed to listen to my songs – such was the beauty and serenity. Even today people listen to my songs but they trouble me so much that they are not allowed to come close, let alone meet or touch me. The trees on the other hand, never did all this. There was a peach tree, in fact, which holds its ground even now. The almond tree and the rest of the orchard are still there. It is just by chance that recently I halted there for sometime while on my way to Shimla. I felt like going there and seeing how things were at the place where I had stayed earlier. Everything else had changed but the trees were still there. The tree never said: 'You once sat under my shade, so at least thank me.'

What I was then, is a carbon copy of what I am now. My troubles at that point of time were negative but now they are positive. That is because if an organisation is formed, you have to look after it and that is exactly what I am doing now. Though fortunately, there are people around the area who do their work with complete efficiency, honesty and faith.

Coming back to the previous point, the young man asked the Zen fakir, "Can I be your disciple?" What one has to do, to become a disciple. A guru is always a guru. He is a guru whether he is alone or in a crowd. At times a bunch of my old disciples get disheartened and say, "You don't come and sit with us the way you did earlier." Well, earlier there were a hundred people but now those hundred have turned into thousands. Hence, problems are inevitable. All of them can't possibly sit together. I told them in reaffirmation, "Your guru has not changed. She is still the same. It is only the circumstances that have changed."

I also feel that those who are closer to me need to understand that even though they can't physically sit next to me, they are as close to me as they used to be. But at times, one doubts his own affection for others. Sometimes, one stops believing in himself. As long as the mind exists, doubts are bound to occur. This implies that Sufism needs to be understood by the heart and not by the mind. Love your guru from your heart. How does it matter how long you sit with your guru? Even a glance is sufficient. They say, in an entire lifetime if your guru looks at you with a full glance even once, it should suffice.

The Zen fakir said to the young man, "Yes, you are accepted. Sit." He was given the task of grinding paddy in the kitchen. That too not the main kitchen; it was in the storeroom in the rear of the monastery. So he would spend the whole day sitting and crushing the paddy. One day, the zen master told him what exactly the path of Zen is. There is only one technique that needs to be followed and that is of awareness. One must always be alert. Now, if the technique meant simply being vigilant, he was happily sitting in the storeroom crushing paddy; however, he was doing it with complete alertness. For him crushing paddy and taking out the rice grain from it became greater than any yoga or pranayama.

Several years passed, but not once did he complain that the guru never called him or asked him anything. He kept pounding paddy in the dark room without any objection. The monastery was quite big and there were many disciples there. Rice was the staple food of the Chinese people; in fact, it is so even today. They need rice for everything. One day news reached his dark storeroom that the master had asked a question to all his disciples and whoever knew the answer to that question would have to go and write it

231

on the rear wall of his house. Whosoever gave the right answer would take the master's seat. There was no need to go and tell him personally, they just had to write it on the wall.

He asked out of curiosity, "What is the question?" People said, "What would a paddy crusher know? You keep pounding your rice." In reply to this he said, "That I am doing in any case. It would be nice if you could please tell me." To this they replied, "Okay, listen if you must. The question is: 'How can one achieve enlightenment?' In addition, the master has said that the answer must come from experience. Only he who answers from experience should bother answering the question. Don't give a mental answer or an answer written in the scriptures." In other words, the master demanded an original answer.

The young man laughed silently. The person who told him the question was probably telling himself: "He is a fool, what would he have understood?" That night the young man was going from the storeroom to his resting place. On the way he thought to himself: "Let me go and write." It was all clear to him, he knew the answer and that is precisely why he had laughed earlier.

Months passed but no disciple could muster up enough courage to go and write the answer. They all feared the master would be able to catch in a moment that they were lying. The young man picked a piece of coal from the storeroom and went and wrote, "Why should there be enlightenment when I myself am the Buddha?" He had not even put the piece of coal down after writing, when a hand stroked him on his shoulder. When he turned he saw the master standing inches away from him. He said to him in a soft but sturdy voice, "Your answer is correct and you are capable of being my heir, but I love you and I want to see you alive, so it is my order that you leave the ashram right now."

In reply to this unexpected statement the young man answered, "I will follow your orders. But I want to ask you a question: "Why are you sending me away? Have I committed any mistake?" The master replied, "No, no mistake at all. In the morning when I tell everybody that the man who has been crushing paddy in the storeroom all these years has given the right answer, all the disciples who have been sitting with me and listening to me, those who have been meditating and practicing with me for years but could not give the right answer will kill you. Hence it is for your own safety that I ask you to leave."

He bowed to his master, went around him thrice and left as discreetly as he had come several years back. After he left, it remained a topic of discussion for several days as to who had actually written the answer. Whenever they asked their master about it he would simply say, "The lotus of whoever's heart had to bloom, has bloomed." But since the man who used to sit in the darkroom pounding rice was not to be seen anywhere, it was evident if not obvious that it was he who had written the correct answer. However, they couldn't understand how an illiterate man who had been sitting in a dark room for several years crushing paddy could possibly have given the correct answer. They wondered: 'What was the use of years of practice and learning?'

The answer to the aforesaid question is simple. Enlightenment doesn't necessarily have to take years to achieve. Whatever is to happen, will happen in a moment. But if one is not deserving of enlightenment, he may keep slogging all his life and yet may never understand the essence of it.

Enlightenment in general can be divided into two parts: Procedural Enlightenment and Sudden Enlightenment. There is a saying among Sufis: 'Anything can happen if God be gracious.' After all, he is the ultimate, the emperor, and the king of kings. In Turkey, Hazrat Jalaluddin Rumi is called either 'Mevlana Rumi' or 'The King'. It is said that the day he left his body and when the preparations for the last rites were on, the whole of Konya city came by crying. It is but obvious that they would cry for the loss of their emperor. And this was no worldly country – Rumi was the emperor of the country of hearts. He was the king of love; it was Shams' love that gave Rumi this precious gift of love.

It is said that one particular day Rumi was going through the marketplace, and a goldsmith was hammering gold in order to mould it into the shape of leaves. He was hammering the heated gold kept on the iron, straightening it up and moulding it. It was a small village, so if somebody hammered heated gold after keeping it on the iron, its sound could be heard across quite a distance. In a small place any sound can be heard at the other end, whether it is the sound of a spinning wheel or that of any other pulley.

The goldsmith was hammering the gold with increasing enthusiasm and renewed vigour – he wanted to give it a shape before it got cold. As soon as the rhythmic sound of the beating reached Rumi's ears, it got synchronised with the palpitating sound of his heartbeat, and he was so captivated by it that he started dancing. He went round and round in circles with spontaneous carefreeness. He raised both his hands, one hand pointing to the sky and the other towards the earth, which meant, from this earth to that sky there is nothing but 'your love'. From this body to my true 'self', there is nothing but 'your love'. The air is filled only with love. His ecstasy, his joy seemed to have no end and he began chanting the phrase 'Ya Hai'.

The goldsmith realised that the sound of 'Ya Hai, Ya Hai' was in tune with his hammering which is why he didn't stop the beating. On seeing the 'Mevlana' dance the way he did in sheer joy, it occurred to the goldsmith that if he kept hammering the gold, it would soon become cold and useless. He would have to heat it up again for moulding and that would cause great loss to his shop. But the effect the dance was having on him cannot be described in mere words. He forgot all about his shop and his profits and kept hammering the gold – on and on and on.

One hour passed, two hours passed; finally six hours passed in the same fashion. Neither his hand nor the 'Mevlana' showed any signs of tiring. He was dancing and singing 'Ya Hai, Ya Hai' with complete abandon. And then all of a sudden, the 'Mevlana' fell on the ground unconscious, as if in a state of trance, and just moments later the goldsmith also fell. It was not only his hammering that had got synchronised with Rumi's dancing, somewhere the strings of their hearts had also got synchronised. Their connection was spiritually deep, to say the least.

When they came to their senses and opened their eyes, they saw that a huge crowd had gathered. The goldsmith got up, walked up to the 'Mevlana' and kissed his feet. The 'Mevlana' held his hand, embraced him and then the zikr started all over again. Earlier he was whirling alone with the sound of 'Ya Hai, Ya Hai', but now he was whirling with the goldsmith in his embrace singing 'Ya Hai, Ya Hai'. Thus Rumi engulfed the goldsmith in his divine love and romance, and the goldsmith was enriched in his first ever meeting with the 'Mevlana' – he was rich with the wealth of love. God gives the wealth of His love to whom he chooses.

Today we see the third name of zikr: 'Hai'. 'Hai' means the 'one who exists', the 'one who is present'. The one who is somewhere in your heart, is the one who has ignited this flame. You have not come here on your own – that flame brought you here. At least in this Sufi camp you have not come on your own. We had to tell a lot of people that there is no more space. Even the ashram has limited space and we can't go beyond a limit. Those who were fortunate enough got a chance to attend the Sufi camp; this flame, this urge that has brought you here is His.

Therefore, one should never say that God is far from one. These bubbles of love that take birth in one's heart are all His gifts. It is He who gave rise to the right emotions and said, "Go." It is He who showed you the way and said, "Go". It is He who told the organisers not to return certain applications. There were four camps in the summer; I spoke morning and evening even though the local crowds asked me not to speak in all the sessions as my throat would pain later on. In reply I said, "How do I stop myself? When He surges down like a flood of water, how can I tell Him to stop? He who has given this body, he who is my true 'self' and who is using this body for His purpose, can keep me in whichever condition He wants; so what if there is pain."

We were thinking of keeping the theme of the December camp, just like the other four, on Sufism, but then I decided against it because I felt that five days were not enough to do justice to a subject as vast as Sufism. As it is, I was already talking about zikr and had not yet been able to touch upon the issue of whirling; I had said that a minimum of ten days would be required for that. The pious Almighty had filled Shams' heart with love, and Shams in turn had filled Rumi's heart with the same love, and the same love had called me there; the same power had given this task to me. So, all the dispirited hearts, which had been selected to get

235

enlightened through me, were only to wait a while longer, before I showed them the true path to the Almighty.

It is said: "You are the king; you are the king of love." Listen to this bhajan (call of heart) with love:

Sultan tu mera, sultan tu mera
Ya Allah, Allah, Hu Hu Allah, Hai Hai
Teri mohabbat par kurban, tu hai mera jaane jan
Zikr hai tera lajawab, rehmat teri behisaab
Sultan tu mera, sultan tu mera

Oh God! You are my emperor
You are the love of my life
And I offer my life to you.
You are my world, O Lord
Thy remembrance is incomparable
Thy grace is infinite

CHAPTER 13
MESSAGE OF LOVE

Ya Allah, Ya Allah, Ya Allah, Ya Allah
Al Bari, Al Khalik, Al Ghaffar, Al Salam
Al Jaami, Al Maalik, Al Aziz, Al Razza
Subhaan Allah! Bismillah!
Al Haalim, Al Karim, Al Maajid, Al Aahad
Al Saamad, Al Qadir, Al Awwal, Al Aakhir
Ya Allah, Ya Allah, Ya Allah, Ya Allah
Bismillah, Bismillah, Haq Bismillah, Bismillah
La Ilaha Illallah, La Ilaha Illallah!

As expressed in the following lines, Hazrat Jalaluddin Rumi Mevlana claimed that his death was his reunion with God:

Is jism ki quaid se azaad
Ab meri rooh jo karegi pravas
Aur hogi ek apne khavind ke saath!

Free from the bondage of my body
My rooh will take flight
And will unite with my husband

'Now my rooh will take flight, and free from this body, it will get united with its husband; the 'Almighty.'

This is the reason why his funeral procession is not called a funeral procession but a wedding procession: This is the night of union – the night of being one. It is Mevlana Rumi who said the following words: "Whenever someone comes to meet me at my grave, he should not come in grief, rather he should come with a bendir in his hands. Depressed people should never get together at my grave." He says: "Come drumming a bendir with your hands, with zikr on your lips and love in your hearts. Only those who love me should come to me."

Now if we were to ask him: "Where are you? Are you inside the grave in Konya? Are you under the tomb?" In reply Mevlana would say: "No, don't look for me, don't ever look for me in the grave, because I will never be buried in the soil. I will be buried in the hearts of those lost in love; in the hearts of Sufis – you may look for me there.

Where does the Mevlana live? Sufis say that the Mevlana lives within them. They claim that Mevlana is the king of love and that one may be saved if one perishes in his unending love.

The process is as follows: Whoever perishes is the one who survives. And the one who saves himself remains the same. He who saves himself is but a human being. But, if the human being perishes, he becomes God – man himself becomes God.

A Sufi will never talk about seeking God. A Sufi's language can never speak of seeking or achieving. Remember, love is the only fundamental element among all the religions of the world. And love never speaks the language of achieving or attaining anything. Love can only speak the language of perishing. Love says 'perish' – don't 'become'. The one who tries to become something actually perishes in the process, and the one who completely obliterates himself, finally becomes God.

There is a tale about Rumi that I have related on several occasions, but I would like to reiterate it once again. A man deeply in love once went and knocked on the door of his beloved. His beloved's voice came from inside, "Who is it?" The lover replied, "It is me, your lover, the one, who has completely fallen for your beauty. In reply to this passionate remark his beloved said, "Go back. You are not ready yet. You are not completely in love as of now."

The lover kept concentrating on his love for several years and then went back. He knocked on the door once again. His beloved asked once again, "Who is it?" The lover replied, "The one who is anxious to see you and whose heart is suffering because of your absence."

Earlier that pain, that anxiousness was not there, now it was there. But again his beloved said, "Go back. You are not ready yet." Again he went back and kept wandering about in the desert. He would keep awake all night and cry, unable to endure the pain; even in the daytime he cried and suffered. He returned after a long time and again knocked on his beloved's door. She asked, "Who is it?" The lover replied, "It is only you." It is said that that day his beloved opened the door!

But in my view, if one were to go a step further, the beloved should have sent him back the third time as well because there was a slight feeling of duality when the lover said: "It is only you". Here the lover still exists thus falsifying the aforesaid statement. If he did not exist, how would he speak? He is present and that is how he is able to speak. And when the word 'you' is used, it means there is an element of 'I' present somewhere.

Therefore the concept of 'I' and 'you' still exists. 'I' means that there is some ego or some notion of the 'self' present even though it may be minuscule or negligible. The expression 'you' never comes without the 'self' existing in some form or the other. The count of 'two' comes only when you first accept the existence of 'one'. If you don't write 'one' at all, you will never be able to write 'two'. If you write one, you will have to write two. If you say 'I', you will have to say 'you'.

When a devotee says: "You are everything. You are the only one who matters," he is only singing a prayer. He is simply doing the zikr. However, it cannot stand by itself as a universal truth.

I personally feel that the lover should have gone back once again in Rumi's story. But this time he should not have come back to his beloved's door. He used to come back because he was aware of the 'self' and he felt a constant itch, which told him that he had to meet his beloved. Thus, there is a lover and there is a beloved. The lover felt that his own 'self' was different from his beloved's 'self' thus perpetuating a duality. The story should

239

finally reach its climax when the lover goes back never to return. Now that the wall of duality has been raised, the question that presents itself before us is: Who should go and where? And why should anyone go at all?

The first destination of love is where 'I' and 'you' fall in love with each other; the second step is when 'I' merges with 'you'; the final step is when both 'you' and 'I' cease to exist and only 'love' is left.

Rumi once told his disciples that Al Hillaj Mansoor had to pay the price of saying An-al-haq with his life. The most surprising thing is that among Mansoor's assassins was an ignorant schoolteacher and a priest as well, but it was his own disciples who cut up his dead body into pieces. Those who killed him only beheaded him; they only chopped his head off and went away. But after that, his own disciples – could not understand his saying 'An-al-haq'.

In addition, after the Mansoor was killed, people started looking for his disciples thinking that if the master had committed a sin by saying 'I am God', his disciples too had committed the sin of being in his company and learning from him. So in this regard, they were equally guilty and liable for punishment. In order to save their lives and to show that they were never with Mansoor, the so called disciples stooped to such a low level. Just to save themselves from the allegations of blasphemy and from getting killed, they went out of their way to show that they were in no way associated with Mansoor. The crowd only saw a beheaded Mansoor, but after that his disciples cut his body to pieces to show how much they hated their guru. Well, in that case, they couldn't possibly have been his disciples in the first place!

However, it is important to note that the same thing that happened to Mansoor happens to most gurus at some time or the other – in whatever way – but it does happen. In most cases the backstabber is not a stranger but someone known. When the Roman Governor and his moral police were searching for Jesus Christ, they were not able to locate exactly where he was hiding as he lived with his twelve disciples and all of them looked alike – they all sported long beards and long hair and wore similar looking gowns. How could one possibly make out whom Jesus

Christ was? Then one of his twelve disciples went and met the rabbi – the Jewish priest – and said, "I have lived with Jesus and realised that he is no messiah."

Do you know why he said this? He had gone to Jesus with some other intention; he wished to bring about a political change through Jesus Christ. Come to think of it, why would Jesus be interested in issues concerning the throne when he had nothing to do with the selection of the king? That disciple never let this desire be known to anybody. He knew for a fact that Jesus had a large following. But his followers remained with Jesus only as long as he kept performing miracles, or, as one may say, as long as miracles kept happening.

Even today when people go to various shrines or tombs of Sufis and tie a thread or offer sheets of cloth, it is always to fulfill their own worldly desires – this is actually a sin. But the Sufi who lies in that tomb cannot say: 'Don't do all this. It is my tomb that you come to and ask for material gains – from me.'

Maybe the Sufi lying in the tomb will not speak, but the Sufi in me will definitely speak up. Sufism is not for those who love their lives and materialistic pleasures more than anything else.

As mentioned earlier, Mullah Nasruddin is a fictitious character created by Sufis. In reality there has never been any character like him. But it is also a fact that there exists a grave with his name engraved on the tombstone. The reality of his existence has remained a mystery to date, but those who create such mysteries and do not even clarify them are called Sufis.

There is a famous story that is attributed to Mullah Nasruddin. It is as follows: One day mullah's wife said to him, "You always say 'I am God's servant; I am his slave'. But look at the poverty we are living in. Who is going to rid us of this poverty? Ask that master of yours to give us something. One should at least be paid if one serves someone. But you never get any money, none at all! Tell your master to give you some money." It is said that mullah went out into the courtyard and started shouting at the top of his voice, "O God, I am your servant. My wife says that if you are my master, you must give me something." At that moment, his neighbour who was a big miser, was sitting and counting his money. He was a big miser who had collected a lot of coins and he was sitting and counting them and putting them in separate bags. God knows what came into his mind, the moment he heard mullah shouting like that, he thought of doing something mischievous. So he put a hundred coins into a bag and threw them into mullah's courtyard.

While mullah was still shouting, the bag full of coins came and fell into his courtyard. When he opened the bag and found a hundred gold coins in it, he told his wife, "Here my noble wife, God has finally given us some money."

"Where have these come from?"

"They have come from above."

It was a joke for the neighbour, but for mullah's wife this was no joke. For her it was a fact, a God send. Now that she had the money, she started buying things and filling up her house. The neighbour who had thrown the money thought that this was going a bit too far and decided it was time he went and told them that the coins were his. So he went to mullah's house and said, "Nasruddin, those hundred coins are mine. I threw that bag into your place."

In reply mullah said, "How would I know. All I know is that they came from above. I had asked God for them and he has given them to me. From where do you come into the picture? It can't be you who gave them to us; there is only one power that gives everything. I have never accepted anything from anybody. And as it is, I was not asking for that money for myself. I was only conveying my wife's message to the almighty."

The miser said to mullah, "I shall go to court."

"Please do", mullah returned the misers threat.

The neighbour lost his nerve and said, "I shall take you along."

"Oh yes, you can take me along. I have no objection."

So the neighbour put on his best clothes and mounted a horse. mullah was walking by his side while the neighbour was riding a horse. After going a distance, mullah said, "Let me give you some advice. The way we are, the magistrate will take pity on my poverty; look at my clothes and look at yours. We must make some changes before the magistrate gets a chance to frame charges against me, or else you will lose the case."

The neighbour asked, "What should I do?"

Mullah said, "Give this expensive gown of yours to me."

He took off the beautifully embroidered gown and gave it to mullah. Mullah put on the gown and then they started walking once again. After walking some distance, mullah said, "Wait a minute. You are going on a horse while I am walking. The magistrate will never give a judgment against me. It does look rather awkward"

The unhappy neighbour said, "Alright. Here, you sit on the horse. You are right; if you go in this condition, the magistrate will take pity on you."

"Yes," said mullah, "Now you can tell him that I have become rich with your hundred gold coins and have made you poor."

They both finally reached the magistrate. The neighbour presented his case saying: "Sir, I threw a bag of hundred coins into his courtyard when he was remembering God. So it is I who gave him the money and now he is refusing to accept my claim to the money. He has come wearing an expensive gown and riding a horse."

The magistrate looked at mullah and marvelled at his impressive style. As it is, judges usually look towards only rich people. Who cares to look at the poor? Mullah dismounted the horse with such style and grace that it seemed the horse actually belonged to him. He deliberately settled his gown so that everybody could take a good look at its gold threaded embroidery! Mullah went close to the magistrate and said, "He is my neighbour, but actually he has gone mad. If you ask him whose gown it is that mullah is wearing, he will say it is his. You can ask him." So the magistrate asked, "The gown that mullah is wearing, whose is it?" The poor man said what he had to say: "Mine."

Mullah threw a sharp glance at the magistrate and said, "Now, if you ask him who the horse belongs to he will give the same answer. Do you think I would take his bag of hundred coins? Just take a look at his condition. He is not in a condition to give even two coins to anybody, leave alone a hundred." The magistrate said, "Alright, I shall ask him who the horse belongs to, but before that I want to ask you if you actually got a hundred coins that day?" Mullah said, "Yes, of course."

"Who gave them to you?"

"They came from above. A higher source. I have very high connections and everything comes from that high source to which I lay claim."

The magistrate began thinking: 'If they have come from a higher source, it means they have come from the king because only the king is higher than a magistrate.' The mullah said, "Just ask him, whose horse it is. He is mad."

"Tell me, whose horse is this?"

The man said proudly, "This horse is mine; this gown is mine. I gave those hundred coins to him." The magistrate ordered the mad man to be put in an asylum!

The gist of the story is that whatever you possess is neither yours nor anybody else's. And if you think it is the neighbour who gave it to you, you are wrong. The power to give lies elsewhere. And whomever 'that' benefactor gives the wealth of love to he alone receives it. Or else the mind remains involved in politics even after getting the company of a mystic like Jesus.

There was a gentleman from Delhi who came to meet me a couple of times. Each time he came he would say just one thing: "I am very troubled after seeing the political leaders of our country. India would prosper if you became the Prime Minister of the country. I am ready to do anything if you just gave your approval."

He then told me the history of his life: "It is I who was behind Indira Gandhi's success." I listened to him once or twice in a lighter vein, but each time I would say just one thing: "Why would anybody like to be the king of a small kingdom, leaving the bigger state? If a person is an uncrowned king of the whole world, why would he be interested in the high chair of just one country?"

It is said that Jesus talked in the same fashion. Whenever he was asked, "Who are you?" He would say, "I am the King." Initially he used to say, "I am the son of the King of Kings." But later on he stopped saying that. Then if someone asked him who he was, he would say, "I am the King." But that foolish Jew thought that since Jesus was a Jew by birth, he was trying to declare himself the King of Jews. They thought he would topple the political power with the help of his supporters.

All the Jewish religious leaders and priests began saying that they had nothing to do with Jesus: "He can never be our king." They could never understand Jesus' language. Who has ever been able to understand the Sufis' language? How can they? They kept swearing by Abraham and Moses who were long dead, but they were not ready to accept Jesus. Because Jesus said, "I am the King," this man came closer to him and became one of his twelve disciples. But later he realised that there was nothing but spirituality that was discussed in the company of Jesus.

Soon enough, shops came up outside 'The House of God' – the place where the Jews went and offered their prayers. Shops supplying articles of daily needs sprang up in no time in the vicinity. One day Jesus went to the temple and got very angry with what he saw; he raised all the shops to the ground saying that no shops supplying worldly goods should be set up near the temple. Soon enough, all the people who had praised him earlier got scared, wondering if he had gone mad.

But that day Jesus' anger knew no bounds. He said, "You people are going to run shops in my father's house now? You want to make it a market place and do business from here?" Seeing him in this rage, the man lost faith in him and went straight to the religious leaders and said, "I know the man you are looking for." He took the soldiers with him and reached the hillock where Jesus was staying with his eleven disciples. The soldiers said, "We have reached the place and are able to see all of them, but who out of all of them is your master? Who is Jesus? How do we recognize him?"

"I shall help you recognize my master. I will go and hug one of them and kiss him on his cheek. That man will be Jesus."

245

No stranger attacked Jesus Christ. It was his own disciple who betrayed him. The disciple went close to Jesus, took him in his embrace and kissed him on his cheek. Even at that time, Jesus was full of love for that disciple. Jesus thought to himself: 'Why is he getting distracted, in spite of being so close?' Jesus' eyes became moist and he said, "You want to cheat, that too with a kiss." Jesus had already got the news that the soldiers were looking for him and during dinner he had told his other disciples: "One of you will be responsible for my death, one of you will betray me."

Peter and Joseph got agitated; Thomas began shouting, "Who is the traitor amongst us? Just point him out. We shall kill him right away." But Jesus said, "No, let his wish be fulfilled. Whatever my master desires, let that happen." As it is, society cannot tolerate Sufis living for very long. If not today, maybe tomorrow they have to be killed. Hence, taking a firm yet surprising stance, Jesus said, "It is all right."

He had sold his master for twenty coins. Just for twenty coins! The thought itself ignites a surge of anger. During the last meal Peter was very annoyed and said, "Please tell us. Who is it that will hand you over to the soldiers? Just tell me and I will kill him immediately." Jesus looked at Peter and said, "Peter, you say you will kill him? Listen, before the night is over and dawn arrives, you yourself will deny thrice that you ever had anything to do with me." Peter replied to this strange remark by inquiring, "How is that possible?"

The glow in Jesus' eyes forced him to remain quiet. But that is exactly what happened. The soldiers apprehended Jesus and tied him with chains. While they were pulling him, a big crowd gathered around. People began shouting, "He is the one who claims to be our king, but he isn't." Suddenly a woman pointed towards Peter and said, "He too is his disciple." Peter was scared for the crowd was huge. He knew for a fact that the crowd would take his life after the soldiers would take Jesus to court. He said to himself: 'they will kill me right here.'

He got so scared that right there, standing in front of Jesus, he said, "I don't know him. I don't even recognize him." And saying this, he mingled with the crowd. He was crying for his master but hiding himself at the same time. While he was anxious to know what treatment would be meted out to Jesus, at the same time he was also feeling scared. It was a winter night and some people were sitting next to a fire; Peter just sat down there. Then a child recognised him: "Isn't he the same man who stayed with Jesus?" Another voice said, "Yes, that's him. Look, he is the same man."

"No. I don't know who Jesus is. Whom are you talking about?"

The third time, someone recognised him: "He is the same man, catch him" Some soldiers were also present there. They were told to arrest the disciple. "Take him to the same place where his master has been taken."

As Jesus had predicted, the disciple denied the crowd's claim for the third time.

When he denied the claim of the crowd for the third time, he heard the cock crowing. Right then, he suddenly remembered Jesus' words: "Even before dawn arrives, you will have denied three times that you ever knew me, leave aside being known as my disciple." Peter cried bitterly, beating his chest in silent disappointment.

Only the brave can be company to living Sufis. Those who lack courage, those who are scared of death, are unfit to be called Sufis. In the Turkish language, benevolence is called baraka. Baraka for whom? For one who has the courage to have his own head cut off, and not for anybody else.

There are several ways of doing zikr, but here in our camp I have told you about three of them: 'Hu', 'La Ilaha Illallah' and 'Hai'. These three names are the three different ways of doing zikr.

The fact remains that after having learnt it for one, two or even three days, you people have not been able to understand anything. Someone was able to go two steps closer and someone went three steps closer, but actually you have to go a thousand steps closer.

Nevertheless, you must very carefully, preserve the seed of zikr that I have sown in your hearts. With the help of memory, one should try and go as deep as possible into zikr.

I would like to reiterate the aforesaid point by saying that zikr is all about love. It is necessary to do it with dum and that too in rhythm. It cannot be done without rhythm.

Why should a Sufi do zikr with dum? It is so because when a Sufi repeats a mantra in harmony with his breath, the sound of 'Hai' should come from within. The flames of 'Hai' that arise in the interiors of the chest, empty out the chest along with the flames. This justifies the tradition of listening to the ney after doing zikr. The zikr will not go deep inside unless and until you give your complete dedication to it; you have to open your heart to it.

Sufi music is not meant only for listening. Sufi music is a means of meditation. As before, it proves to be a means of meditation to the extent that the musical instruments played are not even made by normal musicians. A number of experiments have been done with them and some have even been rejected on the grounds that they are not up to the mark; they lacked that dum, that kind of force and depth that is essential.

Therefore, there should either be dum as in kudum or it should give out a sound like 'Hu' as the ney. When one hears the ney, it is heard with the thought: 'O Ney' – The way divine songs emanate from a person because he or she has become hollow or bare from within, similarly, I should also become clean from inside.

This is what we pray for; zikr means a prayer that empties one from within. All worldly thoughts go from the mind, which becomes clear and pure. The day I get cleared from the inside, divine music starts echoing from within. But the problem is you are not able to empty your insides; you just keep them filled up to the brim.

The one, who gets emptied from the inside, is the one who will be recognised, as a true Sufi. It is not sufficient to just listen to discourses on the topic of Sufi. In order to complete the process of hearing, you will have to become a Sufi yourself. Listening is complete when the person listening to it, himself becomes a

Sufi. This has already happened with a lot of people and will also happen in the future.

I end this discourse with the hope that this love, this truthfulness, this trust and this yearning stirs up your heart as it did mine...

•••

KNOW THYSELF
ANANDMURTI GURUMAA

Anandmurti Gurumaa is an embodiment of love, grace, compassion, understanding and equanimity. At the same time, she is modern and dynamic in her thinking and outlook. Her pragmatic teachings empower the seeker with the wisdom to live with absolute harmony.

"Keep the sword of awareness with you and severe all ties with the mind and the body. These ties are not even real ones. Ties are illusory and so are your bondages. You are chidananda and you will remain that. Nothing can change your being. Be in the being and know that you are the truth. You do not have to do anything to achieve truth — you are the truth! So how can you attain yourself? What can you do to know 'you'? Just wake up and see. The whole journey is the journey of waking up from this sleep."

Anandmurti Gurumaa — a contemporary mystic master — is a beacon of light to those on the path of spirituality, meditation, love and wisdom. With her characteristic humility, Anandmurti Gurumaa says, "I have nothing new to offer in terms of words, but much to offer in terms of the understanding of the truth and its essence."

Gurumaa Ashram

Come to evolve your consciousness

Gurumaa Ashram is a living Buddhafield where a great evolution is taking place - where personalities are being carved out, polished and groomed from raw unconscious states to gracious, aware and enlightened beings. The Master is the magnetic pull that attracts seekers from all over. When this call of love is made, its strength is such that one cannot miss it, but only truly fortunate ones can hear this call. Gurumaa Ashram is one such place where this magic is unfolding.

Every year Gurumaa Ashram welcomes thousands of seekers from all over the world to be part of serene environment of the Ashram. Under the guided presence of Anandmurti Gurumaa they learn and practice different methods of meditation, participate in different activities of ashram, learn self discipline, expand their capacities to create and realize evolution of highest order.

Gurumaa Ashram is a place brimming with the presence of the master where Gurumaa shares the enduring wisdom of life with the seekers. It offers a perfect climate to explore the vastness of inner world and realize the true essence of life. It is a place which must be visited by every individual longing to walk the divine path.

All are invited to be a part of the harmonious environment of Gurumaa Ashram.

Meditation Retreat with Anandmurti Gurumaa

Every year Gurumaa conducts meditation retreats in the ashram and also at various places across the globe. It is usually a five day retreat and offers a wonderful opportunity to learn meditation from Gurumaa and experience the ultimate transformation triggered by the presence of the enlightened master.

The ashram is located on the G. T. Karnal Road (N.H. 1) in Gannaur, Distt. Sonepat, Haryana, India. For details you are welcome to visit www.gurumaa.com.

Books of Wisdom
By Anandmurti Gurumaa

These books are transcriptions of the extempore talks given by Gurumaa from time to time at various places. Books are one of the many ways of chronicling the wisdom that flows from the master and serves as a beacon for seekers.

	Books	Language	Rs.
1	Aatam Bodh	Hindi, Marathi, Telugu	125
2	Antar Drishti	Hindi	125
3	Anhad Ki Dhun Pyaari	Hindi	180
4	Ath Kahe Naarad	Hindi	250
5	Antar Ke Pat Khol	Gujarati, Hindi	90
6	Bhaj Govindam	Hindi	220
7	Chinmaya Ki Aur	Hindi	125
8	Dhamm-Jeevan Aadhaar	Hindi	145
9	Going Beyond The Mind	English	250
10	Govind Naam Mere Praan	Hindi	125
11	Govind Rasdhara	Hindi	125
12	Gyan Shitij	Hindi	125
13	Health & Healing Through Yoga	English	150
14	Karun Hridaya	Hindi	145
15	Kabira Ram Yun Sumariye	Hindi	180
16	Know Thyself	English	295
17	Mind & Sex	English	100
18	Naame Ke Swami	Hindi	125
19	Prema Bhakti - Ek Utsav	Hindi	125
20	Prem Diwani Meera (Hard Bound)	Hindi	295
21	Prem Diwani Meera (Paper Back)	Hindi	150
22	Prem Ka Chhalakta Jaam	Hindi	80
23	Quotes of the Unquotable	English	80
24	Rumi Aur Main- Ek Sufi Prem Katha	Hindi	150
25	Shakti – The Feminine Energy	English, Hindi	80
26	Shakti	Gujarati, Telugu	30
27	Satguru Kaun	Hindi	375
28	Swar - Madhushaala	Hindi	125
29	Shivoham	Hindi	250
30	Satguru Poora Paayo	Gujarati, Hindi, Punjabi	125
31	Truth Exposed	English	200
32	Yuktaahaar	Hindi, Telugu	20

To know more about the books or to buy them online, visit: www.gurumaa.com
Or place your order on call: 09896263821 / 0130 - 2216500 / 0130 - 2216501

Audio & Video Collection of Discourse/Meditation/Sufi/Devotional

By Anandmurti Gurumaa

	Devotional	(Acd/Vcd/Dvd/Mp3)	Language	Rs.
1	Anando	(ACD)		95
2	Baawari Jogan	(ACD)		295
3	Chamkan Taare	(ACD)		95
4	Chants of Krishna	(ACD)		150
5	Desh Begana Hai	(ACD)		95
6	Dilbar Ki Karda	(Set of 2 VCD's)		150
7	Fragrance of Love	(ACD)		100
8	Ishq Hi Maula	(ACD)		150
9	Kahe Kabira	(Set of 2 ACD's)		199
10	Kripa	(ACD)		100
11	Maha-Mrityunjaya	(ACD)		99
12	Mool Mantra	(ACD)		99
13	Nanak Aaya	(ACD)		100
14	Odyssey of Love	(ACD)		295
15	Rangi Re	(ACD)		100
16	Saanwal-Saanwal	(ACD)		150
17	Sajanra	(VCD)		150
18	Sajda	(ACD)		100
19	Samarpan	(ACD)		100
20	Sheikh Farid	(ACD)		99
21	Shiva's Ecstasy	(ACD)		150
22	Shivoham	(Set of 2 ACD's)		150
23	Shoonya	(ACD)		295
24	Shri Rama Stuti	(ACD)		100
25	Wahe Guru Jaap	(ACD)		95
26	Kaisi Aarti Hoye	(ACD)		100

MEDITATION

		(Acd/Vcd/Dvd/Mp3)	Language	Rs.
1	Beyond Boundaries	(ACD)	Eng & Hindi	150
2	Mudra	(ACD)	Eng & Hindi	150
3	Pranav	(ACD)	Eng & Hindi	150
4	Ram Ras	(ACD)		150
5	Sacred Spaces	(ACD)		195
6	Shiv-Naam-Omkar	(ACD)		295
7	Simran	(ACD)	Punjabi	95
8	Sparsh	(VCD)		150
9	Stuti Sutra	(ACD)		150
10	Shwason Ka Vigyan	(VCD)		150
11	Tratak	(ACD)		195
12	Urja	(ACD)	Eng & Hindi	150

13	Yog Nidra for Youth	(ACD)	Hindi	195
14	Yog Nidra Part-1	(ACD)	Eng & Hindi	195
15	Yog Nidra Part-2	(ACD)	Hindi	195
16	Zikr- Call of a Sufi	(ACD)		150
17	Waheguru	(ACD)		99

Poetry

| 1 | Rumi- Love at its Zenith | (ACD) | 150 |

MP-3

1	Jaap Sahib	(MP 3)	245
2	Japji Sahib	(MP 3)	245
3	Ki Jana Main Kaun	(MP 3)	250
4	Rehras Sahib	(MP 3)	250
5	Shankaracharya	(MP 3)	350
6	Shivoham	(MP 3)	350
7	Veetragata	(MP 3)	250

Discourses in Hindi

1	Shrimad Bhagwad Gita	(Set of 71 DVD's)	11000
2	Shrimad Bhagwad Gita	(Set of 136 VCD's)	8100
3	Buddha Sutra	(VCD)	125
4	Guru Gita	(Set of 25 DVD's)	4500
5	Jaap Sahib	(Set of 25 VCD)	1800
6	Jaap Sahib	(Set of 13 DVD's)	2600
7	Jeevan Ka Vigyan	(Set of 8 VCD's)	600
8	Kaisi Aarti Hoi	(VCD)	150
9	Ki Jaana Main Kaun	(Set of 15 VCD's)	1000
10	Krodh Se Karuna Tak	(ACD)	99
11	Kya Hai Sadhuta	(VCD)	100
12	Mann Ka Satvik Ahaar	(VCD)	100
13	Manotantra Vigyan	(VCD)	100
14	Raj Yoga	(Set of 13 ACD's)	520
15	Shankaracharya	(Set of 28 VCD's)	2000
16	Shivoham	(Set of 30 VCD's)	2000
17	Tanaav Ko Kahein Alvida	(Set of 10 VCD's)	750
18	Tu Toh Mann Key Mool Main	(VCD)	100
19	Veetragata	(Set of 14 VCD's)	1000

Discourses in English

1	Shakti: An Ode To Women	(VCD)	199
2	God: Mystery or Reality	(VCD)	150
3	Know Your Mind	(VCD)	150

For more information and comprehensive collection, Please logon to www.gurumaa.com.
Or place your order on call: 09896263821 / 0130 - 2216500 / 0130 - 2216501